跨境电商英语直播实用教程

A Practical Guide to English Live Streaming

主编 ◎ 邬玲琳

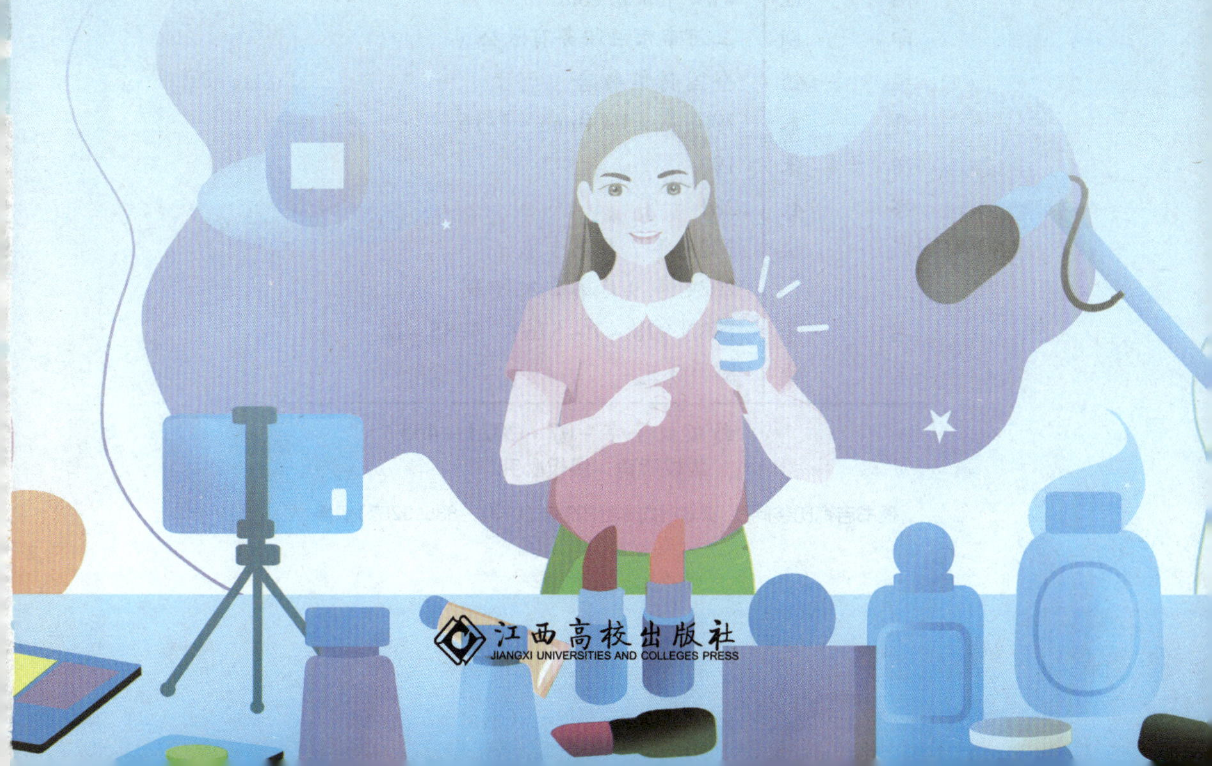

江西高校出版社
JIANGXI UNIVERSITIES AND COLLEGES PRESS

图书在版编目(CIP)数据

跨境电商英语直播实用教程 = A Practical Guide to English Live Streaming/邬玲琳主编. --南昌:江西高校出版社,2023.7(2024.9重印)

ISBN 978-7-5762-3985-0

Ⅰ. ①跨… Ⅱ. ①邬… Ⅲ. ①电子商务—网络营销—英语—教材 Ⅳ. ①F713.365.2

中国国家版本馆 CIP 数据核字(2023)第 119777 号

出版发行	江西高校出版社
社　　址	江西省南昌市洪都北大道 96 号
总编室电话	(0791)88504319
销售电话	(0791)88522516
网　　址	www.juacp.com
印　　刷	三河市京兰印务有限公司
经　　销	全国新华书店
开　　本	700mm×1000mm　1/16
印　　张	19
字　　数	281 千字
版　　次	2023 年 7 月第 1 版 2024 年 9 月第 2 次印刷
书　　号	ISBN 978-7-5762-3985-0
定　　价	88.00 元

赣版权登字 -07-2023-455
版权所有　侵权必究

图书若有印装问题,请随时向本社印制部(0791-88513257)退换

编委会名单

主　编：邬玲琳

副主编：李　琼　张樱子　李　响　侯铁军

编　委：邱　萍　汪珞燃　李福中　张志华
　　　　戴继善　刘群海　郑李娜　彭晓云
　　　　黄　可　程　峰　候嘉宇　李思婷
　　　　朱汶青　邬睿琦　陶宇翔

前　言

2022年，国务院发布了《关于同意在鄂尔多斯等27个城市和地区设立跨境电子商务综合试验区的批复》以促进跨境电子商务等新业态健康、持续、创新发展。近年来，随着经济一体化和全球化的不断发展，跨境电商日渐兴盛，越来越多的海外客户选择通过跨境电商平台购买中国商品，为更多的中国企业和经营者带来无限商机。然而，随着当今用户消费习惯的改变，跨境电商正经历着营销方式的巨大变革。跨境电商英语直播凭借庞大的用户流量基础、巨大的影响力、真实的体验感、实时的互动性，以及低成本、低门槛等特点，成为当前跨境电商重要的营销方式。跨境电商英语直播的快速兴起，使得社会急需既有扎实英语语言基础和产品专业知识，又能有效进行跨文化交流互动，帮助消费者建立信心并激发消费者购买欲望的优秀英语主播，但在此领域尚无体系完整的人才培养教材和课程。

本教材根据行业领域的特点设计了英语直播基础知识、陶瓷产品英语直播、服装产品英语直播、电子产品英语直播、美妆个护产品英语直播、玩具产品英语直播、DIY产品英语直播、家居产品英语直播和宠物用品英语直播等十个单元，包括上千个专业单词和话术句子，几十种产品介绍模板，涵盖了跨境电商英语直播的各个领域。通过学习《跨境电商英语直播实用教程》，学生可以做到轻松学、流利说，在跨境电商英语直播领域游刃有余，从而在未来就业时具有较大的竞争优势。

根据新时代应用型高校教育"三教改革"(教师、教材、教法)和教材"双元开发"(学校和企业)的要求,本书在坚持"实用为主"的前提下,突出以下特色:

1. 服务国家战略。教材设计紧密围绕国家、地方经济发展战略,以不同行业实际需求为出发点,科学设计单元主题,选取当下中国跨境电商畅销产品类目为教学内容,精准对接国家、地方和企业发展需求。

2. 深化"双元"合作。本教材在编写过程中依托校企合作,坚持"行业指导、企业参与"原则。教材编写人员既有高校一线骨干教师,又有国内不同行业的知名企业负责人、培训专家和技术人员。他们的参与使得该教材能紧跟行业发展趋势、反映岗位职业能力要求,从而有效保证教学内容的针对性、科学性和实用性。

3. 编著理念先进。本教材编写以 CBI (Content-based Instruction) 教学理念为指导,将内容课程与语言课程紧密结合,将语言技能教学和特定专业知识教学相结合,使学生通过跨境直播专业知识的学习提升英语语言能力,并在英语直播活动中获得跨境电商相关的专业知识,提高思维能力。

4. 实用特色鲜明。本教材以"必需、实用"为原则,对接跨境直播岗位的职业能力要求,选取实践性强的教学内容,以提升学生在岗位工作中应用行业英语和专业英语的能力。

5. 内容设置科学。为了准确、科学地设置教学内容,我们走访了相关企业,求教了企业管理者、行业专家和一线工作人员,通过调查问卷和电话访问开展了"跨境电商英语直播工作所需技能专题调研",并以此为课程目标科学设置教学内容,为跨境电商英语直播专业人才培养提供有力支撑。

6. 教学资源丰富。 为丰富教学内容、加强学习沉浸感、提高学习自由度，教材编写团队努力开发配套在线课程，打造"立体式"教材，同步建设课程资源，更好地服务师生，助力信息化教学改革。

本书由邬玲琳负责策划和统稿，参与编写工作的老师有邬玲琳、李琼、张樱子、李响。各单元编写分工如下：邬玲琳负责第1至第3单元的编写；李琼负责第4、第6、第10单元的编写；张樱子负责第5、第9单元的编写；李响负责第7、第8单元的编写。侯铁军对本书的框架、体例提供了宝贵的资料和指导建议。汪珞燃负责校稿。武汉市家福园建材有限公司董事长李福中、佛山市云生海机械制造有限公司董事长张志华、佛山市一剪梅彩色印刷有限公司董事长戴善继、广东省佛山市大境陶瓷科技有限公司董事长刘群海、箭牌家居集团澳洲负责人郑李娜、中国国家博物馆藏品征集与鉴定部副研究员彭晓云、深圳市锐铭鑫科技有限公司董事长黄可、东阳市弘萱化妆品有限公司监事程峰（排名不分先后）等为本书提供了大力支持。景德镇陶瓷大学教师邱萍，2022级翻译硕士侯嘉宇、李思婷、朱汶青，2021级翻译专业学生邬睿琦，2018级英语专业学生陶宇翔负责本教材的资料收集和整理工作。

由于编者水平有限，本教材仍存在不足之处，欢迎读者批评、指正。

编　者
2023年5月

目录
CONTENTS

第一章　跨境电商英语直播基础知识　/001

导言　/001

1.1　英语电商直播平台介绍　/001

1.2　跨境直播业务流程　/003

1.3　跨境英语主播应具备的能力　/004

1.4　跨境英语直播流程设计　/006

1.5　英语直播脚本设置　/007

1.6　英语直播口才训练　/010

1.7　跨境直播客服话术　/013

第二章　陶瓷产品英语直播　/019

2.1　建筑陶瓷 Architectural Ceramics　/019

2.2　卫浴陶瓷 Ceramic Sanitary Wares　/028

2.3　日用陶瓷 Household Wares　/038

2.4　艺术陶瓷 Art Ceramics　/048

2.5　实战脚本 Script　/059

第三章　服装类产品英语直播　/061

3.1　服装 Clothing　/061

3.2　鞋类 Shoes　/074

3.3　帽子 Hats and Caps　/081

3.4　实战脚本 Script　/088

第四章　电子类产品英语直播　/091

4.1　消费类电子产品 Consumer Electronics　/091

4.2　办公类电子产品 Office Electronics　/102

4.3　电子元器件及电子产品配件 Electronic Components and Accessories　/110

4.4　实战脚本 Script　/117

第五章　美妆个护类产品英语直播　/120

5.1　油膏类美妆 Oil and Creamy Products　/120

5.2　粉类美妆 Powder Products　/127

5.3 个体护理 Personal Care /135

5.4 实战脚本 Script /143

第六章 玩具产品英语直播 /146

6.1 启蒙及益智类玩具 Educational Toys /146

6.2 运动型体育及户外玩具 Sports and Outdoor Toys /155

6.3 观赏收藏类玩具 Collectible Toys /163

6.4 实战脚本 Script /171

第七章 首饰和饰品类产品英语直播 /173

7.1 金属类首饰和饰品 Metal Jewelry and Accessories /173

7.2 宝石类首饰和饰品 Gemstone Jewelry and Accessories /183

7.3 其他种类的饰品 Other Kinds of Accessories /191

7.4 实战脚本 Script /200

第八章 DIY 类产品英语直播 /202

8.1 DIY 工具 DIY Tools /202

8.2 DIY 玩具 DIY Toys /211

8.3 DIY 工艺品 DIY Arts and Crafts /219

8.4　实战脚本 Script　/227

第九章　家居产品英语直播　/229

9.1　家具用品 Furniture　/229

9.2　电器用品 Household Appliances　/237

9.3　床上用品 Bedding and Lines　/245

9.4　实战脚本 Script　/252

第十章　宠物用品英语直播　/255

10.1　宠物食品 Pet Food　/255

10.2　宠物日常生活及户外用品 Pet Daily and Outdoor Supplies　/264

10.3　宠物清洁及医疗保健用品 Pet Cleansing and Healthcare Products　/273

10.4　宠物服饰及玩具 Pet Apparels and Toys　/282

10.5　实战脚本 Script　/290

第一章
跨境电商英语直播基础知识

导 言

2022年12月,世界直播电商大会在杭州召开,针对直播电商新模式、新场景、新生态等热点议题进行了讨论,并发布了《世界直播电商发展报告(2022)》。据预测,到2025年,直播带货在电商中的份额将达25%,年规模是4.25万亿元,行业复合增长率约达31%。

据浙江省电子商务促进会数字贸易研究院发布的《跨境电商直播研究报告》,自2017年以来,世界各国纷纷加入跨境电商直播领域:2017年,俄罗斯、西班牙和法国等国的主播首次在速卖通进行直播;2018年,美国电商平台Gravy.Live开启互动直播电商模式,千家商家在Lazada开启直播,业务覆盖泰国、越南、菲律宾、马来西亚等国;2019年,亚马逊公司推出直播购物App——Amazon Live Creator,电商平台Shopee开通直播带货,业务覆盖马来西亚、菲律宾和泰国。目前,几乎所有海外主流媒体平台均开通了直播功能,跨境电商直播发展迅猛。

1.1 英语电商直播平台介绍

如果要进入英语电商直播行业,首先要了解当前世界上存在的主要跨境电商直播平台。每个平台都有自身的优势和特点,选择合适的平台尤为重要。目前,全球英语电商直播平台主要包括TikTok、AliExpress Live、Amazon Live、Lazada和Shopee。

(1) TikTok

TikTok是字节跳动旗下的短视频社交平台,2017年夏在全球范围内上线后，迅速受到世界用户喜爱。2017 年 10 月，该平台上线了直播功能，目前业务覆盖全球 150 多个国家和地区，囊括 75 种语言，全球用户数超过 15 亿，是全球最受欢迎的 App 之一。TikTok 页面、设置、功能、产品逻辑、购物车功能等都与抖音相似，因此中国商家具有先发优势。2022 年，TikTok 首次推出"全球年末大促季"，跨境业务整体 GMV 销量增长 136%，订单量增长超 77%，近 6 万商家、超 3 万达人参与其中，相关账号累计开播超 272 万小时。

（2）AliExpress Live

AliExpress 是阿里巴巴面向国际市场打造的跨境电商平台，通过支付宝国际账户进行担保交易，并使用国际物流渠道运输发货，是全球第三大英文在线购物网站。AliExpress Live 于 2017 年上线，直播形式与国内的淘宝直播相似，外国的买家在观看直播的同时可以在页面下方进行选购，实现边看边买的娱乐购物体验。目前，该平台囊括了百余家 MCN 机构、上千位主播和数万名网红。

（3）Amazon Live

Amazon Live 是 2019 年美国最大的一家网络电子商务公司亚马逊在其应用程序中增加的一项直播服务，不再局限于之前的视频发表，而是发展成为亚马逊直播。通过使用 Amazon Live，卖家可以采用直播形式，向消费者展示产品的使用场景，激发消费者的购买行为，买家则可以通过视频下方的链接直接购买商品，从而有效提高转化率。

（4）Lazada

Lazada 是东南亚地区最大的在线购物网站之一，成立于 2012 年 3 月，业务覆盖印度尼西亚、马来西亚、菲律宾、新加坡、泰国和越南，主要经营时尚服饰、家居用品、运动器材、3C 电子类产品。2016 年起，Lazada 成为阿里巴巴集团东南亚旗舰电商平台，2018 年以 27% 的访问额占东南亚电商在线流量排名榜单第一，2019 年当选印度尼西亚年轻一代最受欢迎的购物平台，2022 年平台生日大促期间，销售额为平日的 66 倍。

（5）Shopee

Shopee 是 2015 年在新加坡成立的东南亚及中国台湾地区的电商平台，业务覆盖新加坡、马来西亚、菲律宾、泰国、越南、巴西等 10 余个市场，是东南亚发展最快的电商平台。2022 年第二季度，Shopee 的 GMV 为 190 亿美元，总营收

17亿美元。直播是Shopee手机端推出的引流手段,通过在线互动和实物展示,短时间内聚集大量潜在的顾客,提高转化率和销量。

上述电商平台各有优势,具体见表1-1。

表1-1 英语电商直播平台优势对比①

平台	优点
TikTok	(1)双向标签,可精准定位目标客户 (2)涨粉速度快 (3)商业化程度较低,品牌推广成本可控性强
AliExpress	(1)卖家和达人都可以创建直播间 (2)用户可以将整个视频下载后截取 (3)AliExpress Conncect 的卖家自播模式有平台官方提供的流量支持,不用支付费用
Amazon Live	(1)卖家的直播视频可以永久留存,并且用户可以在直播频道随机看到,有利于增加流量 (2)平台会针对直播卖家,给予相应的站内流量分布 (3)直播结束后,后台会生成详细的直播数据
Lazada	(1)获得阿里巴巴支持,数据中心强大 (2)支付、物流体系完善 (3)对中国产品依赖程度高 (4)推广预算低,平台有流量支持
Shopee	(1)首页入口就可以直播,并且直播带货的卖家有平台提供的流量支持 (2)店铺排名越高,获得的流量越高,可以积累人气和直播积分 (3)卖家开播时间越长,直播时间越早,越有机会被官方推荐到黄金位,直播间最多可展示200款产品

1.2 跨境直播业务流程

跨境电商指的是分属不同关境的交易主体,通过国际电子商务平台达成交易,进行电子支付结算,并通过跨境电商物流及异地仓储送达商品,从而完成交易的一种国际商业活动。作为跨境电商引流和促单的重要方式,跨境直播将英语直播带货与跨境电子商务紧密结合,业务操作流程与跨境电商相似。具体流程如下:

---

① 信息来源:浙江数字电商委。

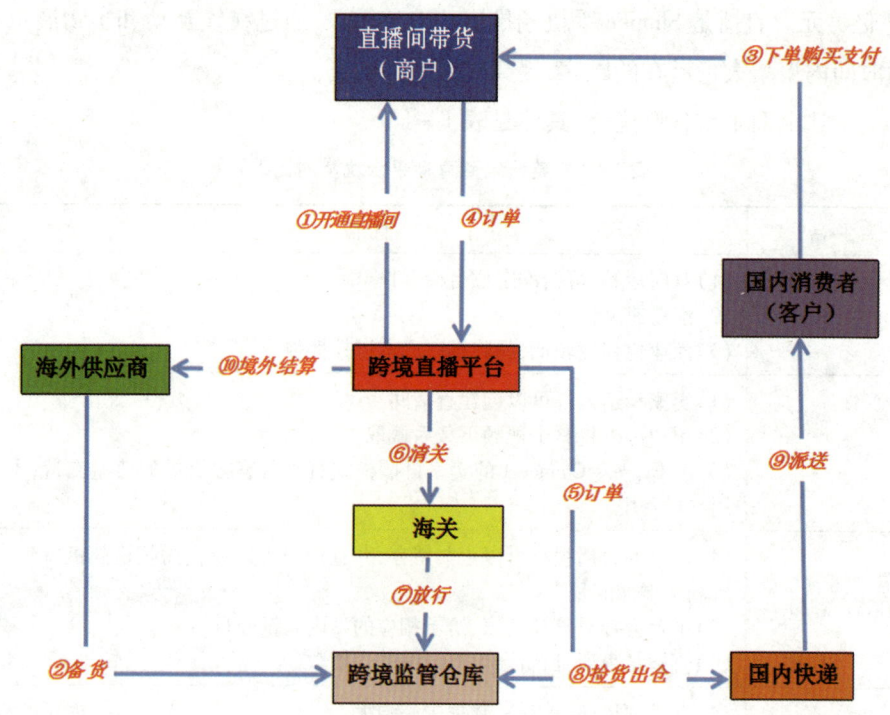

1.3 跨境英语主播应具备的能力

跨境电商直播实质上是围绕"人"和"货"进行的商业行为。与传统营销模式相比,英语主播在跨境电子商务活动中更为重要。英语主播的语言技能、产品专业知识、销售技巧、直播话术,甚至微表情、微引导都将决定一场英语直播最终是否能够实现有效转化。因此,一名优秀的英语主播需要具备多项能力。

(1) 语言技能

一名合格的跨境电商英语主播,首先应当具备的就是较强的英语语言能力。英语主播的主要职责是销售货物,在发音、词语和语法方面并不做太高的要求。英语主播只要能够用英语进行流畅的表达,熟悉所销售产品的专业词汇和常用带货英语表达就可以胜任。英语直播脚本需要提前准备。互动问答中,国外买家主要关注的是主播的个人信息以及产品的相关问题,如尺码、材质等。因此,较好的英语口语基础能够满足英语主播所需的英语语言技能要求。

(2) 专业知识

各行各业都有其专业性,英语直播带货也不例外。英语主播的专业性体现在其必须充分了解直播产品,能够对产品进行准确的介绍,突出产品的特色,对产品有足够的推荐力。主播的专业性直接关系到潜在消费者对主播和产品的信任感,也是潜在消费者购买产品的核心驱动力。

(3)表达能力

英语主播并不是售卖产品的机器,直播带货时重在与国外的消费者进行沟通、交流。英语主播需要在直播过程中与粉丝积极互动,从而提高粉丝的黏性。良好的表达能力包括语言表达能力、丰富的表情和恰当的肢体语言,可以调节直播间的气氛,从而激发消费行为的产生。英语主播要有一套适合自己产品的话术,并能够根据直播间的流量及时调整直播方式,提升消费者的体验感。

(4)直播心态

良好的直播心态是英语主播最需要培养的。由于缺乏流量基础或直播时间段不佳等原因,在整个直播过程中,观看直播的人往往很少,甚至没有任何人参与互动。即使在这样的情况下,主播依然需要保持良好的直播状态。一名优秀的英语主播能够以良好的直播心态灵活应对各种突发事件,承受住直播的压力。

(5)复盘能力

一名合格的英语主播,每次直播结束后都需要及时根据平台数据进行分析。反应较好的直播语言和销售策略,在下次直播中可以沿用;直播过程中效果不佳的地方,在下次直播中要进行调整。此外还需要多观看其他主播直播,取他人之所长,补己之所短。

(6)工作毅力

直播是一场需要耗费大量脑力和体力的工作。直播前,主播需要熟悉产品的各项特性,突出产品的核心卖点,撰写脚本并进行彩排。英语主播还需要对不熟悉的英文单词及时查漏补缺。直播过程中,工作时间很长,特别是跨境直播,需要根据不同国家的最佳直播时段来进行直播,主播时常要倒时差,需要很大的毅力才能坚持下来。从实践来看,很多能力非常强的英语主播因为难以坚持而中途放弃,只有坚持下来的才最终得到市场的认同。

1.4　跨境英语直播流程设计

许多新手直播效果不理想,原因之一是没有预先做好流程规划。只有合理设计英语直播流程,再加上多次实践,才能保证直播活动的顺利进行。英语直播通常包括五个环节:预热环节、开场环节、产品介绍环节、结尾环节和复盘总结环节。

(1) 预热环节

要想在跨境电商直播中增加流量,除了选择黄金时段开播,还需要进行直播前的预热宣传。宣传方式包括以下几种:在官网宣传,即在跨境电商卖家的官方网站、独立站或电商平台提前发布直播预告,获得官方网站的自然流量和推广流量;利用跨境直播平台的预告功能吸引粉丝;在每次直播前发布一段预热视频,从而得到更多的流量;在国外社交平台发布直播预告,对直播间的流量进行加成。

(2) 开场环节

开场环节主要由主播介绍和直播活动介绍两部分组成,这也是粉丝最为关心的两个方面。在直播开场时,英语主播首先需要向粉丝打招呼,亲切的问候容易拉近主播与粉丝的距离;再简单介绍自己和直播业绩,这不仅可以体现自己的人格魅力和专业性,还能让粉丝认同主播,产生信任感;接下来可以给粉丝介绍本次直播活动、福利以及购买流程,重点突出福利内容和形式,激发粉丝观看的兴趣,增加留存率。需要注意的是,开场环节不应太长,5 分钟内必须进入主题,否则容易让粉丝觉得无趣,导致粉丝流失。

(3) 产品介绍环节

产品介绍环节要求英语主播用流利的英语和专业的态度介绍不同产品的材质、规格、功能、卖点和优势,并对咨询率较高的问题进行解答,让粉丝清晰地了解该产品。由于直播往往长达几小时,涉及众多产品,因此主播介绍每个产品的时间不应过长,须控制在 10 分钟以内。为了增加粉丝的留存率,主播需要设计一两款爆品或者特价产品(爆品和特价产品最容易带来转化率)进行重点、深入的讲解。在产品介绍环节,主播还需要引导粉丝及时下单,通常可以采取低价、满减、领取优惠券、发红包、抽奖等形式。这些活动不仅有助于活跃气氛,调动粉丝的积极性，还可以增加转化率。在介绍了产品之后，主播要适时改变话术，体现出紧迫感和限量感，才能更好地促进粉丝下单。

（4）结尾环节

在直播即将结束时，主播可以对本次直播活动进行简单的总结，感谢大家的参与，并向粉丝预告下次直播的时间和主要内容，也可以提及下次直播的福利和低价产品，吸引粉丝前来观看，从而增加直播间粉丝的黏性。

（5）复盘总结环节

复盘总结环节是英语直播中必不可少却又常常被忽视的环节。要想改善直播效果、提高销量，主播就必须在每次直播结束后及时观看回放的直播视频，查看直播数据，进行有效复盘，记录直播过程中存在的问题，并不断进行调整和优化。

1.5　英语直播脚本设置

要有效地完成跨境直播流程，保证每一个环节顺利进行，主播就必须撰写一份详细、清晰、执行度高的英语直播脚本。英语直播脚本也是主播把控跨境直播节奏、规范直播流程、达到预期目标的关键一步。下面先来介绍英语直播脚本设置的步骤：

（1）明确直播主题。英语直播脚本首先需要明确直播主题，即有清晰的直播目的，是新品上市、大型促销、节日主题还是回馈粉丝。这些明确的直播目的可以让粉丝清楚地知道自己在这场直播中可以得到什么，让粉丝更有目标感。

（2）确定直播产品和具体内容。每场直播的主要内容是推荐产品，因此必须提前选品。主播不仅会推荐不同类型的产品，还会销售不同价格区间的产品，以吸引不同层次的粉丝，因此直播前要梳理好各个产品的特点、功能卖点和价格卖点，以更加真实、准确地介绍产品信息。脚本中还需要确定产品的推荐顺序，尤其是重点推荐款。通常同类产品排在一起，起到互相促进的作用。在这个环节中，英语主播的话术显得尤为重要。如何获得粉丝的好感？如何凸显产品的优势？如何提升下单转化率？主播需要针对这些问题事先做好准备。

（3）设置优惠玩法。卖家需要提前设计好能承受的优惠券面额、秒杀活动和赠品支出，以更好地调动直播间的气氛，引导粉丝消费。在英文直播脚本中，"优惠"一定要有所体现，并设置好所在位置和搭配的商品。

此外，在撰写英文直播脚本时，最好细化到分钟，应尽可能详细，包括调度直播分工，对所有参与人员的动作、话术等进行指导，增加互动频率，提高留存率；还需准备突发预案，以保证直播顺利完成，并取得最佳效果。

整场直播脚本：

主题	主题				
	目标				
成本与效果	预期效果	粉丝人数	销售额	观看时长	新增粉丝人数
	预期成本				
促销活动	店铺促销				
	直播促销				
英语直播流程	组成部分	时间	内容	详细信息	技巧	团队合作
	直播开场	3—5分钟	欢迎粉丝入场	主播自我介绍、粉丝互动	1. 主播简单介绍自己 2. 欢迎粉丝入场 3. 简要介绍店铺和品牌	调试设备、准备道具
		5—8分钟	预热	简单介绍直播活动、福利和爆单商品	1. 根据入场粉丝人数确定热场时间 2. 介绍爆单商品，引起粉丝兴趣，增加留存率	客服做好售后服务
	直播主体	15分钟	介绍产品	1. 介绍爆款 2. 秒杀活动	1. 快速推出几款爆款，吸引粉丝关注、留言 2. 鼓励粉丝关注、点赞和留言 3. 及时回复评论	录制、上购物链接、弹券、抽奖
		3—5分钟	介绍福利活动	1. 解读抽奖的操作方法以及优惠券的领取和使用方法 2. 解读抽奖主题，加强与粉丝互动	1. 采用倒计时的方式增强紧张的氛围 2. 预告下一次福利，引导粉丝关注、点赞和留言	客服回复粉丝留言、配合做好抽奖等活动

续表

	组成部分	时间	内容	详细信息	技巧	团队合作
英语直播流程	直播主体	10分钟	介绍产品	1. 介绍产品 2. 回答粉丝提问,引导粉丝下单和评论	1. 根据价格差异调整产品顺序 2. 引导粉丝下单、关注、点赞和留言	弹券、录制产品讲解视频
		3—5分钟	介绍福利活动	1. 对福利活动进行解说 2. 介绍福利活动主题 3. 回答粉丝提问	1. 采用倒计时方式增强紧张的氛围 2. 预告下一次福利,引导粉丝关注、点赞和留言	客服回复粉丝留言、协助抽奖、弹券
		产品介绍与福利活动循环进行				
	直播结尾	5—10分钟	结束话术和下期预告	1. 预告下期直播的时间和主题 2. 介绍下期直播活动、爆款、和福利,预告下期产品	1. 提前策划下期直播 2. 直播前的引流	在屏幕上提示下次直播的时间
材料准备	道具准备	预告封面、奖品				

单品直播脚本:

产品名称	产品图片	产品卖点	产品价格	直播优惠价	促销活动
大号陶瓷咖啡杯		**产品规格**:活性釉杯,每一个都是不同的。杯子容量大(24盎司),满足办公室和家庭需求。 **坚固耐用**:采用坚固的陶瓷结构设计,无铅、无镉,品质高。适合热饮和冷饮。可使用洗碗机清洗,也可用于微波炉。 **易于握持**:大手柄可防止杯子旋转,有助于舒适地享用茶饮。 **光泽独特**:设计简约而经典,采用活性釉技术。每个杯子都是独特的,有五种颜色可供选择,是节日、生日和特殊场合的最佳礼品。	25.99美元	23.99美元	10%的折扣

1.6 英语直播口才训练

一名成功的英语主播不仅要口语流利、专业知识充足,还要有良好的口才,只有学会处理各个环节的典型问题,例如如何开场,如何宣传、介绍产品,如何催单,如何互动,才能高效地完成一场英语直播。因此,英语主播需要结合自身特点,利用不同的英语直播话术控制直播流程、完善直播特色和营造直播氛围。好的英语直播口才不仅可以直接带来利益,促进下单转化,还可以增加粉丝对直播间和主播的信任感,提高留存率和复购率,帮助打造主播人设,组建具有黏性的粉丝群,从而拥有一个稳定的购买团体。

(一)开场话术:热情欢迎粉丝,加强沟通与互动

电商直播与传统营销模式相比最大的优势就是互动。主播是直播间气氛的掌控者,在开场时最重要的是带给大家好心情,拉近与粉丝的距离。具体可以采用以下话术:

(1)自我介绍,突出主播

• Hi guys, thanks for joining us today! I am Audrey, very excited to have you here!

• Hi guys! How are you doing? Welcome to my live. I am Audrey, and with me is Jacob.

• Hi guys, welcome to my live show. This is Audrey from ABC Fashion, China.

• Hello everyone, welcome to Audrey's live. If you like me, like my goods, please give me a "like".

(2)解读粉丝昵称,拉近彼此距离

• Hi Joyce, welcome to my live. I really like your name. Your name reminds me of a spring afternoon with bright sunshine.

(3)寻找共同话题,了解粉丝喜好

• Hi guys, welcome! Can you tell me what is your favorite color?

(4)预告直播爆点,提高粉丝留存率

• Welcome to my live! Today we will sell some best coffee set from Jingdezhen, the capital of porcelain. If you are interested, don't miss it! Just follow us.

(二)宣传话术

跨境电商直播还需要不断宣传,让粉丝了解店铺、品牌、直播时间和直播内容,才更能够获得粉丝的信任,留住高黏性的客户。

(1)宣传店铺和主播

• This is Audrey from ABC porcelain factory in Jingdezhen, China. With experienced technicians and designers, we handle various kinds of tableware of medium grades, such as porcelain tableware, porcelain dinner ware, porcelain drink ware, which are all with high quality and fine workmanship. We continuously provide customers with healthy and quality products. That is why our products are so popular in international market. So if you like Chinese ceramics, you have just come to the right place.

(2)宣传直播内容

• I am Audrey, let me show you some exquisite ceramic vases. See, do you like them? If you like these, don't forget to follow me, and learn more about ceramics. There must be one that you like.

(3)宣传直播时间

• Welcome to my live! We start our live streaming at 7:00 p.m. every day, the same time. My friends, thank you for coming every day. I am so happy. Thanks for your accompany.

(三)带货话术:减少距离感,帮助粉丝决策

直播的最终目的是卖货,直播间的粉丝就是顾客。良好的带货话术可以缩短主播与粉丝间的距离感,让粉丝感同身受,激发购买需求。主播再通过深入介绍产品材质、功效、价格等特色,有效促使粉丝做出购买行为。

(1)设置场景,引起共鸣

• Spring is coming. Do you want to enjoy the afternoon tea with your friends in the yard? So, do you need a nice ceramic tea set? Emblazoned with the distinctive flower pattern, it can help you relax your tired physical and mind by enjoying the afternoon tea with your friends.

(2)引入产品,解决困惑

• This mug is of perfect size to drink your favorite coffee or tea. It is suitable for hot and cold drink. It is safe with dishwasher and microwave, so forget the hassle of washing it manually.

（3）放大话题，刺激消费

- The Christmas is coming. This is the lowest price in history, the bottom price. There will be no second chance for you to have such a price.

（4）详细解说，增加附加值

- Now, I show you the coffee set. What you see, and what you get. It is made of premium quality Bone China Porcelain, lead free, safe and healthy. You don't need to worry about its quality! If you need after-sales, you can message me. We will help you out.

（5）产品对比，增强可信度

- Now I'd like to show you the market price, a box of ten. The market price should be like 35 USD ok? At least. You can just check it by yourself on your phone. You can just find other suppliers. You can just ask them how much it costs. But today in Audrey's live, I'd like to mention, that only cost you 20 USD. Ok?

（四）催单话术：了解粉丝心理，制造紧张气氛

直播是一场即时营销活动，适当的饥饿营销和限时刺激往往能制造出一种紧迫感，营造出抢购的紧张氛围。这对于部分犹豫不决的粉丝来说，具有十分微妙的刺激作用。饥饿营销指的是商家有意控制产品的供应量，通过调控市场供求关系维持品牌形象和较高的售价。

（1）饥饿营销，适时适度

- Anyone just come to my live? Today we have a special discount, buy 3 get 30% off. Only 10 boxes! First come, first served! There will be no more chance for this price.

（2）限时促销，刺激下单

- This price, you know, it is the bottom price. If I have never cooperated with you, I think maybe this is a chance for us to cooperate with each other. Now it is the time, ok? The last 5 seconds. Let's count down. 5, 4, 3, 2, 1. There's no more. Thank you for your trust.

(五)互动话术:关注粉丝,解决问题

直播过程中,主播需要一直与粉丝保持互动,让粉丝感受到被关注。粉丝提出的问题和诉求也需要得到快速回复,这样才能有效了解粉丝,并留住粉丝。

(1)选择型话术:参与简单,互动性强

- These ceramic plates are of two sizes, 10 inches and 12 inches. 10 inches is the standard size as main course serving dinner plate, and the 12-inch one is good for salad. If you want the smaller one, please type "1" on screen; if you prefer the bigger one, type "2".

(2)提问型话术:问题简单,容易回答

- Did you learn the tips I just shared with you? If yes, please type "1".

(3)节奏型话术:增强氛围,留住粉丝

- My friends, please give us some likes. We will do a lucky draw, which is our best seller—round-shaped ceramic vase with stand. 5 pieces for free to our fans for the first 10 thousand likes! Just follow us and hit the "like".

1.7 跨境直播客服话术

词汇积累 Vocabulary

序号	中文名称	英文名称
1	规格	specification
2	参考价	reference price
3	市场价	market price
4	均价	average price
5	现价	present price
6	原价	original price
7	总金额	total volume
8	在线付款	payment online
9	在线购物	shopping online

续表

序号	中文名称	英文名称
10	实体店	brick-and-mortar store
11	条码	bar code
12	说明书	description
13	产地	the point of origin
14	批号	date code
15	公差	tolerance
16	货号	article No.
17	等级	grade
18	一等品	first-class
19	标准	standard
20	检验报告	survey report
21	样品	sample
22	品质	quality
23	中等以上质量	above the average quality
24	中等以下质量	below the average quality
25	良好平均品质	fair average quality(F. A. Q)
26	低劣质量	inferior quality
27	优等质量	superior quality
28	全套样品	full range of samples
29	款式样品	pattern sample
30	色彩样品	color pattern
31	对等样品	counter sample
32	原样	original sample
33	复样	duplicate sample
34	免费样品	free sample

续表

序号	中文名称	英文名称
35	代表性样品	representative sample
36	商品目录	catalogue
37	宣传小册	pamphlet
38	花色搭配	assortment
39	增减	plus or minus
40	个数	number
41	净重	net weight
42	毛重	gross weight
43	皮重	tare
44	以毛作净	gross for net
45	面积	area
46	体积	volume
47	容积	capacity
48	长度	length
49	重量	weight
50	装运重量	shipping weight
51	溢短装条款	more or less clause
52	退款	refund
53	退货	return
54	换货	replacement
55	折扣	discount
56	好评	positive feedback
57	中评	neutral feedback
58	差评	negative feedback
59	取消交易	cancel the transaction
60	取消订单	cancel the order

直播客服英文话术

1. 首次接待

重点：表示欢迎，凸显亲切热情

• Dear friend, thank you for visiting our store. Please feel free to buy anything here. If you have any questions, just tell me, and I will try to help you.

• Hello, my friend, what can I do for you?

• Dear customer, you can place an order directly. Please contact me at any time if necessary.

• Dear friend, thank you for coming to our store. All the goods in the store are available.

2. 回复买家议价

重点：表示拒绝或提供议价条件，凸显客气

• Hi, all the items are of the lowest price. No bargain. Thanks.

• Dear friend, thanks for your message. If you buy more than three items, we can offer you a 5% quantity discount.

3. 关于缺货的问题

重点：表达歉意，提供替代选择

• Dear friend, I am sorry to tell you that the white color you chose has been out of stock. What about trying some other colors? The yellow one is also very popular with our customers.

• Thanks for your order. But the product you selected has been out of stock. Would you mind trying the product in this link? They are quite similar. If you don't need another item, please apply for "cancel the order". In this case, your payment will be returned in 5 business days. Sorry for the trouble and thanks for your understanding.

• If you choose another model, I will send you a free gift or a 5-dollar coupon.

4. 回复如何下单、如何付款、何时发货的问题

重点：提供有效帮助

- Dear, you can click into the page and find BUY NOW.

- You can use the electronic wallet to pay. If you still don't know how, please check it out with the Help Center.

- Your item will be delivered in two days and then the order status will be changed into SHIPPING.

5. 催付款,提醒买家确认订单

重点:表现客气,避免语句生硬带来负面效果

- Dear friend, we have got your order of AW0061. But it seems that the order is still unpaid. If there is anything I can help, please feel free to contact me. After the payment is effected, I will process the order and ship it out as soon as possible. Thanks.

- Please confirm your order, and we can arrange the shipment for you now. Usually, it will take 8 to 10 days for delivery. Please be patient and wait for a few days. Any other needs, please contact us without hesitation. Thank you and best regards.

6. 关于物流信息查询

重点:及时回复,提供最新信息

- Dear friend, your order has been sent out. Please pay attention to the logistic information.

- According to our records, your package has been shipped and is on its way. Please wait for some more time.

- I apologize that your package is delayed. We will contact the shipping company and let you have the latest news.

- Dear friend, your package has been sent out two days before. I apologize for the inconveniences and hopefully you will receive the package soon. If you have any problems, please don't be hesitate to contact me.

- Thank you for your understanding of our service. I will remind the warehouse to send a free gift. Looking forward to having your new order.

- Because we have many orders every day, in order to avoid sending the wrong item, we will ship goods according to the order date of booking. But don't worry.

When goods are sent out, we will send you a message.

7. 关于退换货

重点：积极配合、满足客户要求

• Sorry for the trouble. We accept return or exchange. Please send your item back to No. 504, Changning Road, Gubei District, Shanghai, China. Thank you.

• Ok. You can send it back for exchange. Please send your item back to No. 504, Changning Road, Gubei District, Shanghai, China. We will send you a new one after receiving your parcel. Please be aware that you will bear the cost of return shipping and re-send shipping.

8. 关于是否开具发票的问题

重点：提供发票或表示歉意

• Thanks for contacting us and sorry for keeping you waiting. Please find the invoice with this link.

• Sorry, we don't have invoice service.

9. 关于索要好评

重点：提供鼓励措施

• Dear friend, please give us five-star review if you are satisfied with our product. We will give you a free gift next time when you order.

10. 关于修改差评

重点：提出补偿，语言委婉

• Dear friend, thank you for purchasing items from our store. As per your review, I understand that you are not satisfied with the item. We really feel sorry about that and do hope to make it up for you.

We would like to provide you a full refund, and just hope you can update your review based on the full experience after we refund you. Looking forward to your kind reply. Thank you!

第二章
陶瓷产品英语直播

中国海关总署的统计数据显示，2022年6月，中国陶瓷产品出口数量为176万吨，出口金额为30.2亿美元；2022年1—6月，中国陶瓷产品出口数量为852万吨，出口金额为146.4亿美元。当前中国陶瓷产品出口主要类别包括日用瓷、艺术瓷、建筑卫浴陶瓷及先进陶瓷。

2.1 建筑陶瓷 Architectural Ceramics

词汇积累 Vocabulary

序号	中文名称	英文名称
1	背景墙	background wall
2	地砖	floor tile
3	广场砖	plaza tile/paving tile
4	户外地板	outdoor flooring
5	建筑陶瓷	architectural pottery
6	角砖	angle tile
7	墙砖	wall tile
8	外墙砖	exterior wall tile
9	内墙砖	interior wall tile
10	室内地砖	indoor floor tile
11	室外地砖	outdoor floor tile

续表

序号	中文名称	英文名称
12	腰线	border/decorative border tile
13	异形配件砖	timmers
14	泳池砖	swimming pool tile
15	3D瓷砖	3D ceramic tile
16	半抛光砖	semi polished tile
17	超白哑光抛光砖	porcelain super white matt
18	超感石	I-Touch rustic porcelain tile
19	瓷抛砖	porcelain polished tile
20	大板	big slab
21	大理石瓷砖	marble tile
22	单色砖	single color tile
23	仿古砖	rustic tile
24	浮雕瓷砖、雕纹花砖	embossed tile
25	负离子瓷砖	negative ion tile
26	花岗岩砖	granite tile
27	花色砖	multi-color tile
28	花砖	decoration tile
29	立体花纹砖	stereogram tile
30	六角砖	hexagonal tile
31	马赛克	mosaic
32	木纹砖	wood-look tile
33	耐磨砖	endurable/wearable tile
34	抛光砖	polished tile
35	抛晶砖	polished crystal tile
36	抛釉砖	glazed polished tile

续表

序号	中文名称	英文名称
37	情绪板	mood board
38	柔光砖	soft lustre tile
39	渗花砖	soluble salt tile
40	炻质砖	stoneware tile
41	水泥砖	cement tile
42	陶瓷锦砖	ceramic mosaic tile
43	图案砖	pattern tile
44	无光釉砖	mat glazed tile
45	无釉砖	unglazed tile
46	有釉砖	glazed tile
47	岩板	sintered board
48	复合轻纹瓷砖	composite light texture tile
49	板岩	slate
50	玻璃砖	glass block
51	尺寸	dimension
52	图案	pattern
53	防水的	water resistant
54	防火的	fire resistant
55	室内的	interior
56	室外的	exterior
57	自粘贴纸	self adhesive sticker
58	安装	install
59	瓷砖粘贴胶	tile glue
60	水泥	cement

话术演练 Language Skills①

产品规格介绍：

(1) These are 1.8″×1.8″ ceramic tiles with 15 different pattern designs.

(2) These tiles come with 5 shapes, circle, diamond, triangle, square and rectangle[1].

(3) More than 20 bright colors are mixed in one package.

(4) Red, pink, purple, and orange glass is more expensive to produce, but you will find those colors in equal quantity in our tile assortments[2].

(5) This is a wonderful package to create with. All the different shapes and colors make it easy to complete a project with just one package.

(6) The package weighs 17.6 oz, containing about 700-750 tiles.

(7) It is calcined[3] from high-quality absorbent[4] tiles, with fine texture and good water absorption.

(8) Our ceramic tiles have an ideal size of about 5 inches wide and about 0.4 inch thick.

单词解析：

1. rectangle ['rektæŋgl] n. 长方形（其他常见形状：圆形 circle、半圆 semi-circle、方形 square、三角形 triangle、菱形 rhombus、五边形 pentagon、六边形 hexagon、七边形 heptagon、梯形 trapezoid、平行四边形 parallelogram）

2. assortment [ə'sɔːtmənt] n. 各种各样（近义词：variety）

3. calcine ['kælsaɪn] v. 煅烧

4. absorbent [əb'zɔːbənt] adj. 易吸收（液体等）的

---

① 话术部分的例句中，带有下划线的内容表示主播可根据直播需要替换相应的内容。下同。

产品质量介绍：

(9) The glass tiles were cut from stained[5] glass sheets, so their vibrant[6] color will last nearly forever!

(10) Our pieces are quality cuts with smooth edges.

(11) There were no cracks[7] or chips[8].

(12) The rest are in excellent shape, and all are usable.

(13) The glazing is fine with no mars[9] or blemishes[10].

(14) They are clean, shiny, and ready to be used!

(15) Our tiles are made of durable ceramic.

(16) The ceramic tiles have a cork backing[11] to protect against unwanted damage and ensure stability on wood, glass, or even metal surfaces.

(17) The tiles themselves have a nice weight, and all seem to be pretty uniform and smooth.

(18) Nice and sturdy[12], it's ready for painting or whatever you want to do with it.

(19) This product is fired at high temperature.

(20) These arrived nicely packed in a box with foam around them.

(21) Its mysteriously shining surface brings this delightful play of light and shadow to an interior look, which makes it look significantly different with different lighting scenarios[13].

(22) This tile naturally looks good with modern and minimalism[14] styles, but its stylish[15] combination with other materials like glass or stone allows mixing it into various styles, from vintage[16] to country.

(23) Tiles may present slight variations on colors, designs and sizes due to its handmade process.

(24) The glaze is smooth and colorless.

(25) This tile has a high gloss[17] finish.

单词解析：

5. stained［steɪnd］*adj.* 沾有污渍的

6. vibrant［'vaɪbrənt］*adj.* 鲜艳的；明亮的（近义词：bright、lively、luminous）

7. crack［kræk］*n.* 裂纹（近义词：flaw、fissure）

8. chip［tʃɪp］*n.* 缺口；缺损处

9. mar［mɑː］*n.* 斑点

10. blemish［'blemɪʃ］*n.* 瑕疵（近义词：flaw、defect）

11. cork backing 软木衬垫

12. sturdy［'stɜːdi］*adj.* 结实的；坚固的（近义词：strong、not easily damaged）

13. scenario［sɪ'nɑːrɪəʊ］*n.* 情况（近义词：situation）

14. minimalism［'mɪnɪməlɪzəm］*n.* 极简主义

15. stylish［'staɪlɪʃ］*adj.* 时尚的；高雅的；雅致的（近义词：fashionable、elegant、exquisite）

16. vintage［'vɪntɪdʒ］*adj.* 最佳的；典型的；优质的（近义词：premium）

17. gloss［ɡlɒs］*n.* 光泽（近义词：luster、shine、burnish）

产品功能介绍：

（26）You can use the regular ceramic installation method such as ceramic tile glue or cement to install the tiles on the wall.

（27）All quality high temperature tiles are good for wet areas, pools, fountains and showers.

（28）They are good for both high and low temperatures.

（29）We offer available warehouse[18] designs for your projects.

（30）Our tiles are specifically designed to be used for arts and crafts with all sides perfectly smooth and with a matte finish[19].

（31）This tile is perfect for interior design, adding a premium[20] feel to installations.

（32）The pattern is applied to the top surface and can be cleaned with a mild detergent[21].

(33) You can use the tiles for many DIY decoration projects.

(34) Unglazed ceramic tiles are perfect for creating your own coasters with alcohol ink, markers, crayons[22], acrylic[23] paint, resin[24] and more.

(35) Design, create, decorate and customize your own coasters as gifts for family and friends.

(36) Tile set makes a great gift for any crafter[25] or hobby enthusiast!

(37) They are excellent applications for bathroom wall and floor, shower enclosure[26], bathtub surround, kitchen backsplash[27], and in-home accent wall[28].

(38) This tile backsplash is perfect for developing unhackneyed[29] and highly individual design.

(39) This tile can be used both as a creative focal[30] point to strike the eye immediately and a trendy[31] background to support the main design idea.

(40) It can be used on both sides, allowing you to draw on it, or stick personalized stickers on to create multiple styles.

(41) These coaster tiles with cork meet your various needs, which can not only protect your tabletop from scratching[32] but also are unique decorative coasters that will be a decent[33] gift for friends, family, lovers or craft enthusiasts.

(42) These absorbent stone coaster blanks are also super nice for painting and crafts.

(43) The application scenarios of composite[34] light pattern slabs are background wall, living room, study room, restaurant, balcony and commercial space.

(44) Blank smooth solid ceiling panel[35] is a universal fit to all kinds of interior decoration.

单词解析：

18. warehouse ['weəhaʊs] n. 仓库；货栈；货仓

19. matte finish 无光表面

20. premium ['priːmiəm] adj. 优质的（近义词：superior、high-quality、high-class、good、prime、choice）

21. detergent [dɪ'tɜːdʒənt] n. 洗涤剂

22. crayon [ˈkreɪən] n. 彩色铅笔（或粉笔、蜡笔）（近义词：colored pencil、chalk）

23. acrylic [əˈkrɪlɪk] adj. 丙烯酸的

24. resin [ˈrezɪn] n. 树脂；合成树脂

25. crafter [ˈkrɑːftə] n. 手工制作者

26. shower enclosure 整体淋浴房

27. backsplash [ˈbækˌsplæʃ] n. 壁砖

28. accent wall 特色墙

29. unhackneyed [ʌnˈhæknɪd] adj. 崭新的

30. focal [ˈfəʊkl] adj. 中心的；很重要的（近义词：central）

31. trendy [ˈtrendi] adj. 时髦的

32. scratching [ˈskrætʃɪŋ] n. 划损

33. decent [ˈdiːsnt] adj. 得体的；像样的

34. composite [ˈkɒmpəzɪt] adj. 复合的；合成的；混成的

35. panel [ˈpænl] n. 嵌板；镶板；方格板

产品服务介绍：

(45) We offer the self adhesive[36] stickers to you, which make your decor work so easy!

(46) We are professional at providing what you need for a better and happier life with affordable prices and amazing quality.

(47) We always aim at providing better design and more satisfying service.

(48) We have responsive after-sales service and professional customer service.

(49) We promise to make your purchase worry-free!

(50) We offer full service 24/7 for our customers for any product related issues, 1-year warranty.

单词解析：

36. adhesive [ədˈhiːsɪv] adj. 黏合的

直播模板 Template

_____ are high-fired ceramic tiles. They are polished, durable and glossy finished. _____ will not fade.

These tiles range in size from _____ to _____, with most being somewhere in the middle. The tile are _____ thick and cover approximately _____ square foot per bag.

The ceramic tiles for crafts come in at least _____ eye-catching colors including _____, _____, _____, _____ and _____. This ceramic are _____ different textures including the more expensive _____ and _____.

These ceramic tiles are highly glazed and durable! Smooth edges make them safe for use. _____ and _____ make them suitable for exterior applications. They are also great for _____ projects too.

Assorted shapes and textures allow for a high amount of variety when it comes to placement and need very little, if any, nipping to complete your _____ projects.

We provide self adhesive sticker together with the tiles, put the sticker to the tile, then stick tiles to your decor project.

2.2 卫浴陶瓷 Ceramic Sanitary Wares

词汇积累 Vocabulary

序号	中文名称	英文名称
1	卫生陶瓷	ceramic sanitary ware
2	花洒	shower
3	龙头	faucet
4	角阀	angle valve
5	感应龙头	automatic faucet
6	台式龙头	basin faucet
7	浴缸龙头	bathtub faucet
8	净身器龙头	cleaner faucet
9	暗式龙头	concealed faucet
10	四通冲洗阀	cross-joint flush valve
11	双把龙头	double handle faucet
12	快开龙头	fast on faucet
13	厨房龙头	kitchen faucet
14	脸盆龙头	lavatory faucet
15	淋浴龙头	shower faucet
16	恒温龙头	thermostat faucet
17	延时龙头	time-lapse faucet
18	脚踏式龙头	pedaled faucet
19	地漏	floor filler
20	淋浴器	shower fitting
21	脚踏式淋浴器	pedaled shower fitting
22	淋浴喷头	shower nozzle
23	脚踏式角阀	pedaled valve

续表

序号	中文名称	英文名称
24	面盆	wash basin/hand basin
25	落水管	sink drain
26	存水弯	trap
27	水箱盖	tank lid
28	浮球	float ball
29	浮球阀	ball-cock assembly
30	进水管	inlet tube
31	厕纸架	toilet paper holder
32	皂碟	soap dish
33	双碗厨房水槽	double bowl kitchen sink
34	水槽壁挂式小型半浴室角面盆	wall mount small half bathroom corner basin
35	陶瓷控制台水槽	ceramic console sink
36	碗形水槽	round vessel sink
37	小便器	urinal
38	浴缸	bathtub
39	浴室梳妆台陶瓷水槽	bathroom vanity ceramic vessel sink
40	智能坐便器	smart toilet
41	马桶盖	toilet cover
42	马桶座圈	toilet seat
43	低水箱	tank
44	置物吊柜	storage shelf
45	卫生间镜箱	bathroom cabinet
46	毛巾架	towel rack/rail
47	白色釉面陶瓷浴缸	white glazed ceramic tub
48	扁平陶瓷镊子	flat ceramic tweezers
49	灰色大理石陶瓷蜡烛碗	gray marble ceramic bowls for candle making

续表

序号	中文名称	英文名称
50	家用陶瓷涂层喷雾套件	home ceramic coating spray kit
51	尖头陶瓷镊子	pointed ceramic tweezers
52	宽齿陶瓷推刀头	coarse ceramic cutter
53	毛巾杆釉面陶瓷浴室配件套装	towel bar glazed ceramic bathroom accessory kit
54	实用刮刀	utility scraper
55	带过滤器和烧烤架的陶瓷厨房水槽	ceramic kitchen sink with strainer and grill
56	陶瓷马桶刷	ceramic toilet brush
57	陶瓷阀	ceramic valve
58	陶瓷加湿器	ceramic humidifier
59	陶瓷剃须皂碗/马克杯	ceramic shaving soap bowl/mug
60	陶瓷替换喷嘴	ceramic replacement nozzle
61	陶瓷香氛加热器	ceramic fragrance warmer
62	陶瓷圆顶滤水器	ceramic dome water filter
63	弯曲的陶瓷镊子	bend ceramic tweezers
64	专业陶瓷剪刀刀片	professional ceramic clipper blades
65	LED 夜灯	LED nightlight
66	热水器	water heater
67	除臭剂	deodorizer
68	暖风机	warm air dryer
69	自动的	automatic
70	近距离传感器	proximity sensor
71	自动冲洗	automatic flushing
72	多功能的	multi-function
73	不锈钢喷嘴	stainless steel nozzle
74	预冲洗	pre-rinse

续表

序号	中文名称	英文名称
75	冲水系统	flushing system
76	自动冲水系统	automatic flushing system
77	备用电池	backup battery
78	保暖座椅	heated seat
79	实时水温	real-time water temperature
80	座椅高度	chair height

话术演练 Language Skills

产品规格与特色介绍：

(1) The bathroom corner sink dimension is 12 inches long, 10 inches wide, 6 inches high.

(2) This soap dish measures 5.8×3.05×3.05 inches.

(3) The sink is packed with extra-thick foam on all sides in the strong corrugated[1] cardboard box[2] against shock and vibration[3].

(4) The drain hole center is 5 inches from the width edge.

(5) It is 6 inches from the faucet side edge and 4 inches from the opposite side edge.

(6) The package includes the wall mount sink and mounting hardware only.

(7) This item is of superb flushing operation with a 4-inch flush valve[4] and 3-inch fully glazed trapway[5] for an effective flush.

(8) Using only 1.25 gallons per flush, this toilet is WaterSense certified, which means you utilize 20 percent less water.

(9) 16-3/4″ rim height offers chair-height seating which makes sitting down and standing up easier for most adults.

(10) When properly installed, this toilet will sit less than 1 inch from the wall, at its closest point.

(11) The toilet is included, but it is not a slow close seat.

(12) Full/Half flush (1.6 GPF/1.1 GPF) is more energy efficient.

(13) A full suite of convenient features includes heated seat, nightlight, deodorization, instant warm water, warm-dryer, LED display, auto flush, and a remote control.

(14) Dual-flush technology allows you to choose between a full or partial flush.

(15) Upgraded to a 16″ seating height, it meets ADA code requirements, and makes sitting down and standing up easier for most adults.

单词解析:

1. corrugated [ˈkɔrəgeɪtɪd] *adj.* 起皱的
2. corrugated cardboard box 瓦楞纸箱
3. vibration [vaɪˈbreɪʃn] *n.* 振动
4. valve [vælv] *n.* 阀门
5. trapway [ˈtræpweɪ] *n.* 排污通道

产品质量介绍:

(16) The sink is made of premium quality ceramic, with lasting beauty and exceptional durability.

(17) Our sinks are made from the finest materials combined with one of the most advanced manufacturing operations in order to provide you with functional designs.

(18) This sleek[6] vessel sink has a smooth, non-porous[7] surface with a baked-on glaze for added durability and a high-gloss finish.

(19) Simply wipe the sink surface with a damp cloth to keep it look beautiful with minimal maintenance.

(20) We check the sink prior to shipping to make sure it has not been cracked or chipped.

(21) Durable and smooth ceramic wall mounted sink is easy to clean from every angle, inside, outside and even underneath.

(22) This small sink is made from vitreous[8] china, and white high gloss glaze finish.

(23) This small bathroom sink uses high quality kaolin and adopts unique 1280 ℃ high temperature clay grinding[9] technology, which ensures the uniformity[10] and durability of the porcelain body.

(24) The three-layer spray[11] glaze technology makes the color of the ceramic vessel sink brighter.

(25) Smooth and not rough, the surface is full of luster, and will not crack.

(26) The glaze with baking adds durability and high gloss.

(27) With low water absorption, dirt is not easy to adhere[12], so just wipe the surface of the sink with a damp cloth to maintain its beauty.

(28) This intelligent toilet has a fashionable appearance, which complements[13] your fashionable decoration style.

(29) The dual[14] flush square one-piece toilet is designed for luxury and performance.

(30) It features a concealed trapway with a sleek skirted design that is both visually appealing and makes for easy cleaning.

(31) This toilet has passed the ADA Compliant & IAPMO EGS & CUPC certification, safer to use and with quality assurance[15].

(32) This toilet seat is made of a durable plastic material.

(33) This one-piece toilet pairs minimalist style with the comfort.

单词解析：

6. sleek [sliːk] adj. 光滑的;线条流畅的;造型优美的

7. non-porous ['nəʊn'pɔːrəs] adj. 无孔的

8. vitreous ['vɪtriəs] adj. 玻璃质的;透明的

9. grind ['ɡraɪnd] v. 碾碎

10. uniformity [juːnˈfɔːməti] n. 统一(性);一致(性)

11. spray [spreɪ] v. 喷洒

12. adhere [ədˈhɪə(r)] v. 黏附

13. complement ['kɔmplɪmənt] v. 补足;使完美

14. dual ['djuːəl] adj. 双重的

15. assurance [əˈʃʊərəns] n. 保证;担保

产品功能介绍：

（34）This sink which allows just enough space to wash hands and brush teeth without wasting space is perfect for cloakrooms or bathrooms with limited space.

（35）Sink can either be mounted[16] to the wall or a place above a counter.

（36）The simple and elegant ceramic basin is with a bright white luster, providing modern and charm to any bathroom or bar dressing table.

（37）The sink with a unique U-shape, which can be installed in any corner, fully use your extra space, meet the needs of small and medium-sized apartments and create an ideal bathroom space.

（38）Our wall mount bathroom sinks make full use of every corner, and can be widely used in small bathrooms, half bathrooms, cloakrooms, washrooms, etc..

（39）The package includes a pop-up drain with ceramic surface which perfectly matches the size and color of the vessel sink.

（40）The sink drains quickly and effectively filters debris[17].

（41）Integrated[18] simple Nordic[19] style. you don't need to spend time and money to find a suitable drain. Just install and use it directly.

（42）The enlarged water storage area and rounded corner protection treatment bring you a comfortable feeling of use.

（43）You don't need to spend time and money to find a suitable drain and installation kit[20]. Just install and use it directly.

（44）Seat fastening system is easy to install with just a wrench[21].

（45）Heated seat can be adjusted to temperatures.

（46）Automatic flush when you walk away from the seat.

（47）It comes ready to install with bowl, tank, seat, wax ring[22] and floor hardware.

（48）ADA compliant[23] means it is ideal for the elderly and individuals with disabilities.

（49）Convenient nightlight function is convenient for you to find the toilet quickly and accurately at night.

（50）The powerful flushing function and self-cleaning function can meet your daily life needs.

(51) The heated seat cushion[24] will not make you feel cold in the toilet in cold weather.

(52) The product adopts a more energy-saving design, which is more water saving than the general toilet.

(53) Quick-release seat can be unlatched[25] from the toilet for easy removal and convenient cleaning.

(54) The strong dual flush function is very dependable, offering a never-failing performance.

(55) The seat and cover come with the toilet. There is no bidet[26] with this fixture[27].

(56) All intelligent designs are designed with comfort and convenience, like the automatic cleaning nozzle to bring you a different spa feeling, instant warm water, warm dryer, intelligent nightlight, heated toilet seat, remote control, deodorization[28], and LED display.

(57) With siphonic[29] jet[30] TECH, it can reduce waste accumulation and keep the toilet clean.

(58) Self-cleaning arc wand offers adjustable position, water pressure, and temperature.

(59) Front and rear wash modes provide warm water for cleansing.

(60) ECO energy savings mode ensures that electricity is never wasted.

(61) With heated seat and warm air drying, you will not feel cold in winter.

(62) Backup battery ensures normal flushing operation in case of a sudden power outage.

(63) One flush will create 2 siphons in toilet, emptying waste in toilet twice in a row to achieve no residual[31] flushing, which can meet the first and second water efficiency requirements of national standard.

(64) The super adsorption force of diatom[32] can not only adsorb odorous[33] particles[34] but also convert[35] harmful particles into oxygen particles, keeping a fresh bathroom environment at all times.

(65) When the toilet seat detect that the user is seated, the pre-wetting function will be pulse-on[36].

(66) The pre-wetting function will make the bowl cleaner and easier to clean.

(67) The soap dish drains quickly, effectively preventing the soap from becoming mushy[37].

单词解析：

16. mounted ['maʊntɪd] adj. 安装在……上的

17. debris ['debriː] n. 残渣

18. integrated ['ɪntɪɡreɪtɪd] adj. 集成的；综合的

19. Nordic ['nɔːdɪk] adj. 北欧国家的

20. kit [kɪt] n. 成套设备

21. wrench [rentʃ] n. 扳手；扳钳

22. wax ring 蜡环

23. compliant [kəm'plaɪənt] adj. (与系列规则相)符合的

24. cushion ['kʊʃn] n. 软垫；坐垫

25. unlatched [ʌn'lætʃt] adj. 未拴的

26. bidet ['biːdeɪ] n. 坐浴盆

27. fixture ['fɪkstʃə(r)] n. 固定设施(如房屋内安装的浴缸或抽水马桶)

28. deodorization [diːəʊdəraɪ'zeɪʃn] n. 除臭

29. siphonic [saɪ'fɔnɪk] adj. 虹吸式

30. siphonic jet 虹吸式喷射

31. residual [rɪ'zɪdjuəl] n. 残余物

32. diatom ['daɪətəm] n. 硅藻

33. odorous ['əʊdərəs] adj. 有气味的

34. particle ['pɑːtɪkl] n. 颗粒

35. convert [kən'vɜːt] v. (使)转变

36. pulse-on 启动

37. mushy ['mʌʃi] adj. 糊状的

产品服务介绍：

（68）As brand manufacturer, it's our great honor to give you enjoyable experience of this product.

（69）We're confident that you'll love this small vessel sink with pop up drain.

（70）We always adhere to the pursuit of original design and innovation, and customers' satisfaction is our responsibility.

（71）We hope that you have a pleasant shopping experience.

（72）We manufacture and provide ceramic sink and smart integrated toilets.

（73）3 years warranty for residential application and 2 years warranty for commercial application.

（74）We have been in business for more than 15 years and is a global leader in vitreous manufacturing working with some of the most recognizable OEM[38] brands in the world.

单词解析：

38. OEM (original equipment manufacturer) 代工（生产）

直播模板 Template

_____ is the ultimate expression of design paired with next generation technology. Its _____ and _____ belies its powerful functionality and advanced features.

With an ultra low profile and striking design features like _____ and _____, _____ becomes the centerpiece of any bathroom.

_____ is with advanced _____, _____, _____, and so much more.

_____ features an _____ seat and lid with automatic flushing, and a multi-function foot sensor for a hands-free toileting experience. Utilizing a two stage flushing system with an initial jet that circulates the bowl and then more powerful jet down the drain, _____ effectively and quietly removes waste. Its WaterSense certified flush can be automatic, or manually controlled via _____, _____, or _____.

With an _____ shaped stainless steel nozzle that minimizes splashback, air plasma bowl freshener, and an automatic bowl pre-rinse, _____ takes cleanliness to new heights. _____'s unique pre-rinse system sends a small jet of water around your toilet bowl to moisten the surface when you sit down. This prevents waste from sticking and keeps your bowl cleaner.

_____ programmable user presets, shortcut functions, and adjustable automations make _____ the most customizable yet user friendly smart toilet on the market.

2.3 日用陶瓷 Household Wares

词汇积累 Vocabulary

序号	中文名称	英文名称
1	茶杯	ceramic cup
2	茶杯碟	tea saucer
3	茶罐	caddy
4	茶壶	tea pot
5	茶碗	tea bowl
6	餐具套装	tableware set
7	茶具	tea set

续表

序号	中文名称	英文名称
8	咖啡具	coffee set
9	炒锅	saute pan
10	大浅盘	platter
11	饭碗	bowl
12	盖碗	bowl with cover
13	手绘瓷匙	hand painted ceramic spoon
14	工夫茶具	kung fu tea set
15	胡椒瓶	pepper jar
16	陶瓷马克杯	ceramic mug
17	花艺茶杯	ceramic cup with flowers blooming
18	带陶瓷涂层的绝缘咖啡旅行杯	insulated coffee travel mug with ceramic coating
19	把杯	handled cups
20	白茶盏	white teacup
21	不粘陶瓷切盘	non-sticky ceramic quiche plate
22	餐巾盆	nappy
23	餐具柜	buffet
24	奶壶	milk pot
25	奶油碟	butter disk
26	奶油缸	creamer
27	盐瓶	salt shaker
28	平盘	flat plate
29	深盘	deep plate
30	鱼盘	oval plate
31	水果盘	fruit plate
32	汤盘	soup plate

续表

序号	中文名称	英文名称
33	圆形瓦楞馅饼盘	round corrugated tart dish
34	糖罐	sugar pot
35	陶瓷搅拌碗	ceramic mixing bowl
36	大号陶瓷服务碗	large ceramic serving bowl
37	沙拉碗	salad bowl
38	陶瓷浆果篮	ceramic berry basket
39	陶瓷蜂蜜罐	porcelain honey jar
40	陶瓷刀具	ceramic knife
41	陶瓷剪刀	ceramic scissors
42	蒸锅	steamer
43	带盖平底锅	saucepan with lid
44	煎锅	frying pan
45	电动陶瓷钛煎锅	electric ceramic titanium skillet
46	陶瓷馅饼平底锅	porcelain pie pan
47	健康陶瓷不粘锅	healthy ceramic nonstick frying pan
48	带盖汤锅	stock pot with lid
49	陶瓷内锅	ceramic inner pot
50	电陶瓷茶壶	electric ceramic tea kettle

话术演练 Language Skills

产品规格介绍：

(1) This mug has a large capacity (21 oz), which will definitely meet your needs for office and home.

(2) A choice of 8 stylish colors makes it a great gift for holidays, birthdays and special occasions.

(3) This mug is simple but classic and we offer you 10 colors to choose from.

It's a great gift for your friends, family and colleagues on birthday, Christmas and more.

(4) This coffee mug holds up to 21 ounces[1], so you can fill it up and get to work on your next big project.

(5) This exquisite[2] tea set has 1 teapot, 4 cups, 4 saucers, 4 spoons, and 1 spray shelf.

(6) This tea set includes 1 teapot with stainless steel filter, 6 teacups, and 1 wooden tea tray.

(7) The weight is 3.8 pounds, and the dimension is 13.4×4.8×8.1 inches.

(8) The ceramic travel tea set is of a normal small size and exquisite for traditional kung fu tea ceremony.

(9) This size is suitable for business trip, outdoor picnic, with travel bag, and then you could enjoy your tea time at any time and place.

(10) The 13-pc ceramic tea set includes a teapot, 6 small teacups and 6 saucers with a beautiful floral pattern.

(11) Porcelain dinnerware sets for 6 include 9.7-inch dinner plates, 7.4-inch dessert plates, 8 oz soup plates, 7 oz cups, and 5.7-inch saucers.

(12) Dinner plate measures approximately 10 inches across. Bowl measures approximately 7 inches across and holds approximately 18 fluid ounces. Mug measures approximately 4 inches tall and holds approximately 12 fluid ounces.

单词解析：

1. ounce [aʊns] n. 盎司（重量单位，1盎司约等于28.35克）

2. exquisite [ɪkˈskwɪzɪt] adj. 精致的；精美的（近义词：artistic、delicate、fine）

产品质量介绍：

(13) Designed with strong ceramic construction, it is made of lead-free[3] and cadmium-free[4] high quality ceramic.

(14) They are dishwasher and microwave safe.

(15) Every mug is unique because of the special glaze technique.

（16）If you're looking for a well-made and sturdy coffee mug with a special design and big capacity, this coffee mug will be your great choice!

（17）Clean them up easily in the dishwasher without worrying about the finish wearing.

（18）The wide mouth makes it easy when you handwash it.

（19）It is prettier in person than in the pictures.

（20）This mug has a wonderful design while also being sturdy.

（21）After 1250 ℃ to 1400 ℃ high-temperature fire-forming and using Chinese millennium pottery production process, the use of high-quality raw materials help to create extraordinary quality.

（22）The glaze is smooth, elegant and relaxing, with a particularly simple and elegant aesthetic[5] design.

（23）It is made of durable high quality ceramic, fine texture[6], hard and durable, beautiful, simple and practical.

（24）For the protection of the pattern on the appliance, please do not place it in the dishwasher or microwave oven.

（25）The handle adopts traditional hand-woven rope, which is retro[7] and anti-hot, so you will feel comfortable when gripping[8] it.

（26）The tea set is made of natural high grade kaolin, durable and high quality.

（27）It is cadmium-free and lead-free, and has passed SGS test.

（28）Each component[9] is strictly made by experienced workers and inspected by our professional QC team[10].

（29）The package is with deep Asian culture presence.

（30）Our packaging is using the moulded PE foam to protect the cups well.

（31）Made of quality porcelain, our dinnerware sets are non-toxic and harmless, compatible[11] with cold and hot food, and safe for daily meals.

（32）High-temperature firing makes our dish set harder and crack-resistant.

（33）This gorgeous ceramic tableware, with exquisite color matching, gives a refreshing feeling.

(34) With a safe underglaze color process, it can directly touch the food, and the color is bright and lasting, giving you peace of mind.

(35) This set is made from high-fired earthenware and is microwave and dishwasher safe.

(36) It is Jingdezhen high white porcelain, and we also use a few kinds of colored clays by mixing various raw materials with locally available clays.

(37) This collection is made by using an environmentally friendly coloring agent, which is added in the clay.

(38) This collection products are made by using special materials for special processes.

(39) It is formed by adding a variety of oxides[12] to the base glaze formulation[13], as well as highly refined metals, quartz[14] pigments[15] and rare metallic[16] elements.

(40) These styles pay more attention to the safety and environmental protection performance.

(41) The body is casted[17] in a plastic mould.

(42) we must bisque fire[18] it and then we glaze it and fire it one more time.

(43) We do an overglaze paint for these gold specks.

(44) By firing at high temperatures in a kiln and keeping the heat in reasonable amounts, the reaction produces rich colors that are layered on top of one another.

(45) These glazes make use of specific materials such as magnesium oxide, a highly refined aluminium oxide.

(46) They are made by using high-temperature boron[19] solvents[20] and high-temperature calcium materials in the glaze.

(47) 3D printing technology uses contactless digital technology to control the spraying of decorative patterns.

(48) The entire set of products adopts underglaze color process.

单词解析：

 3. lead-free 无铅的

 4. cadmium-free 无镉的

 5. aesthetic [iːsˈθetɪk] adj. 美学的（近义词：esthetic、artistic）

6. texture ['tekstʃə(r)] n. 质地

7. retro ['retrəʊ] adj. 再度流行的

8. grip [ɡrɪp] v. 紧握；紧抓（近义词：hold fast、clutch）

9. component [kəm'pəʊnənt] n. 组成部分（近义词：part）

10. QC team 质检小组

11. compatible [kəm'pætəbl] adj. 兼容的

12. oxide ['ɒksaɪd] n. 氧化物

13. formulation [fɔːmjuˈleɪʃn] n. 配方

14. quartz [kwɔːts] n. 石英

15. pigment ['pɪɡmənt] n. 色素；颜料

16. metallic [mə'tælɪk] adj. 金属的

17. cast [kɑːstid] v. 浇注成型

18. bisque fire 素烧

19. boron ['bɔːrɒn] n. 硼

20. solvent ['sɒlvənt] n. 溶剂

产品功能介绍：

(49) This is a reactive glaze mug and every one is different.

(50) It is suitable for hot and cold drinks.

(51) Big handle can keep it from rotating when you try to hold the mug, which helps you enjoy your coffee comfortably.

(52) There's nothing quite like the smell of fresh brewed[21] coffee in the morning. If you like a little caffeine boost, this mug is the first thing you'll need.

(53) The cup conducts quite a bit of heat but the handle is large enough, so you can drink from it without touching the sides of the mug.

(54) This beautiful tea set comes with a beautiful gift box, you can give it as a gift to your friends and beloved ones on Valentine's Day, Father's Day, Mother's Day or birthday.

(55) This tea set brings both visual and taste enjoyment and is full of collector's value.

(56) It can be an eye-catching decoration for your living room, kitchen or study.

(57) With simple and elegant style, this Chinese tea set is suitable for afternoon tea, family gathering or friends gathering.

(58) This tea set with exquisite patterns can be used for drinking tea and coffee at home.

(59) The beautiful pattern design can add to the taste of life.

(60) This tea set is a perfect companion for enjoying your tea time.

(61) If you are a tea lover or looking for a Chinese tea set, this must be the smart choice for you.

(62) Built-in[22] density stainless filter[23] helps tea separation well, so that you can drink conveniently.

(63) A smooth spout helps water flow smoothly.

(64) This tea set which is cute and quaint[24] can be used as a decorative piece in your kitchen or living room.

(65) This tea set is aimed to provide an easy and healthy lifestyle—When you are travelling around, make a cup of tea, take a sip, enjoy your relaxed afternoon time with inner peace.

(66) It's also suitable for business trip, picnic, office, party, household and outdoor.

(67) The removable metal-mesh[25] tea infuser[26] cup can be placed in the top opening of the teapot to allow you to brew loose-leaf tea.

(68) Each plate bowl set is versatile[27] and suited for various dining environment. It brings a delightful dining experience for your family.

(69) The glazed dinner set is easy to clean and saves much dishwashing time.

(70) The low profile edges of dinnerware allow for a stackable[28] and space-saving.

(71) The dinnerware sets for 6 are matched with any kitchen style, ideal for a family gathering, restaurant, formal banquet, etc..

(72) Beautiful design and great quality will be present on your table with these

dinnerware sets.

(73) These shaped bowls are multi-purpose, perfect for displaying mousse[29], sauce, souffle[30], dipping, rice, pudding, oatmeal[31], and soups.

(74) The glaze is smooth and delicate, saving time and effort for cleaning.

(75) A variety of models are available to meet different living needs and can be used in microwave ovens and dishwashers.

(76) This classic design will complement traditional and contemporary tastes, which has made it a popular gift for weddings, holidays and other special occasions.

(77) Chinese tea ceremony culture is profound and has a long history.

(78) Chinese tea culture has a profound history.

(79) Our tea set is made from Jingdezhen, China, the Capital of Porcelain.

(80) All Chinese kung fu tea culture is for tasting, relaxing and relieving stress.

(81) Our porcelain dinnerware set with classic natural element style never goes out of fashion.

(82) It has always devoted itself to integrating modern ideas with traditional aesthetics for elegant porcelain with superb craftsmanship.

(83) Our designs range from classic to modern.

单词解析：

21. brewed [bruːd] *adj.* 煮的

22. built-in 内置的

23. filter [ˈfɪltə(r)] *n.* 过滤器

24. quaint [kweɪnt] *adj.* 古色古香的（近义词：antique、vintage）

25. metal-mesh 金属网

26. infuser [ɪnˈfjuːzə] *n.* 浸煮器

27. versatile [ˈvɜːsətaɪl] *adj.* 多功能的（近义词：multifunctional、multi-purpose）

28. stackable [ˈstækəbl] *adj.* 可叠起堆放的

29. mousse [muːs] *n.* 慕斯

30. souffle [ˈsuːfl] *n.* 蛋奶酥

31. oatmeal [ˈəʊtmiːl] *n.* 燕麦片

产品服务介绍：

（84）We are committed to providing our customers with high-quality tea sets.

（85）If you received any broken pieces, we guarantee to give you new replacement or full refund[32] including the shipping cost.

> **单词解析：**
> 32. refund [rɪˈfʌnd] n. 退款

直播模板 Template

The _____-piece porcelain ceramic coffee tea gift sets include _____ teapot, _____ sugar bowl, _____ creamer, _____ teacups, _____ saucers, and _____ teaspoons.

The teapot is of _____ oz, _____ inches by _____ inches by _____ inches; the teacup is of _____ oz, _____ inches by _____ inches; the sugar bowl is _____ oz, _____ inches by _____ inches; and the creamer is _____ oz, _____ inches by _____ inches.

The coffee sets are made of premium quality _____, lead free, safe and healthy. Besides, you can continue to buy exquisite _____ that make the coffee set easy to store, and space saving to keep your table neat and tidy.

Perfect contrast of _____ and _____ reflects the luxury of deep elegance. Delicate pattern with _____, _____ as well as _____ creates a high-grade and inviting atmosphere, making it a unique addition to any tea party or your cabinet.

Gorgeous _____-piece tea set is packed with an exquisite gift box, which makes it always be the best gift for your friends, family, tea or coffee enthusiasts, whether there is wedding, birthday, family reunion or any other party.

Emblazoned with the distinctive _____ pattern creating a peaceful ambience, which can help you relax your mind while enjoying afternoon tea with your friends.

2.4 艺术陶瓷 Art Ceramics

词汇积累 Vocabulary

序号	中文名称	英文名称
1	耳杯	winged cup
2	高柄杯	goblet
3	高足杯	stem cup
4	高足转杯	revolving stem cup
5	莲实吸杯	lotus-shaped sucking cup
6	荷叶形碗	lotus leaf-shaped bowl
7	鸡心碗	chicken heart-shaped bowl
8	菊瓣盘	chrysanthemum-shaped dish
9	瓷板	porcelain panel
10	薄胎瓷	eggshell porcelain
11	陈设瓷	ornamental porcelain
12	仿古瓷	imitation antique porcelain
13	克拉克瓷	kraak porcelain
14	八仙	eight immortals of ancient figures
15	挂毯	arras
16	壁画	mural painting

续表

序号	中文名称	英文名称
17	雕塑	sculpture
18	寿星	God of longevity with lad
19	本色釉	colorless glaze
20	变色釉	photo-chromic glaze
21	冰裂纹	ice crackle
22	茶叶末	tea dust
23	大观釉	Daguan glaze
24	斗彩	contrasting-color
25	珐琅彩	enamel decoration
26	仿石釉	imitation stone glaze
27	粉彩	famille rose
28	粉青	powder green
29	高白釉	brilliant white glaze
30	古彩	antique color
31	钴蓝釉	cobalt blue glaze
32	黑釉	black glaze
33	花釉	variegated glaze
34	祭红	sacrificial red
35	霁红	bright red
36	结晶釉	crystalline glaze
37	钧窑茄皮紫	Jun Kiln-eggplant purple
38	钧釉	Jun glaze
39	郎窑红	Langyao red
40	郎窑绿	Langyao green
41	裂纹釉	crackle glaze
42	琉璃釉	Liuli glaze
43	卵白釉	egg-white glaze
44	玛瑙釉	agate glaze

续表

序号	中文名称	英文名称
45	秘色	secret color
46	墨彩	ink-painted decoration
47	青花	blue-and-white
48	青花玲珑	underglaze blue decoration with rice grain pattern
49	青釉	green glaze
50	乳浊釉	opacified glaze
51	软彩	soft color
52	素三彩	plain three-color
53	唐三彩	three-color glazed wares of the Tang Dynasty
54	天蓝釉	clair-de-lune
55	天青釉	light sky-blue glaze
56	铜红釉	copper-red glaze
57	透明釉	transparent glaze
58	兔毫釉	hare's fur glaze
59	乌金釉	mirror black glaze
60	无光釉	matt glaze
61	五彩	five-color
62	新彩	new color
63	颜色釉	colored glaze
64	洋彩	foreign color
65	窑变釉	transmutation glaze
66	硬彩	hard color
67	釉里红	underglaze red
68	釉下五彩	underglaze five-color decoration
69	边沿	rim
70	口沿	mouth

话术演练 Language Skills

产品规格与造型介绍：

(1) The entire sculpture is elegant and luxurious[1], and the shape is exquisite and unique.

(2) The size of the ceramic abstract art decoration sculpture is 7.67 × 2.36 × 8.26 inches.

(3) The plate depicts a baby wearing a waistcoat[2] crawling in the midst of flowers, revealing an air of innocence.

(4) This piece is characterized by the rim on the round mouth and tapered[3] globular[4] body with unglazed base and mouth.

(5) The shoulders of the jar are painted with a black circular band of pomegranate[5] branches and two bands of swirling[6] patterns sandwiching[7] a band of dots.

(6) The center section is inscribed[8] with two verses of a poem in cursive[9] calligraphy[10]: "Wind of the Yangtze River urges the guest to set sail, but the rain retains the traveler in the lonely house."

(7) This piece is characterized by the flared dish-shaped mouth, narrow neck, and flattened globular body.

(8) It is covered in blue enamel[11] with a slight revealing of the bone in the ring base, which stands on triangular spikes[12].

(9) The enamel was intricately[13] applied to create a perfect fuse[14] to the bone, and the glowing saturated[15] color reveals the elegance of royalty.

(10) This piece is characterized by its flared mouth, narrow neck, and round body.

(11) The symmetric[16] line drawing is arranged into a diamond shape totem[17] of peony[18].

(12) The flower petals are decorated with combed lines[19] to create an effect of paper-cutting art.

(13) Contrast of black and white reveals glamour[20] in subtlety[21], and

sophistication in simplicity.

(14) A ewer[22] is a wine container with a handle and a spout[23] designed for pouring.

(15) The design of the ewer was mostly in the shape of a near sphere or flattened sphere without a lid, and the spout was large and short in hexagonal[24] or octagonal[25] shape.

(16) The large and short spouts are sculpted into the shape of a chicken head.

(17) Lines were drawn into the monochrome[26] bone piece in symmetric design and highly characteristic style.

(18) The lines were intricate and fluid, and the composition was symmetric and well-balanced.

(19) Celadon[27] is different from the powder jade green[28] wares of the Song Dynasty and is considered as the forerunner of the jade green color of official wares made by the Longquan Kiln.

(20) Regardless of the changes of green, the iron-brown spots are the distinctive[29] feature of celadon vases.

(21) The shape and size of these iron-brown spots are changeable, bringing out whimsical[30] and different feelings.

(22) These iron-brown spots are carefully designed and laid based on the makers' experience to display their skillful techniques and esthetic views.

(23) The tonal[31] harmony between the iron-brown spots and celadon background is the source of beauty.

(24) Portions of the mouth and ring base are unglazed, revealing the red color and solid construction of the bone.

(25) The vase is glazed in celadon, a gentle and pleasing green.

(26) A sculpture of a dragon girdles[32] the neck, waving its claws and staring into the space ready to fly.

(27) Along the rim of the niche[33], there are carved clouds and entwining[34] branches patterns.

(28) On the beam, there is a long-bead fortune crane[35] pattern.

(29) Over the pond, lotus leaves and branches are erecting[36] in the shape of plates for holding offerings[37].

(30) The neck is an octagonal cylinder[38] with the shoulders slightly tapered, the body is an octagonal sphere[39], and the slighted flared base has marks of sand.

(31) The full ewer is glazed in olive green.

(32) Inside, the lid and body is unglazed, revealing the grayish white bone.

(33) An octagonal spout with smooth edges is placed at the front shoulder position and a patterned curve at the rear side of the shoulder as the handle.

(34) The body is carved with floral patterns, the upper portion decorated with double banana-leaf impressions and the lower portion with double lotus-petal patterns.

(35) The transitional spaces between two smooth edges are decorated with begonia[40] patterns, and the gaps are filled with impressions of vines[41] and small flowers.

(36) The ground is glazed in brown and engraved with floral patterns.

(37) The back is unembellished and the base is glazed.

(38) The left side of the bottom has an irregular pattern of the bone covered with saggar[42] base soil[43].

(39) The rim is decorated with combed patterns of semi-swirls, and the wall is engraved[44] with patterns of waves.

(40) In the shape of a Chinese crab[45] (flower) at the edge, the potholder has a straight abdomen[46] and a flat bottom.

(41) The top of the eel-yellow[47] blank is coated with a brownish blank foundation, ash plaster[48], and lacquer[49], one on top of another.

(42) This sculpted figurine is characterized by unglazed pure white cavities and pressing finger marks.

(43) Without overwhelming embellishment, this sculpture presents a well-proportioned form and the demeanor[50] of spirituality with a touch of humanity.

(44) Our home decor vase sets of 3 feature different sized ceramic vases are available in 3 different sizes.

(45) The thinker sculpture has a simple and powerful shape, and adopts the

design method of abstract expression, which is suitable for various decorative styles and enhances the overall taste of the decorations.

单词解析：

1. luxurious [lʌɡˈʒʊəriəs] *adj.* 奢侈的（近义词：extravagant）
2. waistcoat [ˈweɪskəʊt] *n.* 背心
3. taper [ˈteɪpə] *v.* （使）逐渐变窄
4. globular [ˈɡlɒbjələ(r)] *adj.* 球形的；球体的
5. pomegranate [ˈpɒmɪɡrænɪt] *n.* 石榴
6. swirling [ˈswɜːlɪŋ] *v.* （使）打旋（swirling patterns 旋纹）
7. sandwich [ˈsænwɪtʃ] *v.* 把……夹在……之间
8. inscribe [ɪnˈskraɪbd] *v.* 在……上写（词语、名字等）；题；刻
9. cursive [ˈkɜːsɪv] *adj.* 草书的
10. calligraphy [kəˈlɪɡrəfi] *n.* 书法
11. enamel [ɪˈnæml] *n.* 搪瓷；珐琅
12. spike [spaɪk] *n.* 支钉
13. intricately [ˈɪntrɪkətli] *adv.* 错综复杂地（近义词：complicatedly）
14. fuse [fjuːz] *v.* 融合
15. saturated [ˈsætʃəreɪtɪd] *adj.* 饱和的
16. symmetric [sɪˈmetrɪk] *adj.* 对称的
17. totem [ˈtəʊtəm] *n.* 图腾
18. peony [ˈpiːəni] *n.* 牡丹
19. combed line 篦纹
20. glamour [ˈɡlæmə(r)] *n.* 吸引力
21. subtlety [ˈsʌtlti] *n.* 微妙
22. ewer [ˈjuːə(r)] *n.* 水壶
23. spout [spaʊt] *n.* （容器的）嘴
24. hexagonal [heksˈæɡənl] *adj.* 六角形的
25. octagonal [ɒkˈtæɡənl] *adj.* 八边形的
26. monochrome [ˈmɒnəkrəʊm] *adj.* 单色的；黑白的

27. celadon [ˈsɛlədɔn] n. 青瓷

28. powder jade green 粉青色

29. distinctive [dɪˈstɪŋktɪv] adj. 独特的（近义词：unique、typical）

30. whimsical [ˈwɪmzɪkl] adj. 异想天开的

31. tonal [ˈtəʊnl] adj. 色调的

32. girdle [ˈɡɜːdl] v. 围绕；环绕

33. niche [niːʃ] n. 壁龛

34. entwining [ɪnˈtwaɪnɪŋ] adj. 缠绕的

35. fortune crane 祥鹤

36. erecting [ɪˈrektɪŋ] adj. 竖立的

37. offering [ˈɔfərɪŋ] n. 祭品；供品

38. cylinder [ˈsɪlɪndə(r)] n. 圆柱

39. sphere [sfɪə(r)] n. 球体

40. begonia [bɪˈɡəʊnɪə] n. 秋海棠

41. vine [vaɪn] n. 藤蔓

42. saggar [ˈsæɡə] n. 匣钵

43. base soil 垫土

44. engrave [ɪnˈɡreɪv] v. 在……上雕刻（字或图案）

45. Chinese crab 海棠

46. abdomen [ˈæbdəmən] n. 腹部

47. eel-yellow 鳝鱼黄

48. plaster [ˈplɑːstə(r)] n. 灰泥

49. lacquer [ˈlækə(r)] n. 漆

50. demeanor [dɪˈmiːnə] n. 风度；举止；行为

产品质量介绍：

（46）White vases for decor are made from high-quality ceramic so that the vases have a good ability of corrosion resistance[51].

（47）In order to prevent damage during transportation, we have made a comprehensive foam protection.

(48) Tests have verified[52] the vase packaging can withstand multiple drops from a height of 1.8 meters without any damage.

(49) The process of electroplating ceramics makes the elegant ceramic abstract art sculpture more shiny, with green as the overall basic color, and gold as the embellishment[53].

(50) All these decorative vases are carefully made by hand with selected ceramic, so you will see how smooth and delicate they are.

(51) Our products are safety tested and certified[54] in the top laboratories.

(52) The statues are made of high-quality ceramic in elegant black and white.

(53) Such fine china is fired under extremely high temperature, and the sheer bone produces a crisp sound when clanked[55].

(54) The fine craftsmanship and the characteristics of glazed base testify[56] to its authenticity[57].

(55) The clay is fine and delicate.

(56) The entire ware is lustrous[58] and smooth, reflecting a majestic flavor.

单词解析:

51. corrosion resistance 耐腐蚀

52. verified ['verɪfaɪd] *adj.* 被证实的;被核实的

53. embellishment [ɪm'belɪʃmənt] *n.* 装饰;渲染(近义词:ornamentation、decoration)

54. certified ['sɜːtɪfaɪd] *adj.* 被证明了的;鉴定的;持有证明书的

55. clank [klæŋk] *v.* 发出叮当声

56. testify ['testɪfaɪ] *v.* 证明;证实

57. authenticity [ˌɔːθen'tɪsəti] *n.* 真实性;确实性

58. lustrous ['lʌstrəs] *adj.* 有光泽的(近义词:shiny、glossy、sheeny、glistening、shining)

产品功能介绍:

(57) The white vases can make your interior much more elegant and exquisite with one or two flowers.

(58) Simply put a flower in the vase now and make your home look warmer and brighter.

(59) Art is much less important than life. But what a poor life without Art!

(60) Even if you know nothing about floral[59] arrangement, this vase is the perfect choice to make your place much more exquisite and elegant.

(61) The vase is in a quite small size and can be suitable for many occasions, like candlelight dinner, family party, entrance decoration and so on.

(62) It is very suitable for living room decoration, bedroom decoration, study decoration, kitchen decoration, library, exhibition hall decoration.

(63) Ceramic abstract art decoration sculptures are eye-catching desktop decorations and are excellent gift ideas.

(64) The white ceramic vase has a very stylish design and is the perfect centerpiece for all rooms and occasions.

(65) Simple design creates affordable decorative lighting designs for your home.

(66) This table lamp is sized perfectly for your living room, dining room, bedroom, or foyer[60]!

(67) The ewer is used for serving not only wine but also soup and tea.

(68) This is a "pot holder" for court display purpose, made in a classic and elegant style.

单词解析：

　　59. floral [ˈflɔːrəl] *adj.* 花的

　　60. foyer [ˈfɔɪeɪ] *n.* (私宅或公寓的)前厅

产品服务介绍：

(69) Simple designs knows the value of practical lighting solutions, and our mission is to provide a wide selection of lighting designs you'll love.

(70) We follow all local and federal product regulations to keep your home and family safe.

直播模板 Template

_____ measures _____ inches high by _____ inches long and _____ inches wide and is just the right size to blend in perfectly with most home decor. It can be a decorative piece for a _____ or _____ or _____, or it can be an addition to any home decor.

This _____ is beautiful and eye-catching, presenting the artistic beauty of _____. This _____ can be perfectly combined with most home decor and can be used as decoration for your dining room, living room, office, coffee table, fireplace, TV cabinet, etc. .

_____ is made of ceramic material, not easy to break, comfortable to touch, and easy to clean. The bottom of _____ is designed with _____, which can be placed steadily without slipping and also protects the furniture.

_____ is a great holiday gift choice, which can be given as a precious gift to relatives, family, friends, art lovers on birthdays, Christmas, Thanksgiving and other special days. We guarantee that those who receive this _____ will be happy and impressed.

And our products are packaged with customized foam, plus a layer of carton packaging. Double-layer protection helps to avoid damage during transportation, so rest assured that the product will be delivered to you in perfect condition.

2.5　实战脚本 Script

Live Streaming Script of Household Ceramics

Hi guys, welcome to my live show. This is Joyce from ABC porcelain factory in Jingdezhen, China. If you would like to enjoy our live benefits, you can just follow our livestream. Best prices are all in Joyce's live.

First of all, I'd like to bring you this nice high-white glaze blue-and-white small handleless wine cup. Ten in one gift box. As you can see here, it is a small wine cup, the size is 3.5 cm high and 4.5 cm in diameter, taking about 45 ml liquor. Its high-white glaze is soft, transparent and delicate.

On the surface, it is painted with a lotus. I think you may know lotus stems up from mud but keeps itself clean; even the root is snow-white though it has been buried in the silt for a long time. So Chinese people believe lotus symbolizes a noble and unsullied personality. It is a perfect product for yourself or a gift for your friends. Now I'd like to show you the market price for a box of ten.

As you can see, it is 35 dollars. You can check on your phone, maybe find other suppliers and compare the prices if you want. But if you buy it in a retail store, the price will double or even higher. But today in Joyce's live, I'd like to mention, the price is 20 dollars. And we only have 100 boxes in stock. Because of this price, you know, it is the bottom price, so we only have a limited stock. Yeah, you still could join us. Now it is the time, ready? We are sold out! Thank you for your trust.

    Now I will show you our best sellers, cute cartoon mouse coffee mugs. It is great for collecting and gifting. This 11 oz ceramic mug is the perfect way to say "I'll be there for you" in this graduation season. This mug is unique and designed by our professional designer. It is the perfect size to drink your favorite coffee or tea. It is suitable for hot and cold drink. It is safe with dishwasher and microwave, so forget the hassle of washing it manually. Patty says, it is especially good for young people. Yeah, you are right. I think all girls will like it. The price for it is only 5.2 dollars each. The discount for today's live is buy 3 get 30% off. The lowest price ever! There are only 50 pieces left. Wish you good luck. Wow, we are sold out!

    Ok that would be all for today's live. You can follow me, follow Joyce, and subscribe to our channel, ABC ceramic factory. Ok, so have a nice day, bye bye, see ya.

第三章
服装类产品英语直播

中国海关总署的统计数据显示,2022年1—11月,服装(包括服装及衣着附件)累计出口额为1607亿美元,同比增长4.30%。2022年10月,中国帽类出口数量为9.02亿个,同比增长0.20%;出口金额为5.16亿美元,同比增长4.50%。2022年1—10月,中国帽类出口数量为93.79亿个,出口金额为56.16亿美元。2022年1—9月,中国鞋靴累计出口金额为430亿美元,同比增长27.50%。

3.1 服装 Clothing

词汇积累 Vocabulary

序号	中文名称	英文名称
	职业装	Business Wear
1	西装	business suit
2	修身版西服	slim fit suit
3	西装外套	blazer
4	西装套装	suit set
5	领带	tie
6	长裤	pants
7	直筒裤	straight leg pants
8	弹力裤	stretch pants
9	微喇长裤	bootcut pants
10	正装长裤	dress pants
11	裙子	skirt

续表

序号	中文名称	英文名称
12	连衣裙	dress
13	齐膝短裙	knee-length skirt
14	长裙	full-length dress
15	铅笔裙	pencil dress
16	裹身裙	wrap dress
17	衬衫	shirt
18	女士衬衫	blouse
19	polo 衫	polo shirt
20	大衣	(over) coat
21	带袖扣的男士衬衫系列	cufflinks
22	制服	uniform
23	工装裤	work pants
24	连体工作服	coveralls
25	厨师服	chef's jacket
26	外科手术服	scrubs
27	燕尾服	tuxedo
28	晚礼服	evening gown
	休闲服	Casual Wear
29	皮夹克	leather jacket
30	防风夹克	windbreaker
31	机车夹克	biker coat
32	（男子在非正式场合穿的）粗花呢西装外套	sports jacket/sports coat
33	派克大衣	parka
34	羽绒背心	down vest
35	羽绒服	down jacket
36	毛衣	sweater
37	开襟毛衣	cardigan sweater

续表

序号	中文名称	英文名称
38	套头毛衣	pullover sweater
39	针织衫	knit top
40	牛仔上衣	denim jacket
41	牛仔背心	denim vest
42	马甲	vest
43	套头衫	pullover
44	休闲裤	slacks
45	背带裤/工装裤	overalls
46	牛仔裤	jeans
47	保暖内衣	thermal undershirt
48	长款内衣	long underwear
49	睡衣裤	pajamas
50	睡袍	nightgown
51	家居服	loungewear
52	polo 裙	polo dress
53	长衬裙	full slip
54	半身短衬裙	half slip
55	打底裤/紧身裤	leggings
56	塑身裤/紧身衣	body shaper/girdle
57	毛巾袜	terry socks
58	长袜	stockings
59	短袜	ankle socks/anklets
60	水手式短袜/男士半腿袜	crew socks
	运动服	Activewear
61	运动套装	sweatsuit
62	运动裤	sweatpants/athletic pants
63	田径服	track suit
64	慢跑服	jogging suit

续表

序号	中文名称	英文名称
65	慢跑裤	jogging pants
66	跑步短裤	running shorts
67	女紧身裤/七分裤	capris
68	运动衫/连帽衫	sweatshirt/hoodie
69	卫衣	badge of sport
70	泳衣	swimsuit/bathing suit
71	男式泳裤	swimming trunks
72	瑜伽服	yoga outfit
73	瑜伽裤	yoga pants
74	运动文胸	sports bra
75	运动背心	active tank
76	背心	tank top
77	短裤	shorts
78	冲锋衣	interchange jacket
79	速干衣	dry-fit T shirt
	服装图案	**Apparel Pattern**
80	动物印花	animal print
81	菱形花纹	argyle
82	迷彩	camouflage
83	卡通	cartoon
84	方格	checkered
85	V形图案	chevron
86	花卉	floral
87	水果	fruit
88	几何图形	geometric
89	心形	heart
90	千鸟格	houndstooth
91	人字形花纹	herringbone

续表

序号	中文名称	英文名称
92	字母印花	letter print
93	摩尔纹/水波纹	moire
94	佩斯利(羽状)图案	paisley
95	格纹	plaid
96	波点	polka dots
97	星形	star
98	条纹	stripe
	服装材质	**Clothing Material**
99	棉	cotton
100	亚麻	linen
101	羊毛	wool
102	羊绒/开司米	cashmere
103	丝绸	silk
104	皮革	leather
105	牛仔布/蓝粗棉布	denim
106	蕾丝	lace
107	缎面	satin
108	网纱	mesh
109	天鹅绒	velvet
110	灯芯绒	corduroy
111	尼龙	nylon
112	马海毛	mohair
113	骆马绒	vicuna
114	聚酯纤维/涤纶	polyester
115	维纶	vinyon
116	氨纶	spandex
117	腈纶	acrylic
118	腈氯纶	modacrylic

续表

序号	中文名称	英文名称
119	人造丝	rayon
120	丙纶	polypropylene fiber
	颜色	**Color**
121	黑色	black
122	深灰色	charcoal
123	灰色	gray
124	白色	white
125	粉红色	pink
126	紫红色	fuchsia
127	红色	red
128	梅红色	plum
129	紫色	purple
130	藏青	navy
131	蓝色	blue
132	奶油色/米色	cream
133	珊瑚色	coral
134	杏色	beige
135	绿松石色	turquoise
136	蓝绿色	teal
137	祖母绿	emerald
138	深棕色	dark brown
139	棕色	brown
140	橄榄绿	olive
141	锈红	rust
	特殊服装尺码	**Special Clothing Size**
142	高大款	big&tall
143	健壮款	husky
144	小号	juniors

续表

序号	中文名称	英文名称
145	瘦小款	petite
146	加大款	plus size
	服装版型	Apparel Fit Type
147	宽松	loose
148	修身	fitted
149	直筒	straight

话术演练 Language Skills

产品材质介绍：

（1）Rayon and polyester, these materials are thick and comfortable, keeping you warm in the fall and winter.

（2）The long sleeve[1] shirt is made with high quality flannel[2].

（3）The flannel fabric is thick, wear-resistant, and has good warmth retention.

（4）Filled with 700 FP[3] 80% down, this men down puffer jacket[4] is both lightweight and warm.

（5）Completed with 100% nylon construction with a durable water-repellent[5] finish, full front zip closure[6] and elastic[7] binding[8] cuffs[9], this down puffy jacket performs well for wind and rain protection.

（6）The fabric[10] is soft, stretchy[11] and comfortable.

（7）Do not bleach and hang dry.

（8）Its material is breathable, flowy[12], lightweight, soft and stretchy.

（9）The color of fibers for undyed[13] white and undyed natural come completely from cashmere goat so the color of each piece might be slightly different.

（10）Superior soft, ultra warm and lightweight extra long staple fiber from Inner Mongolia[14] can ensure highest anti-pilling[15] performance.

（11）All of our collections get their start with happy, healthy Inner Mongolian goats.

（12）When you pay for 100% cashmere, you should get 100% cashmere.

（13）These are the essential and best-selling styles of 100% pure cashmere collection that you won't want to miss.

（14）These women's hoodies are made of 55% cotton and 45% polyester.

> **单词解析：**
>
> 1. sleeve [sliːv] *n.* 袖子
>
> 2. flannel [ˈflænl] *n.* 法兰绒
>
> 3. FP(filling power) 蓬松度
>
> 4. down puffer jacket 羽绒服（puffer 是河豚的意思，用来形容羽绒服应该是因为穿着羽绒服容易显胖）
>
> 5. water-repellent [ˈwɔːtə rɪpelənt] *adj.*（材料等经处理后）防水的（近义词：water-resistant）
>
> 6. zip closure 拉链
>
> 7. elastic [ɪˈlæstɪk] *adj.* 有弹力的；有弹性的
>
> 8. binding [ˈbaɪndɪŋ] *adj.* 捆绑的
>
> 9. cuff [kʌf] *n.* 袖口（cuffs = handcuffs）
>
> 10. fabric [ˈfæbrɪk] *n.* 织物；布料（近义词：material、cloth、textile）
>
> 11. stretchy [ˈstretʃi] *adj.* 有弹性的（近义词：stretchable）
>
> 12. flowy [fləʊɪ] *adj.*（尤指头发或衣物）松垂的；飘逸的
>
> 13. undyed [ʌnˈdaɪd] *adj.* 未染色的；天然色的（近义词：unbleached、uncolored、natural color）
>
> 14. Inner Mongolia [ˈɪnə(r) mɔŋˈɡəʊliə] 内蒙古
>
> 15. anti-pilling [ˈænti ˈpɪlɪŋ] *adj.* 抗起球的

产品规格与特征介绍：

（15）US SIZE，Small =（US 4-6），Medium =（US 8-10），Large =（US 12-14），X-Large =（US 16-18）.

（16）It accommodates[16] extensive range size chart from size 00 to size 22.

（17）Jacket length is 22-25 inches and skirt length is 29-30 inches.

（18）This formal suit set is slim fit[17] cut style from 3D draping[18], and thus it will be a little tighter than regular suits.

(19) This design perfectly reveals the navel[19], and is equipped with a high-waist[20] belt design to trim the waist line and visually[21] elongate[22] the waist ratio[23].

(20) This long sleeve shacket[24] jacket is featured with plaid[25] print, shacket, button down, soft fabric, loose fitting and casual style.

(21) Cold-weather style is easy with this versatile[26] water-resistant lightweight puffer jacket featuring a full-zip front and stand-up collar.

(22) With 80% down, this men down puffer jacket is both lightweight and warm. The quilted design can better lock the warmth and also keep you from being bulky[27].

(23) 2 secure zip pockets and 2 inner pouch pockets[28] can store your essentials and warm your hands.

(24) The lightweight and flowy material with simple and fashion design makes this dress suitable for most women.

(25) This women's cocktail dress[29] features with classic round neck and 3/4 sleeve.

(26) The length comes right above the knee.

(27) We are in love with its comfortable fit and pretty floral print.

(28) This casual plain sweater top featuring short sleeves, make you an elegant and fashion look.

(29) It is simple in layering[30] and styling.

(30) We design our trendiest pieces with your feeling comfortable in mind.

(31) Our collections deliver sophisticated[31] looks that you will love.

(32) This men zip up hoodie is fade resistant and supports machine wash and tumble dry[32].

单词解析：

16. accommodate [əˈkɔmədeɪt] v. 容纳；为……提供空间

17. slim fit 修身款

18. draping [ˈdreɪpɪŋ] n. 立体裁剪

19. navel [ˈneɪvl] n. 肚脐

20. high-waist [haɪ weɪst] adj. 高腰的（近义词：high-waisted）

21. visually ['vɪzjuəli] adv. 视觉上

22. elongate ['iːlɔŋgeɪt] v.（使）变长；伸长；拉长（近义词：lengthen）

23. ratio ['reɪʃiəʊ] n. 比例

24. shacket [ʃækɪt] n. 结合衬衫的挺阔外形和夹克外套休闲感的新款上衣（shirt + jacket = shacket）

25. plaid [plæd] n. 格子图案

26. versatile ['vɜːsətaɪl] adj. 多功能的

27. bulky ['bʌlki] adj. 笨重的

28. pouch pocket 囊袋型口袋；钱包型口袋

29. cocktail dress（正式社交场合穿的）短裙

30. layering ['leɪərɪŋ] n. 层次

31. sophisticated [sə'fɪstɪkeɪtɪd] adj. 复杂巧妙的

32. tumble dry 烘干

产品功能介绍：

(33) This ultra-soft, moisture-wicking[33] knit[34] fabric provides a versatile layer with a loose and light fit for maximum range of motion.

(34) This is an athletic fit that sits close to the body for a wide range of motion, designed for optimal[35] performance and all day comfort.

(35) You can pair this shirts with a variety of tank tops, bodysuit, jeans, denim shorts, jeggings[36], sneakers[37] or boots to complete your casual look.

(36) It is perfect for casual daily life, shopping, street wear, working, office, school, holiday, vacation, night out, and outdoor.

(37) Flare[38] leg allows you to move without restriction, effectively helps hide the defects of the calf[39], and creates the contour[40] and slender appearance of the popular line.

(38) This fall fashion hoodie is the ideal choice in your wardrobe, and one of the best choice for autumn and winter outfits.

(39) So versatile is our flannel button down pocket top that can be worn open as

a jacket or closed as a top!

(40) It can be tied at the waist or wrapped around waist.

(41) The ultra light short winter jacket can be layered over your shirts in chilly days.

(42) It will keep you warm at home or on a morning jog around your neighborhood.

(43) Classic elegant simple style with knee length and round neck is great for baby shower, casual, wedding, photography and parties during pregnancy[41].

(44) This dress is loose and casual, comfortable and cool for summer.

(45) Pair this cute dress with your fave[42] sandals and accessories[43].

(46) Made with durable and comfortable flex denim for added ease of movement, these versatile jeans are made to last through everyday wear.

> 单词解析:
>
> 33. moisture-wicking ['mɔɪstʃə(r) 'wɪkɪŋ] adj. 快干的
>
> 34. knit [nɪt] n. 针织衫
>
> 35. optimal ['ɔptɪməl] adj. 最优的,最佳的（近义词:optimum、the best）
>
> 36. jeggings ['dʒegɪŋz] n. 牛仔打底裤
>
> 37. sneakers ['sniːkəz] n. 运动鞋
>
> 38. flare [fleə(r)] n. 喇叭型
>
> 39. calf [kɑːf] n. 小腿肚（身体部位:neck 脖子、shoulder 肩膀、arm 胳膊、elbow 肘部、forearm 前臂、wrist 手腕、abdomen 腹部、hip/buttocks 臀部、thigh 大腿、knee 膝盖）
>
> 40. contour ['kɔntʊə(r)] n. 外形;轮廓
>
> 41. pregnancy ['pregnənsi] n. 怀孕（近义词:maternity）
>
> 42. fave [feɪv] adj. 特别喜爱的
>
> 43. accessory [əkˈsesəri] n. 附件

产品服务介绍:

(47) This high waist yoga pants are sold with a 30-day, full-money-back warranty[44] and can be returned with no questions asked.

(48) This item may run small. Please size up if you prefer a loose fit model.

(49) Your satisfaction is our top priority[45].

(50) We sincerely hope that you would be completely satisfied with our suits and service!

> 单词解析：
>
> 44. warranty ['wɔrənti] n. 担保；（商品）保用单
>
> 45. priority [praɪ'ɔrəti] n. 优先事项；当务之急；首要事情；重点

直播模板 Template

模板一

Premium _____ has been brushed on both sides for a luxuriously soft and plush feel. Made with _____ and _____, its coziness is perfect for lounging inside or for layering outside in cooler weather.

Its shape has been fitted for the ultimate relaxed look. With dropped shoulders and a _____ pocket, _____ should be a staple in every woman's wardrobe. You can pair it with jeans for a laid-back look, or your matching sweatpants for ultimate comfort. And _____ is sewn at the _____ to adhere to your body better than the regular _____.

This timeless classic comes in _____, _____, _____, and _____ (different colors). They are available in sizes _____ to _____.

Our model is _____ and wears size _____.

模板二

The next item is what I am wearing today. You see, it is a bodycon dress. You must have a look at its material and designs. Its material is _____, so it has a good breathability but will not cause any shrink. It is of good quality and I can check it out for you. When I pull the sleeve, like this, you see it's stretchy and flexible. Now let me show you the design. It is of _____ style. You can see its _____ patterns make this _____ classy and timeless. And here the sleeves are of _____ length. It is great for showing off your _____ and _____, like this. And have a look at its neck. A _____ neckline paired with a _____ length makes me modesty while looking sexy. _____ says it looks wonderful. Thank you, _____. In fact, I am only _____ feet high and weigh about _____ pounds. If you have a better figure than me, this one will perfectly show your curve and make you look hot. Trust me, girls, it is a must have in your wardrobe. If you like it, hurry up, the stock of this one is not too much.

3.2 鞋类 Shoes

词汇积累 Vocabulary

序号	中文名称	英文名称
1	靴子	boots
2	过膝靴	thigh high boots
3	及膝靴	knee high boots
4	雨靴	Wellington boots
5	牛仔靴	cowboy boots
6	雪地靴	ugg boots
7	罗马靴	gladiator boots
8	绷带靴	bondage boots
9	坡跟靴	wedge booties
10	马丁靴	Dr. Martens
11	切尔西靴	chelsea boots
12	洞洞鞋	crocs
13	罗马鞋	gladiators
14	木底鞋	clogs
15	拖鞋	mules
16	露跟女鞋（后帮为窄带）	slingbacks
17	僧侣鞋	monk
18	乐福鞋	loafer
19	帆布鞋	converse
20	牛津鞋	oxford
21	芭蕾鞋	ballerina flats
22	一脚蹬	slip-on
23	软帮皮鞋	moccasin

续表

序号	中文名称	英文名称
24	帆船鞋	dockside
25	锥形跟	cone heel
26	多尔赛鞋	d'orsay
27	踝带	ankle strap
28	T带	T-strap
29	露趾	open toe
30	坡跟	wedge
31	粗跟	chunky heel
32	果冻鞋	jelly
33	细跟	stiletto
34	猫跟	kitten heel
35	水台	platform
36	鱼嘴鞋	peep toe
37	平底无带女鞋	pump
38	尖头鞋	scarpin
39	玛丽珍鞋	Mary Janes
40	人字拖	flip flops
41	运动鞋	trainers/sneakers
42	慢跑鞋	running shoes
43	足球鞋	football boot
44	篮球鞋	basketball shoes
45	网球鞋	tennis shoes
46	鞋带	lace
47	鞋底	sole
48	鞋舌	tongue
49	鞋面	vamp
50	鞋跟	heel

话术演练 Language Skills

产品材质介绍：

(1) Our women's flat shoes have 2x memory foam foot-bed, making you feel like walking on the clouds.

(2) Textile sponge[1] lining[2] allows your feet to breathe all day.

(3) This product is made with a series of high-performance recycled materials.

(4) Our shoes select high-quality real leather upper, soft lining, breathable insole and anti-skid[3] and wear-resistant[4] rubber sole to bring you the ultimate[5] experience.

(5) Each pair of shoes is strictly handmade and painted by experienced craftsmen.

(6) With breathable and soft lining, our men's dress shoes can reduce foot friction[6] and keep your feet odor free and dry every day.

(7) Our ankle boots are modeled on classic Chelsea styles, but given a twist with chunky block heels[7].

(8) The rubber outsoles are cleverly framed with reinforced toe caps for practical wear.

(9) Classic snow boots are made of suede[8] leather upper.

(10) Anti-skid rubber outsole allows you to enjoy yourself well.

(11) They feature premium quality stretchy faux suede, almond toe[9], high chunky heel and partial side zip closure.

(12) The pumps for women of upper material is an artificial[10] PU leather, and the sole is made by anti-slip rubber.

(13) Our shoes are fully ASTM F2913-11 tested, and CE certified.

(14) Using a combination of leather, synthetic[11] leather and rubber, our design draws inspiration from mid-1980s basketball shoes.

单词解析：

1. sponge [spʌndʒ] *n.* 海绵
2. lining [ˈlaɪnɪŋ] *n.* 衬层；内衬；衬里
3. anti-skid [ˈænti skɪd] *adj.* 防滑的
4. wear-resistant [weə(r) rɪˈzɪstənt] *adj.* 抗磨损的
5. ultimate [ˈʌltɪmət] *adj.* 终极的；最好的（近义词：best）
6. friction [ˈfrɪkʃn] *n.* 摩擦
7. block heels 方跟
8. suede [sweɪd] *n.* 绒面革；仿麂皮（faux suede 绒面革）
9. almond toe 杏仁鞋头
10. artificial [ˌɑːtɪˈfɪʃl] *adj.* 人工的；人造的
11. synthetic [sɪnˈθetɪk] *adj.* 人造的；（人工）合成的（近义词：man-made、artificial）

产品规格介绍：

（15）These modern dress shoes for men come in various classic colors, such as black, brown and dark brown, suitable for formal, wedding, work, business and casual.

（16）The sexy high heel women's pumps has an approximately 3.28 inches stiletto heel, so they can perfectly show off your sexy figure.

（17）If between sizes, please order 1/2 size down from your usual size.

（18）Classics are unisex[12]. Ladies, please order two sizes down from your normal street shoe size.

（19）Ankle snow boots are with the boot height of about 8.8 inches.

（20）These over-the-knee boots are available in several colors and you can wear them with leggings[13] or jeans for your everyday look.

（21）The heel height of uniform dress shoes is about 1.96 inches.

（22）The gorgeous platform pumps are featured by ankle strap, mid chunky heel, platform, round toe, and buckle[14].

（23）Please check our size chart and choose your correct size before order, ensuring you could receive comfortable shoes.

(24) Because of the various shoe sizing systems between different manufacturers, it is never a good idea to buy shoes based solely on the shoes size you usually wear.

(25) These men's and women's crocs offer a roomy fit and we recommend ordering a size down to the next largest whole size.

(26) Heel height is approximately 1.18 inches and shaft[15] measures approximately 11.4 inches from arch.

(27) Women PU working loafer flats are true to size.

> 单词解析：
> 12. unisex ['ju:nɪseks] adj. 男女皆宜的；不分性别的
> 13. legging ['legɪŋ] n. 打底裤
> 14. buckle ['bʌkl] n. 搭扣
> 15. shaft [ʃɑ:ft] n. 鞋筒

产品特征与功能介绍：

(28) Special ankle protection design, is not only comfortable, but also sweet and warm like lover's hug.

(29) These women's flats offer a minimalist, sophisticated solution for easy fashion, matching all outfits and occasions.

(30) These selected synthetic sole is solid enough to wear from spring to winter, and the soft microfiber makes women's dress flats flexible and lightweight.

(31) These flats shoes with sponge cushion can protect your ankles. You do not need to spend extra $5 or even $10 to buy a sticker which can drop off sometimes.

(32) Thick cushioned latex[16] insoles make walking more comfortable.

(33) The rubber outsole of men's oxford shoes is flexible, lightweight and wear resistant, providing good cushioning, adding shock absorption and relieving foot fatigue.

(34) Back zipper is for easy slip on and take off.

(35) The adjustable crossed straps are designed with buckle and elastic[17] to create a custom fit and provide support for the feet and ankle.

(36) Our closed toe heeled sandals are particularly different in generous

cushioning and a wider toe box, which provide all-day comfort walking.

(37) The pair of criss-cross[18] strappy[19] pumps are the most classic design but never go out of style and will be sure turn heads wherever you go.

(38) Update your personal style with a pair of classic black high heels, or elegant nude high heels.

(39) Such a pair of women's ankle strap high heels is not only a fashion must-have for modern wardrobes, but also a perfect gift for your loved ones.

(40) Short winter boots with warm lining and soft insole can keep your feet warm all day.

(41) These fitted thigh high boots will give the lengthening look to your legs.

(42) These over-the-knee boots feature a comfortable cushioned insole that snuggles[20] your feet to provide comfort with every step.

(43) The crocs for men and women feature lightweight iconic crocs comfort.

(44) These slip-on clogs are easy to take on and off, while being extremely durable.

(45) The classic clogs are not only the most comfortable shoes for women and men but also easy to clean.

(46) These shoes can be worn all year round. They're so versatile, you can wear them for jogging, bike riding, hiking, or for your workout at the gym, you can also wear them for parties and other occasions.

(47) This canvas loafer is lightweight, foldable and comfortable to wear.

(48) We always adhere to the concept of manual color process, so as to contribute the shoes with elegant color and high quality.

单词解析：

16. latex ['leɪteks] n. （天然）乳胶；（尤指橡胶树的）橡浆；人工合成的乳胶（用于制作油漆、黏合剂等）

17. elastic [ɪ'læstɪk] adj. 有弹力的；有弹性的

18. criss-cross ['krɪs krɔs] adj. 十字交叉的

19. strappy ['stræpi] adj. 有带子的

20. snuggle ['snʌgl] v. 紧贴

产品服务介绍：

(49) Our goal always remains the same: to provide the perfect shoes that cater to all your needs.

直播模板 Template

If you are looking for a pair of _____ for _____ which is _____, _____ and _____, these _____ are for you. The super soft upper made with _____ is _____, _____ and _____, making standing and walking an enjoyment.

To offer you the best _____ and _____ experience, we designed our _____ with _____ and _____ outsoles, which is of _____ and _____ at the same time. The soles of our _____ have _____ patterns on the bottom to improve slip and wear resistance while also preventing fatigue due to long-time walking or standing.

Our shoes are equipped with _____ that offers _____ to the feet, which enhances the stability of your each step while walking or jogging, preventing ankle sprains and promising a comfortable wearing experience.

Constructed of high-quality _____, these _____ are built to last. You can wear these _____ with confidence knowing that they're wear resistant while improving your performances.

These _____ are available in stylish colors that are perfect to match with your daily outfits. Available in whole sizes only. If between sizes, please order 1/2 size down from your usual size.

3.3 帽子 Hats and Caps

词汇积累 Vocabulary

序号	中文名称	英文名称
1	帽子	hat/cap
2	运动帽	sports cap
3	棒球帽	baseball cap
4	太阳帽	sun hat
5	卡车帽	truck cap
6	高尔夫球帽	golf cap
7	草帽	straw hat
8	巴拿马帽	panama hat
9	钟形女帽	cloche hat
10	软呢爵士帽	fedora hat
11	大檐帽	large brimmed hat
12	护耳帽	earcuff hat
13	礼帽	bowler hat
14	针织帽	knitted hat
15	时装帽	fashion hat
16	盆帽	bucket hat
17	贝雷帽	beret
18	鸭舌帽	flat cap
19	羊毛帽	fleece hat
20	渔夫帽	bucket hat
21	安全帽	hard hat
22	毛皮帽子	fur hat
23	童帽	kid hat

续表

序号	中文名称	英文名称
24	泳帽	swimming cap
25	帽边	hat brim
26	帽檐	cap peak
27	帽顶	top of hat
28	帽舌	peak/visor
29	舌面	upper peak
30	舌底	under peak
31	弯帽舌	curled peak/curved brim
32	平帽舌	flat peak/brim
33	帽护耳	earflap
34	帽里	lining
35	全里	full lining
36	半里	half lining
37	气眼	eyelet
38	锁眼	sewn eyelet
39	帽扣	buckle
40	帽片	panel
41	魔术贴	velcro
42	吸汗带	sweatband
43	拉链扣	zipper buckle
44	弹性带	elastic band
45	伸缩扣	stopper
46	帽围/头围	circumference/perimeter
47	顶纽	top-button
48	帽饰流苏	cap tassel
49	帽饰绒球	cap pompon

话术演练 Language Skills

产品材质与特点介绍：

(1) This fisherman's beanie[1] is made of 60% merino wool[2] and 40% acrylic[3], which is stretchy, soft and no shading, giving you comfy[4] wearing experience.

(2) This sailor watch cap is finished by hand.

(3) The rib-knit[5] cuff[6] fisherman hat adds comfort and style to any outfit.

(4) Mesh provides ultimate air flow and moisture-wicking[7].

(5) Our hats are 6-panel and contain a mid-profile[8] wool-like texture that provides the perfect combination of durability and comfort.

(6) A hard buckram[9] sewn into the front of the crown[10] provides excellent structure while a silver undervisor provides an additional dose of style.

(7) The baseball hat are made of soft and breathable cotton, designed to keep you comfortable in the summer all day long.

(8) Vintage and classic washed style will never be out of style.

(9) This fedora[11] hats for women are made of 55% cotton, 45% polyester[12], soft and comfortable to wear.

(10) This women's hats are breathable, lightweight and comfortable for all-day wear.

(11) The hat is made of polyester, lightweight, comfortable and foldable.

(12) The hat is constructed from weaved straw, featuring a wide brim, lined headband and adjustable chin strap.

(13) The hat is constructed of 100% rafia[13] straw fiber and should not be submerged[14] in water or kept stored where the integrity[15] of the hat crown is compromised.

(14) Original washed cotton sweatband is consistent with the appearance.

(15) You can make any curvature[16] of the brim to fit your forehead and keep the shape constant.

(16) 6 embroidered eyelets make the hat breathable and comfortable.

(17) Maximum breathability is achieved with Dri-FIT moisture management

technology and perforated[17] mid and back panels.

(18) The trademark is embroidered on the center back.

(19) This 6-panel cap has an unstructured[18] low profile design with a hook and loop[19] closure.

> **单词解析：**
>
> 1. beanie ['biːni] *n.* 无檐小便帽
> 2. merino wool 美利奴羊毛
> 3. acrylic [ə'krɪlɪk] *n.* 丙烯酸纤维
> 4. comfy ['kʌmfi] *adj.* 舒服的；舒适的（近义词：comfortable）
> 5. rib-knit [rɪb nɪt] *n.* 螺纹组织
> 6. cuff [kʌf] *n.* 袖口
> 7. moisture-wicking ['mɔɪstʃə(r) 'wɪkɪŋ] *n.* 快干
> 8. mid-profile [mɪd'prəʊfaɪl] *adj.* 中头的（high profile cap 高头帽，mid profile cap 中头帽，low profile cap 低头帽）
> 9. buckram ['bʌkrəm] *n.* （旧时用作书皮或衣服衬里的）硬棉布；硬麻布；硬衬布
> 10. crown [kraʊn] *n.* （某物的）顶部
> 11. fedora [fɪ'dɔːrə] *n.* 浅顶卷檐软呢帽
> 12. polyester [ˌpɒli'estə(r)] *n.* 聚酯纤维；涤纶
> 13. rafia ['ræfɪə] *n.* 拉菲草
> 14. submerge [səb'mɜːdʒ] *v.* 淹没；（使）潜入水中
> 15. integrity [ɪn'tegrəti] *n.* 完整
> 16. curvature ['kɜːvətʃə(r)] *n.* 弯曲；曲度
> 17. perforate ['pɜːfəreɪt] *v.* 打孔；穿孔；打眼
> 18. unstructured [ʌn'strʌktʃəd] *adj.* 结构凌乱的
> 19. loop [luːp] *n.* 环；环形

产品规格介绍：

(20) A wide range of colors lets you choose your favorite one or you can pick several colors to go with your clothes.

(21) The circumference of the black beanie is 21 – 23 inches(53 cm – 58 cm).

(22) This short beanie is made from highly stretchable materials, making it a perfect choice for average size head of men, women and teens.

(23) Whether it's baseball season or a special company event you've got approaching, take your pick from a variety of colors and sizes to find the perfect cap for you and your team.

(24) With a rounded athletic shape and stretch band to fit all sizes, this cap is ideal for all of your team sports needs.

(25) Choose from one of our versatile[20] colors to ensure your team rocks these hats with impeccable[21] style and finesse.

(26) Suitable for the head perimeter of 17.7 – 26.5 inches, this men knit hat beanie can be small, medium and large size.

(27) The adjustable back ensures a perfect for your head, and makes it one size fit most women, men, youth and teens.

(28) The hat circumference section is 22 – 23½ inches.

(29) This women's hat is only one size, but fits most women.

(30) This hats for women using classic retro[22] design with buckle belt are so classic, giving your outfit an elegant and charming touch.

(31) This hat can be folded to small and easily packed inside a suitcase or purse.

(32) This hat is 22 – 22.8 inches. It fits almost everyone, from teenagers to adults.

(33) One size fits all.

(34) The crown is measured 4 inches high, and the brim is measured 3 inches long and 7½ inches wide. The hat circumference is 22 – 23½ inches (56 cm – 60 cm).

单词解析：

20. versatile [ˈvɜːsətaɪl] *adj.* 多功能的；多用途的

21. impeccable [ɪmˈpekəbl] *adj.* 无可挑剔的；完美的（近义词：perfect）

22. retro [ˈretrəʊ] *adj.* 再度流行的

产品功能介绍：

(35) Short plain roll-up edge knitted skullcap[23] is the most fashionable hat in autumn and winter now.

(36) Our beanie hat is designed with everyday use in mind.

(37) The cuffed beanie cap keeps your head warm and snug[24] in autumn and winter.

(38) Precise knitting fashion beanie creates a nice and fashionable look design.

(39) The beanie hat is great for outdoor sports like snowboarding, running, skating, biking, snowshoeing, skiing, hiking or any outdoor activities and travel.

(40) It's the best present for men and women in birthday/anniversary/New Year.

(41) This hat offers UPF 50 sun protection to guard you against the sun's most harmful rays.

(42) Wide large floppy[25] brim provides a perfect shade to your face, helping protect you from the hot sunshine.

(43) It is an essential accessory for your outdoor travel, holiday and beach playing.

(44) Its folding packable design is for easy storage in a handbag or backpack when it is not in use.

(45) This cap fit for a variety of occasions such as: sporting events, hiking, picnics, family outings, beaches, sports, birthday parties, theme parks, or anything under the sun.

(46) These perfect unisex bucket hats make an excellent gifting idea for your friends and loved ones!

(47) The classic lifeguard hat is perfect for any day at the beach, working in the yard or adventuring outdoors.

(48) This hat features an adjustable draw cord chin strap with a toggle[26] to customize[27] your fit along with a lined headband for comfort.

(49) Our sun hats help keep you protected while you enjoy the outdoors.

(50) It will be very suitable for the fall and winter, providing you with warmth

and comfort.

> 单词解析：
> 23. skullcap ['skʌlkæp] n. 无檐便帽
> 24. snug [snʌg] adj. 舒适的；贴身的；保暖的
> 25. floppy ['flɔpi] adj. 松软的；下垂的
> 26. toggle ['tɔgl] n. 套索扣
> 27. customize ['kʌstəmaɪz] v. 订制；定做

直播模板 Template

　　This _____ is made of _____, and the _____ is very soft. It will be very suitable for the fall and winter, providing you with warmth and comfort. _____ is stretchy and stretches from _____ to _____, which makes this hat fit most women's heads. So you don't have to worry that it won't fit your head and you won't be able to wear it.

　　_____ is the new trending fashion statement of the _____ season. It completely covers your ears without having to yank it down all the time, and also helps keep the sun out of your eyes because of visor. _____ keeps you warm and looking good in the cold weather.

　　_____ is knitted with _____. You can get different colors like _____, _____, _____ and use it with every outfit matching the colors or going with contrast. Our beautiful _____ is suitable for your every colorful clothes. This _____ can perfectly reflect your fashionable and elegant style.

　　_____ is an ideal gift for your family members, friends and loved ones. It is a holiday gift, great for the cold winter. Be ready for _____ in this winter, and your noggin will be warm, cozy and stylish.

3.4 实战脚本 Script

Live Streaming Script of Clothes

Hi girls, welcome to my channel. This is Christy from ABC Fashion, China. We have professional design teams, experienced pattern making teams and also our own factory. Today I will bring you various kinds of clothes because today is our big sale day. All things like sweaters, shirts, pants, jeans of different kinds and different styles. And each live we offer certain benefits, and we will just send them to you for free. If you would like to enjoy our live benefits, just follow our livestream.

The first item for today is a lightweight yoga crop top. It is made of 95% cotton and 5% spandex, so it will not have any odor and will not cause allergies. This is of great quality and you can check it out. It is stretchy and very soft, super comfy and lightweight but not too sheer. Its breathable fabric retains shape and does not shrink.

Now let me show you the design. The unique design is very versatile. It is slim fit but not too tight. The short top stays right above your belly button and makes you look taller. It is perfect to wear as base layer and match with any fashion items. You can pair it with high waisted leggings. You can wear it to the gym, do yoga, or just hang out. It is a must-have item for your wardrobe. I like it. I really like the color and it is really flattering.

And the price, the original price, as you can see on the tag, is 69 pounds, but today in Christy's live, I promise you that I'm going to give you the best deal ever. Listen carefully, because this price is only for our livestream, 13.99 pounds. We have many colors, like black, beige, grey, white, hot pink, blue, coffee and coral. If you'd like to get two, that's 25 pounds for two pieces. Come on, guys, where can you find this material, this flexibility with such low price? I promise we are giving you the bottom price today. Because we have our own factory and we are the manufacturer. 25 pounds, 2 pieces of different colors, you can contact our customer service. Don't miss the chance, guys. Believe me, that will be 25 pounds well spent for these beautiful and flattering yoga tops. Girls, what are you waiting for?

Now I'll show you our best sellers, bell bottom jeans. It is made of our high quality denim that is soft and breathable. It's hand wash only. Now let's have a look at its design. This flared leg can cover the whole shoe. The high waist design enhances your waist line. The design on the back accentuate the curve of the butt. So these are a pair of pants that will highlight your figure. Here you can see 1, 2, 3, 4, 5 pockets. It is the classic 5-pocket jeans style, and you can wear it on most occasions. It can be matched with shirts, vests, sweatshirts, jackets, and you can pair with high heels, sports shoes or casual shoes. It is so versatile. We have sizes ranging from 0 to 20. But remember, because this is made by stretchy fabric, some clients say they're a little bit loose. If you don't like loose feelings on wearing, please select one size smaller.

The list price for it is only 49.99 pounds. The discount for today's live is 20% off, just 39.99 pounds. That is the price you can never imagine. There are only 100 pieces left. Wish you good luck. Wow, we are all sold out.

Ok and that's for today. You can always follow Christy, follow ABC Fashion. Ok, so have a nice day, bye bye, see ya.

第四章
电子类产品英语直播

近年来,人们逐渐将生活场景从线下转移至线上,日益增长的线上需求推动着电子产品市场的蓬勃发展。数据显示,全球消费电子线上销售额在2018年超过2800亿美元,预计在2023年将达到4060亿美元,年增长率可高达7.6%。我国是世界第一大电子产品出口国,我国电子信息制造业外贸进出口双双保持较快增长。从海关总署的统计数据来看,2021年,我国高新技术产品出口总额9795.8亿美元,比上年增长26.2%,增速比2020年提高19.9个百分点;进口总额8373.3亿美元,比上年增长22.8%,增速比2020年提高15.8个百分点。从主要产品看,出口电脑及零部件2552.9亿美元,比上年增长21.0%;出口手机1463.2亿美元,增长16.6%;出口集成电路1537.9亿美元,增长32.0%;出口液晶显示板277.7亿美元,增长39.8%。2022年,锂电出口总额3426.5亿元(人民币),同比增长86.7%。此外,电子技术、投影仪、智能手表、充电宝等产品海外需求旺盛。

4.1 消费类电子产品 Consumer Electronics

词汇积累 Vocabulary

序号	中文名称	英文名称
1	数码产品	digital product
2	智能手机	smartphone
3	全面屏	full display
4	曲面屏	curved surface screen
5	触摸屏	touch screen

续表

序号	中文名称	英文名称
6	屏幕尺寸	screen size
7	操作系统	operating system
8	续航能力	battery life
9	前/后置摄像头	front/rear camera
10	双镜头	dual camera
11	广角镜头	wide-angle lens
12	微距镜头	micro lens
13	像素	pixel
14	分辨率	resolution
15	处理器	processor
16	手机内存	storage capacity
17	延时摄影	time-lapse photography
18	指纹感测器	fingerprint sensor
19	数字变焦	digital zoom
20	光学防抖	optical image stabilization
21	射频芯片	radio frequency chip
22	面部识别	facial recognition
23	无线充电	wireless charging
24	液晶电视	LCD TV
25	等离子电视	plasma TV
26	数字移动电视	digital mobile television
27	激光电视	laser TV
28	超高清	ultra-high definition
29	超薄	ultra-thin
30	电视面板	TV panel
31	IPS 硬屏	in-plane switching panel
32	VA 软屏	vertical alignment panel
33	背光	backlit

续表

序号	中文名称	英文名称
34	刷新率	refresh rate
35	接口	interface
36	防蓝光	anti-blue light
37	亮度	brightness
38	对比度	screen contrast
39	色域	color gamut
40	立体声	stereo
41	声控	voice control
42	遥控器	remote control
43	壁挂式	wall-hung
44	数码相机	digital camera
45	单反相机	single lens reflex camera
46	拍立得相机	instant camera
47	卡片机	compact camera
48	相机机身	camera body
49	取景器	viewfinder
50	自动曝光	automatic exposure
51	光圈	aperture
52	镜头卡口	lens mount
53	快门	shutter
54	变焦镜头	zoom lens
55	胶卷	film
56	备用电池	back-up battery
57	镜头盖	lens cap
58	保护盖	protective cover
59	相机带	wrist strap
60	图像稳定器	image stabilizer
61	拍摄模式	shooting mode

续表

序号	中文名称	英文名称
62	人像模式	portrait mode
63	风景模式	landscape mode
64	单张/连续拍摄	single-frame/continuous shooting
65	长宽比	aspect ratio
66	全画幅	full frame
67	自动对焦	autofocus
68	焦距	focal length
69	景深	depth of field
70	闪光灯	flash
71	三脚架	tripod
72	智能音箱	smart speaker
73	智能眼镜	intelligent glasses
74	健身追踪器	fitness tracker
75	智能手表	smart watch
76	智能手环	smart band
77	充电宝	portable charger
78	入耳式耳机	in-ear headphone
79	头戴式耳机	headset
80	电子词典	electronic dictionary
81	VR/AR眼镜	VR/AR glasses
82	可穿戴扬声器	wearable speaker
83	蓝牙自拍杆	bluetooth selfie stick
84	电子书阅读器	e-book reader
85	智能服务机器人	intelligent service robot
86	路由器	WIFI router
87	航拍无人机	drone for aerial photography
88	摄像机	video camera
89	按摩仪	massager

续表

序号	中文名称	英文名称
90	电动牙刷	electric toothbrush
91	剃须刀	electric razor
92	电动除尘器	electric air duster
93	掌上游戏机	handheld gaming device
94	电子玩具	electronic toy
95	电子宠物	digital pet
96	智能体温计	smart digital thermometer
97	智能电子秤	intelligent electronic scale
98	血氧仪	oximeter
99	智能猫眼	digital peephole viewer
100	车载吸尘器	car vacuum cleaner
101	无线充电支架	wireless charging stand
102	家庭投影仪	multimedia home projector
103	智能门锁	intelligent door lock
104	可穿戴设备	wearable device

话术演练 Language Skills

产品规格介绍：

（1）Max speed of motor[1] compressed air duster is 100000 RPM[2] and the blowing force is between 1.86－2.51 oz.

（2）It has 3 speed modes and more than 10 nozzles and brush.

（3）The electronic air duster measures 5.6×2.5×7.4 inches and weighs approximately 1.08 pounds.

（4）It has a 256 GB[3] large storage.

（5）The product box comes with a phone, a charger, a USB cable[4], a SIM[5] card and one manual[6].

（6）The door video bell adopts industrial color image sensor 3.5-inch LCD color screen.

(7) Door hole range is between 14 to 28 mm; door thickness range is 35 to 100 mm.

(8) Digital door viewer supports a maximum of 32 G TF card[7].

(9) The movie projector provides a watching size from 30″ to 200″ with the distance from 2.62 ft to 14.8 ft.

> 单词解析:
>
> 1. motor ['məutər] n. 发动机;马达
> 2. RPM (revolutions per minute) abbr. 每分钟转速
> 3. GB (GigaByte) abbr. 千兆字节
> 4. cable ['keɪb(ə)l] n. 电缆
> 5. SIM (subscriber identity module) abbr. 用户识别模块
> 6. manual ['mænjuəl] n. 使用手册;说明书
> 7. TF card (trans-flash card) abbr. 快闪存储卡

产品质量与特色介绍:

(10) Gaming headset features quantum[8] sphere 360 technology with integrated head-tracking sensor.

(11) Large 50-millimeter speaker unit drivers combined with neodymium[9] magnets deliver dynamic bass[10], which is great for DJing[11], mixing[12], monitoring, or listening to music.

(12) Memory foam[13] ear cushions[14] on the headset are covered in soft leather, providing comfort for long marathon[15] sessions, and USB connection is suitable for multi-platform gaming.

(13) Our cordless[16] air duster has a built-in large capacity of 7500 mAh lithium[17] battery and allow this duster to run nearly 25 – 40 minutes continuously.

(14) It can be charged by computer, mobile power, car charger, adapter[18].

(15) Compared with the compressed air can, the dust blower[19] will not produce chemicals, liquids or freezing during cleaning.

(16) This phone launches apps fast, pages and images load quickly, and everything runs smoothly.

(17) Auto-adjusting display provides the best viewing experience regardless of lighting conditions.

(18) Octa-core processor[20] and 6 GB of RAM[21] will provide you a smooth experience.

(19) Coming with a 48 MP[22] high-res AI camera and 16 MP front-facing selfie camera, ××× android phone helps you capture crisp[23] and vivid pictures.

(20) Whether you're going out for a run or getting caught in a little rain, a water-repellent[24] design keeps your phone protected inside and out.

(21) This compact digital camera for indoor/outdoor can be used for making video features with full HD 1080P video resolution[25].

(22) This digital camera supports 16 times of digital zoom[26].

(23) When it comes to your personally identifiable health data, no one can view it without your permission.

(24) 4K ultra HD, HDR[27] 10, and HLG[28] deliver a clearer and more vibrant picture with brighter colors compared to 1080P full HD.

(25) This speaker can operate up to 12 hours at half volume for every single charge.

(26) The high-power motor will bring 3600 strikes[29] per minute, and after using 20 minutes, it will automatically stop to prevent the massager from overheating.

(27) Adopted the latest color reproduction technology, every detail on the screen is accurately restored[30] to ensure a real and color-vibrant viewing effect.

(28) The projector is equipped with the latest cooling system which cuts the fan[31] noise by half, provides a quieter environment for your movie time.

(29) WiFi 6 technology achieves faster speeds, greater capacity and reduced network congestion[32] compared to the previous generation.

(30) The coverage is up to 1,500 square feet for more than 20 devices.

单词解析：

8. quantum [ˈkwɔntəm] n. 量子

9. neodymium [ˌniːəʊˈdɪmiəm] n. 钕

10. bass [beɪs] n. 男低音

11. DJ (Disc Jockey) *v.* 打碟

12. mix [mɪks] *v.* 混音

13. foam [fəʊm] *n.* 海绵橡胶

14. cushion [ˈkʊʃ(ə)n] *n.* 软垫

15. marathon [ˈmærəθən] *adj.* 马拉松式的；耗时费力的

16. cordless [ˈkɔrdləs] *adj.* 无电线的

17. lithium [ˈlɪθɪəm] *n.* 锂

18. adapter [əˈdæptər] *n.* 适配器

19. blower [ˈbləʊər] *n.* 吹风机

20. octa-core processor 八核处理器

21. RAM (random access memory) *abbr.* 随机存储器

22. MP (megapixel) *abbr.* 百万像素；分辨率

23. crisp [krɪsp] *adj.* 清晰分明的

24. water-repellent [ˈwɔtər rɪˈpelənt] *adj.* 防水的

25. resolution [ˌrezəˈluʃ(ə)n] *n.* 分辨率；解析度

26. zoom [zum] *n.* 可变焦镜头

27. HDR (high dynamic range) *abbr.* 高动态范围

28. HLG (hybrid log-gamma) *abbr.* 混合对数伽马

29. strike [straɪk] *n.* 击打

30. restore [rɪˈstɔr] *v.* 修复；还原

31. fan [fæn] *n.* 风扇

32. congestion [kənˈdʒestʃ(ə)n] *n.* 拥堵

产品功能介绍：

(31) Gaming headset <u>incorporates</u>[33] true active noise cancellation which actively monitors your environment and blocks out unnecessary noise so that you can focus on the game in front of you.

(32) The soft <u>padded</u>[34] ear cushions are designed for <u>monitor headphones'</u> comfort and noise isolation.

(33) Air duster creates a concentrated, super-strong airflow to remove <u>debris</u>[35]

and dust from any crevices.

(34) You can clean off crumbs[36], hairs, dust from PC, keyboard, sofa, air conditioner, camera lens or car and burning the charcoal[37] in BBQ, inflating[38] a swimming pool, a yoga ball. You can also take it as vacuum sealer[39] to pump[40] air out of storage bags to save your space.

(35) ×××'s fast-charging all-day battery adapts to you and saves power for the apps you use the most.

(36) With ××× cell phone you can store and access massive photos, videos, music, books and files, and you don't have to worry about the storage running out.

(37) Smaller than cell phones, portable camera is small enough to fit your pocket, easy to carry at anywhere, indoor/outdoor like travelling, camping.

(38) ××× includes access to basic features like steps, heart rate, on-demand blood oxygen level, sleep time, and sleep tracking.

(39) It is built with privacy protections and controls, including a switch[41] that electronically disconnects the microphones.

(40) This bluetooth wireless neck speaker leaves your hands free and allows you to make calls that are crystal clear.

(41) All the classic retro[42] games built-in are coming from the 1980s and 1990s, which will recover your childhood memory.

(42) Our deep tissue massager is built with the percussion[43] technology that can help relax feet, calf, shoulders, neck, back, muscle, arms, and legs.

(43) After the massage gun hits the muscles, it can promote blood circulation[44], decompose[45] lactic[46] acid[47], and relieve muscle soreness[48] after exercise.

(44) This smart fitness scale provides 13 body composition measurements, including body fat ratio, muscle mass, BMI[49], and more, so you can pinpoint[50] areas of improvement and finetune your fitness goals.

(45) 4K dual dash camera can simultaneously[51] record videos in front 4K and rear[52] 1080P resolution, clearly capturing license[53] plates[54] and road signs.

(46) The 1080P HD video doorbell enables you to see, hear, and speak to visitors from anywhere.

单词解析：

33. incorporate [ɪnˈkɔrpəˌreɪt] v. 包含

34. pad [pæd] v. (用垫子)覆盖

35. debris [ˈdebriː] n. 碎片；残骸

36. crumb [krʌm] n. 食物碎屑

37. charcoal [ˈtʃɑrˌkəʊl] n. 碳

38. inflate [ɪnˈfleɪt] v. 使充气

39. sealer [ˈsilər] n. 封口器

40. pump [pʌmp] v. 用泵输送

41. switch [swɪtʃ] n. 开关

42. retro [ˈretrəʊ] adj. 前不久刚流行过的

43. percussion [pərˈkʌʃ(ə)n] n. 打击乐器

44. circulation [ˌsɜːkjəˈleɪʃ(ə)n] n. 循环

45. decompose [ˌdikəmˈpəʊz] v. 分解

46. lactic [ˈlæktɪk] adj. 乳的

47. acid [ˈæsɪd] n. 酸

48. soreness [ˈsɔrnəs] n. 疼痛

49. BMI (body mass index) abbr. 体质指数

50. pinpoint [ˈpɪnˌpɔɪnt] v. 精准定位

51. simultaneously [ˌsɪməlˈteɪniəsli] adv. 同时进行地

52. rear [rɪə] adj. 后面的

53. license [ˈlaɪs(ə)ns] n. 执照

54. plate [pleɪt] n. 车牌

产品服务介绍：

(47) If you have any issues regarding the item, please feel free to contact us, we'll send you a replacement right away.

(48) If there is any issue about the duster blower, please do not worry and free to contact with us, our service team will give you a satisfying solution.

(49) All products are covered by a one-year warranty.

(50) We provide <u>5</u> years return and lifetime repair.

直播模板 Template

　　This is a new smartphone released by _____ company. This phone has a _____ inch full _____ display. The maximum display resolution is _____. It features a _____ body design and comes with multiple color options, including _____, _____, _____...

　　It runs smoothly and securely, powered by a _____ processor and has a _____ GB RAM. The phone is equipped with _____ rear camera setup that includes _____ megapixel and _____ sensors with optical image stabilization technology. With stabilization, this smartphone easily records daytime outdoor adventures or those spur-of-the-moment _____ at night. Video recording capabilities include _____ video recording with _____ sound. It comes with a _____ mAh battery with fast charging support and runs on the latest version of _____ system. _____'s fast-charging all-day battery adapts to your charging habit and saves power for the apps you use most.

　　It supports _____ G, WiFi, _____ SIM and bluetooth. It also protects your data and privacy with _____ security technology.

4.2 办公类电子产品 Office Electronics

词汇积累 Vocabulary

序号	中文名称	英文名称
1	个人电脑	personal computer
2	笔记本电脑	laptop
3	超极本	ultrabook
4	上网本	netbook
5	台式电脑	desktop computer
6	一体机	all-in-one computer
7	电脑终端机	computer terminal
8	平板电脑	tablet
9	掌上电脑	palmtop
10	交换机	switch
11	电脑主机	computer host
12	多媒体	multimedia
13	计算器	calculator
14	移动硬盘	mobile hard disk drive
15	U 盘	USB flash disk
16	录音笔	voice recorder
17	复读机	language repeater
18	电子词典	electronic dictionary
19	无线充电鼠标	wireless charging mouse
20	翻译笔	language translation device
21	语音服务机器人	service robot
22	移动电源	portable power source
23	数码电子相框	electronic digital photo frame

续表

序号	中文名称	英文名称
24	麦克风	microphone
25	光盘驱动器	CD-ROM
26	激光打印机	laser printer
27	喷墨打印机	ink-jet printer
28	多功能一体机	multi-function printer
29	扫描仪	scanner
30	传真机	fax machine
31	复印机	photocopier
32	标签打印机	label printer
33	票据打印机	receipt printer
34	条码打印机	barcode printer
35	碎纸机	paper shredder
36	过塑机	laminator machine
37	收款机	cash register
38	点钞机	money counting machine
39	切纸机	paper cutter
40	刻字机	cutting plotter
41	电动订书机	electrical stapler
42	电子白板	electronic whiteboard
43	LED 显示屏	LED display screen
44	网络拓展器	WiFi extender
45	监控摄像机	surveillance camera
46	考勤机	attendance machine
47	门禁一体机	integration access control
48	监视器	monitor
49	硬盘录像机	hard disk video recorder
50	对讲机	interphone

话术演练 Language Skills

产品规格介绍：

（1）The processor of the computer is 11th Gen Intel Core i3-1115G4 Dual-Core 3.0 GHz processor.

（2）The computer has a 15.6″ HD touchscreen[1] display.

（3）The portable tablet is 1.05 pounds light weight and 0.9 cm thin, also has a 2-in-1 working mode.

（4）It features a 4800×1200 dpi[2] (black and color) print resolution quality and 600×1200 dpi scan resolution quality.

（5）The screen size of the digital photo frame is 10 inches.

（6）Whiteboard has an overall size of 36×24 inches (frame included), and the size of writing surface is 34×22 inches.

> 单词解析：
>
> 1. touchscreen [tʌtʃ skrin] n. 触摸屏
>
> 2. dpi (dots per inch) abbr. 每英寸点数

产品质量介绍：

（7）Memory is 8 GB high-bandwidth[3] RAM[4] to smoothly run multiple applications and browser tabs[5] all at once.

（8）Hard drive is 256 GB PCIe solid state drive which allows to fast bootup[6] and data transfer.

（9）The 1920 plus 1080 resolution boasts impressive color and clarity.

（10）It supports up to 12 hours of reading, browsing the web, watching videos, and listening to music.

（11）Battery life may vary depending on network environment, usage patterns and other factors.

（12）The latest ××× tablet has already pre-installed[7] basic Google apps.

（13）This calculator features 3 operating modes: Angular Measurement, Calculation, and Display modes.

（14）User-friendly buttons are comfortable, durable[8], and well-marked for easy use by all ages, including kids.

（15）This home and office printer offers faster printing at 20 pages per minute, includes fax and scan-to-USB capabilities, and is 14% smaller.

（16）This wireless printer comes with a code to redeem[9] 8 months of instant ink based on printing 100 pages per month.

（17）It can protect sensitive data with built-in security essentials like basic encryption[10], password protection, WiFi security, and document protection.

（18）This ink-jet[11] printer is made from recycled plastics and other electronics, up to 15% by weight of plastic.

（19）Digital voice recorder comes with high-quality recording microphones, a DSP[12] noise reduction system, and built-in voice detection function.

（20）Fax transmission[13] speeds is up to 3 seconds per page.

（21）Equipped with 1280×800 high resolution IPS touch screen, ××× digital picture frame shows your photos with rich and vibrant colors and superior image quality.

（22）The crosscut[14] shredder with 3.4-gallon[15] wastebasket can hold 180 sheets of A4 paper for less frequent and easy emptying.

（23）Two roller system provides precise heat and pressure to ensure high quality lamination[16].

（24）This thermal laminator machine won't be too hot with an intelligent temperature control system, which would be safer to protect your machine and make it last longer.

单词解析：

3. bandwidth ['bænd,wɪdθ] *n.* 带宽；频宽

4. RAM (random access memory) *abbr.* 随机存储器

5. tab [tæb] *n.* 标签

6. bootup ['butʌp] *v.* 启动

7. pre-install [pri 'ɪnstɔl] *v.* 预装

8. durable ['djʊərəb(ə)l] *adj.* 耐用的；持久的

> 9. redeem [rɪˈdim] v. 兑换
> 10. encryption [ɪnˈkrɪpʃ(ə)n] n. 加密技术
> 11. ink-jet [ˈɪŋk dʒet] adj. 喷墨式
> 12. DSP (digital signal processor) abbr. 数字信号处理器
> 13. transmission [trænzˈmɪʃ(ə)n] n. 传输；传递
> 14. crosscut [ˈkrɔsˌkʌt] n. 横切；横锯
> 15. gallon [ˈɡælən] n. 加仑（液量单位）
> 16. lamination [ˌlæməˈneɪʃən] n. 层压；叠合

产品功能介绍：

（25）The perfect combination of performance, power consumption, and value helps your device run smoothly.

（26）This ultra-compact[17] memory system is ideal for mobile devices and applications, providing enhanced storage capabilities, streamlined data management.

（27）It can tackle any task—from basic computing to multimedia entertainment.

（28）Driven by a 12th Intel Core i5 processor, it has the speed, power and storage to do more.

（29）The reliability and superior performance that this desktop computer offer make it ideal for business use, gaming, photography and video editing, and for a multitude of applications that require heavy computer use.

（30）Do more with your notes with ××× connectivity[18] that automatically synchronize[19] everything from to-do lists to school work, whether you're on your tablet, phone or watch.

（31）The tablet supports split screen operation, which will not interfere with each other in a new parallel vision, multiple apps used at the same time.

（32）You can flexibly turn the tablet into a laptop.

（33）The long-lasting battery life and lightweight design allow you to enjoy your tablet anywhere, anytime.

（34）This is a scientific calculator that is able to show graphs of formulas[20].

（35）It features a screen large enough to be able to display graphs and equations simultaneously, allowing you to see calculations and corrections in high detail.

（36）It has 6 functions, including addition, subtraction[21], multiplication, division, percentage, square root[22], and more.

（37）It can easily print, scan, and copy everyday documents from your smartphone, using ×××smart app.

（38）With full battery, this voice recorder can store 2324 hours of recording, or 10,000 songs, up to 54 hours of continuous recording.

（39）This recorder device can set voice decibels[23] at 6 different levels.

（40）It's a wonderful voice recording device for lectures, meetings, and conversations.

（41）The device will auto-detect voice to prevent recording silence, wasting valuable device space.

（42）This audio recorder allows writing while recording, just one button to start recording and saving.

（43）Digital picture frame can instantly receive photos and videos via a WiFi network.

（44）Strip cut shredder can shred paper with staples[24] and credit cards/CDs (one at a time), receipts, bills and important documents.

（45）×××home paper shredder, shreds up to 6 sheets of paper at one time into tiny pieces measuring 13/64 × 1-37/64 inches (5 × 18 mm).

（46）This is truly a heavy-duty unit and can take on large stapling tasks.

（47）This easy-to-use electric stapler holds a full strip of staples and fastens up to 20 sheets of paper.

（48）It laminates max to 9 inches wide (230 mm/A4 size), and compatible[25] with any 3 and 5 mil[26] laminating sheets, like the letter, legal, business card, and photo-size papers.

（49）The whiteboard is perfect for play counting, guided reading, learning, presentation, drawing, education and grocery list etc., without paper wasting.

（50）The fingerprint and password verification[27] mechanisms[28] are available on the smart time clock, and employee hours are automatically calculated.

单词解析：

17. ultra-compact [ˈʌltrə kəmˈpækt] *adj.* 超紧凑的
18. connectivity [ˌkɔnekˈtɪvəti] *n.* 连通性；结合性
19. synchronize [ˈsɪŋkrəˌnaɪz] *v.* 使同步
20. formula [ˈfɔrmjələ] *n.* 公式
21. subtraction [səbˈtrækʃən] *n.* 减法
22. square root 平方根
23. decibel [ˈdesɪˌbel] *n.* 分贝
24. staple [ˈsteɪp(ə)l] *n.* 订书钉
25. compatible [kəmˈpætəb(ə)l] *adj.* 兼容的；可共存的
26. mil [mɪl] *n.* 密耳（千分之一英寸）
27. verification [ˌverɪfɪˈkeɪʃ(ə)n] *n.* 验证；检验
28. mechanism [ˈmekəˌnɪzəm] *n.* 机制

产品服务介绍：

(51) We offer free lifetime tech support.

(52) The tablet supports 6 months free replacement and 2-year warranty.

(53) We support 24-month free warranty to ensure your 100% satisfied purchasing experience.

(54) With professional customer service team, we will quickly respond within 24 hours.

(55) Our laminator comes with a 30-day money-back guarantee for any reason and 12-month warranty for quality-related issues warranty.

直播模板 Template

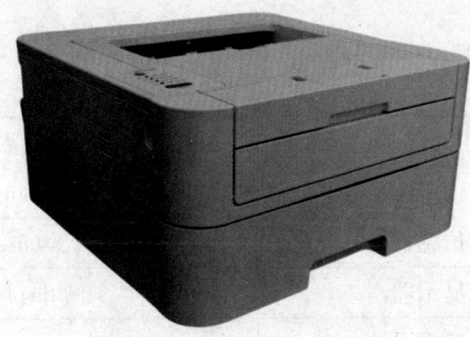

Today we will introduce a multifunction printer from the brand _____. It can print _____ color documents like _____, _____, _____. It gets started fast on any device with the _____ app that guides you step by step. Main functions of this _____ printer include printing, _____ and _____, _____. You can print documents from your phone or tablet through the _____ app, whenever and wherever. It supports multiple media sizes and media weight up to _____. The size is _____ mm, which fit nicely in any workspace.

This printer has a _____ frame structure built for long time use. The ergonomically designed print heads apply ink quickly, so you will never run out of ink. It supports multiple systems.

_____ printer has excellent performance and are widely used in both home and office. _____ advanced technology produces _____ prints with sharp lines and smooth transitions. With the _____ software, users can easily customize their printing by adjusting _____ and color to achieve the desired output. _____ printer also equipped with a range of features, such as _____, _____ to make it easier for users to complete their printing tasks. The package comes with a _____ page starter cartridge. And we offer _____ year standard warranty from the date of purchase. Online customer service is also available.

4.3 电子元器件及电子产品配件 Electronic Components and Accessories

词汇积累 Vocabulary

序号	中文名称	英文名称
1	芯片	chip
2	传感器	sensor
3	显示器	display
4	锂离子电池	lithium-ion battery
5	键盘	keyboard
6	充电器	charger
7	电脑主板	computer mainboard
8	电源适配器	power adapter
9	镍氢电池	nickel-metal hydride battery
10	读卡器	card reader
11	内存卡	memory card
12	处理器	processor
13	显卡	display card
14	笔记本拓展坞	laptop dock station
15	电源连接线	power cord
16	手机充电线	phone charging cable
17	遥控器	remote control
18	打印机墨盒	printer cartridge
19	相机镜头	camera lens
20	电机马达	electric motor
21	电脑桌面开关	computer desktop switch
22	散热器/片	heatsink
23	硒鼓	toner cartridge

续表

序号	中文名称	英文名称
24	转换接头	adapter substitute
25	投影幕布	projector screen
26	游戏机手柄	video game controller
27	游戏机摇杆	game console joystick
28	手持稳定器	handheld stabilizer
29	电子产品收纳包	electronics storage bag
30	充电头	charger plug
31	调速器	speed controller
32	继电器	relay
33	电子模块	electronic module
34	开关元件	switching element
35	电阻器	resistor
36	混合集成电路	hybrid integrated circuit
37	高密度印刷电路板	high-density printed circuit board
38	机电元件	electromechanical component
39	半导体装置	semiconductor
40	电子元器件	electronic parts and components
41	光电子器件	optoelectronic device
42	片式元器件	chip component
43	电子产品外壳	electronic product shell
44	电力电子器件	power electronic device
45	电容器	capacitor
46	二极管	diode
47	整流器	rectifier
48	三极管	triode
49	电感器	inductor
50	电子产品维修工具组	electronic product repair kit

话术演练 Language Skills

产品规格介绍：

(1) It has an input voltage[1] range of 4.5 to 40 V[2].

(2) The package contains 12-pack AAA rechargeable performance-capacity batteries.

(3) This full-sized keyboard offers 104 keys, including navigational[3] controls, full functions and a 10-key keypad.

(4) ×××resistor assortment kit contains 1350 pieces of resistors with variety values.

(5) The repair toolkit contains a precision bit driver set, tweezers[4], flex extension, opening tools, and anti-static wristband[5].

(6) This is a toroid[6] ferrite[7] core inductor with 13 mm outer diameter, 5 mm width and 0.5 wire diameter.

(7) The 12 V relay harness base contains 3 × 12 AWG and 2 × 16 AWG cables, which have higher load-bearing capacity and more stable performance.

单词解析：

1. voltage [ˈvəʊltɪdʒ] *n.* 电压

2. V(Volt) *abbr.* 伏特

3. navigational [ˌnævɪˈɡeɪʃənl] *adj.* 导航的；航行的

4. tweezers [ˈtwizərz] *n.* 镊子；小夹钳

5. wristband [ˈrɪstˌbænd] *n.* 腕带；腕套

6. toroid [ˈtɔːrɔɪd] *n.* 环状物

7. ferrite [ˈferaɪt] *n.* 铁氧体

产品质量与优势介绍：

(8) The regulator is simple to use and include internal frequency compensation and a fixed-frequency oscillator[8].

(9) Power transistors can be internally optimized, with excellent circuit and load regulation.

(10) High density fins design increases more surface area and performs effective heat transfer.

(11) Copper heatsink[9] has nearly double the thermal conductivity[10] than aluminum[11].

(12) Rechargeable batteries are delivered pre-charged and ready to use.

(13) They can be recharged up to 1000 times with minimal power loss and maintain 80% capacity for 24 months.

(14) This rainbow backlit[12] keyboard is designed with an aluminum alloy[13] panel, which not only improves the overall texture of the USB keyboard but also greatly improves the durability and water resistance.

(15) Switch life of each key withstands[14] up to 3,000,000 keystrokes.

(16) The fast charger can provide a maximum of 20 W output power to charge your phone, which can reach up to 3 times faster than the standard 5 W charger.

(17) These fast wall chargers have multipotent[15] safety system ensures complete protection for phone devices.

(18) Our fast charger protects your devices and avoid appearing overcurrent[16], overcharge, overload, surge and short circuit phenomenon.

(19) It uses high-quality ABS material and high-quality PC fireproof[17] material.

(20) The surface of the card reader is covered with a protective film to prevent it from being scratched or damaged.

(21) Card reader supports data transfer speed up to 5 GB per second.

(22) The cartridge[18] combines the toner[19], drum, and development all in one piece.

(23) It is configured a professional chip inside, which is compatible with your print machines, makes it work fluently, improve printing work quality.

(24) The ×××　fan motor has a built-in thermal protector and the protection disconnection temperature is 257 ℉.

(25) With precision winding technology, the geared motor power instant increased by 30%.

(26) The stator winding of the motor is made of pure copper wire, low heat

generation, low loss.

(27) The resistor is resistant to short-term overload, low noise, no change in resistance over the years.

(28) Featuring an easily removable fuse, this device is protected in the event of power surges and item malfunction[20].

(29) All chips are made of advanced materials, rather than being dismantled[21] or refurbished[22].

(30) The weight of this × × × is light, ergonomic[23], comfortable and fashionable, non-slip material, long-lasting effective anti-sweat.

(31) The toroid[24] core inductor has less working frequency impedance[25], high magnetic permeability[26], less magnetic-leakage loss.

(32) The car relay adopts waterproof sealing technology at the bottom and a fixed back strip on the back, which is suitable for various complicated installation environments.

(33) Projection curtain is soft and can be folded, or placed in a backpack or a portable handbag that can be easily taken away.

(34) This projection screen has punching[27] holes on the top, which is very easy to install, can usually be hung on the wall or tied to the frame.

单词解析：

8. oscillator [ˈɒsɪˌleɪtər] n. 振荡器

9. heatsink [hɪtsɪŋk] n. 散热器

10. conductivity [ˌkɒndʌkˈtɪvətɪ] n. 传导性

11. aluminum [əˈlumɪnəm] n. 铝（同 aluminium）

12. backlit [ˈbækˌlɪt] n. 背景光

13. alloy [ˈælɔɪ] n. 合金

14. withstand [wɪðˈstænd] v. 承受；经受住

15. multipotent [mʌltɪˈpəʊt(ə)nt] adj. 多功能的

16. overcurrent [ˈəʊvərˈkʌrənt] n. 过载电流

17. fireproof [ˈfaɪəˌpruf] adj. 防火的

18. cartridge [ˈkɑːtrɪdʒ] n. 墨盒

第四章 电子类产品英语直播

19. toner ['təʊnər] n. 墨粉；碳粉
20. malfunction [mæl'fʌŋkʃ(ə)n] n. 故障；失灵
21. dismantle [dɪs'mænt(ə)l] v. 拆卸
22. refurbish [riː'fɜːbɪʃ] v. 翻新；整修
23. ergonomic [ˌɜːgə'nɒmɪk] adj. 人类工程学的
24. toroid ['tɔːrɔɪd] n. 环状物
25. impedance [ɪm'piːd(ə)ns] n. 阻抗
26. permeability [pɜːmɪə'bɪlətɪ] n. 渗透性；导磁性
27. punch [pʌntʃ] v. 打孔

产品功能介绍：

(35) It sucks the heat away, thus can reduce the risk of hardware failure due to overheating.

(36) Heatsinks are widely used for electronics, computer, LED, power transistor, power amplifier[28], voltage regulator, etc..

(37) With low-profile keys, this keyboard offers a comfortable, quiet typing experience.

(38) It easily connects you to your PC or laptop right away so you can get working or playing.

(39) It provides you with an ergonomic typing angle (7°) and wrist support during use.

(40) with 3 USB-C ports and 3 USB-A ports, this charging station can simultaneously charge multiple devices, such as laptops, cellular[29] phones, tablets, headphones, smart watches, and other devices, which is very suitable for home, office, travel, etc..

(41) This universal remote works with all major brands and supports thousands of the latest audio and video equipment.

(42) The anti-shake technology allows you to shoot incredibly stable and smooth with multi-scene shots.

(43) This motor is capable of rotation in either the clockwise[30] or

counterclockwise direction by reversing the motor's power wires.

(44) Double dock stand[31] is capable of supporting two laptops simultaneously.

(45) Using the power button with long cable helps you control your computer from the comfort place in the room, making PC power switch ON and OFF much easier.

> 单词解析：
>
> 28. amplifier ['æmplɪfaɪə] n. 放大器
> 29. cellular ['seljələ] adj.（无线电话）蜂窝状的
> 30. clockwise ['klɔk,waɪz] adj. 顺时针的；右旋的
> 31. stand [stænd] n. 支架

产品服务介绍：

(46) 3-year warranty is provided when you purchase from the manufacturer or authorized reseller.

(47) We offer 180 days refund or replacement and a free-time warranty for the quality problem.

(48) ABC team will always standby with 7 days and 24 hours service.

(49) Every product purchased from us comes with 24-hour friendly customer service and 1 year product service.

(50) This laptop charger cord is backed for life, including free lifetime multilingual technical assistance.

直播模板 Template

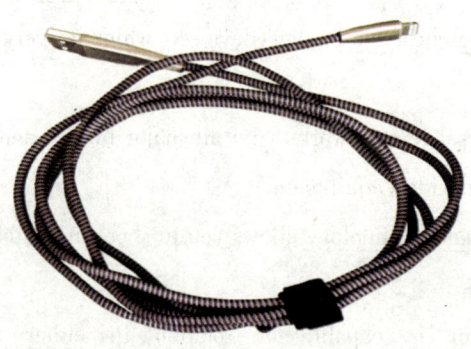

Today we will talk about _____ charging cables. Charging cables are essential for any mobile phone users, as it allows them to keep their device powered up when not in use. This is a fast charger cable. It is compatible with many types of phones like _____, _____, _____, and any device equipped with a _____ port. This cable allows for charging speed up to _____ Mbps, which is faster than most standard cables.

The connector material is formed using _____ to ensure durability and superior toughness. Reinforced stress points with a _____ and _____ bend lifespan make many times more durable than other USB cables. The length of _____ charger is _____ feet/meters, which meets all your needs and keeps your devices connected a much greater distance at home, on sofa, _____, _____.

4.4　实战脚本 Script

Live Streaming Script of Sports Watch

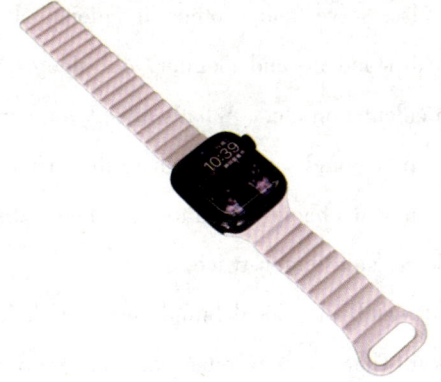

Hello guys, how are you doing? Welcome to Joyce's live streaming from ABC company! We have specialized for nearly 20 years in sportswear manufacturing. Today's main parts are for some best-sellers and of course we have also prepared some discounts for you. Today, we bring one of our best-selling sports watches within amazing price to our new followers. It is just released a few weeks ago. If you love sport accessories, don't forget to follow us and we will update new style every month. Now follow my lead and let's begin with the first item.

The first item is a digital sports watch from ABC company. Let me show you more details. It looks so fashionable and is of good quality. The thickness of the case is around 1.8 cm. The dial of our watch is made of high-quality organic glass. It has two watch movements imported from Switzerland. It has metal frame with soft strap made of PU.

It's the perfect choice for young people who love stylish sportwear and trendy sneakers. Imagine that, when you wear the off-white clothes and Nike shoes, you definitely need a cool watch to match your outfit. And as you can see, each watch comes in many colors and design which offers you multiple options.

The watch is waterproof and shock resistant, and has multiple sports modes. When you do outdoor exercises, like running, it's convenient for you to wear a sports watch and turn on running mode. It will keep track of your movement and it can resist moisture from sweat. And if you like swimming, surfing, cycling, or skipping, it will also be a great choice for you to wear our watch, cuz it's waterproof and shockproof. You can even see the time clearly even in a dark place.

This watch can also serve many other functions. It can help find your cellphone, remind you to stand up and monitor your sleep. You can also use it to check the weather, do calculation etc.. What's more, you can change the wallpaper by connecting it to your phone and select from more than 1000 kinds of wallpapers in the gallery for free. You can change the interface theme display style and adjust brightness by just click the side button twice.

If you buy a smart watch in a local brand store, it definitely costs a lot. But today, you are so lucky! This is newly released, that's why we bring this amazing watch with such incredible price. Only 30 pieces in stock for today. Just go and check our yellow shopping cart link below.

Our watch movement is guaranteed for one year, battery life is around 5 years. You can use it for a long time. If you have any other questions, feel free to leave your comments right here, I will answer all the questions in my live streaming channel, or you can contact our customer service to get more info.

Some of you may worry about shipping problem. There is nothing to worry about cuz we have been doing import and export business for over 20 years. We cooperate with professional shipping company. If the goods are lost during transit, we will send you a new one immediately.

Let's go for next item...

第五章
美妆个护类产品英语直播

中国海关总署的统计数据显示,2022年9月,中国美容化妆品及洗护用品出口数量为92490吨,同比增长1.2%,出口金额为5.35亿美元,同比增长5.9%;2022年1—9月,中国美容化妆品及洗护用品出口数量为783766吨,出口金额为43.22亿美元。

5.1 油膏类美妆 Oil and Creamy Products

词汇积累 Vocabulary

序号	中文名称	英文名称
1	唇膏	lip balm
2	唇笔	lip pencil
3	唇彩	lip gloss
4	润唇膏	lip balm
5	唇线笔	lip liner
6	染唇液	lip stain
7	丰唇液	lip plumper
8	唇部打底	lip foundation
9	固体口红	solid lipstick
10	液体口红	liquid lipstick
11	光泽感口红	shine lipstick
12	奶油口红	creamy lipstick
13	哑光口红	matte lipstick

续表

序号	中文名称	英文名称
14	水感口红	lacquer lipstick
15	缎光口红	satin lipstick
16	金属光泽口红	metallic lipstick
17	珠光口红	frosted lipstick
18	眼线胶	eyeliner gel
19	眉胶	eyebrow gel
20	遮瑕膏	concealer
21	修容膏	contour
22	粉条棒	stick foundation
23	粉底膏	cream foundation
24	睫毛膏	mascara
25	质地	texture/finish
26	颜色	pigment/tint/hue
27	裸色	nude
28	红色	red
29	深红色	deep red
30	珊瑚色	coral
31	猩红色	scarlet red
32	玫红色	rose red
33	橘红色	orange red
34	豆沙色	dusty rose
35	枫叶色	burny orange
36	蜜桃色	peach
37	死亡芭比粉	babydoll pink
38	低遮瑕	Light/sheer coverage
39	中等遮瑕	medium coverage
40	高遮瑕	full coverage
41	中高遮瑕	medium to full coverage

话术演练 Language Skills

产品规格介绍:

(1) Butter gloss is available in a wide variety of sumptuous[1] shades[2].

(2) This lipstick is available in 20 hydrating[3] shades.

(3) Slim lip pencils come in a variety of dashing[4] shades from auburn[5] to orange.

(4) The lipstick has 35 super-saturated[6] shades ranging from classic red liquid lipstick to nude and bold bright lipstick shades.

(5) It contains 4 colors velvet liquid lip stick set, full-size lip gloss of the most popular colors.

(6) Go for super-shiny[7] color in 23 unique shades from nudes, to pinks, to reds, and more.

(7) This eyebrow gel has the size of $0.8 \times 0.7 \times 3$ inches, and a capacity of 0.12 ounce[8].

(8) The original 6pcs red-toned lipstick set includes 5 colorful lip sticks and 1 smooth lip plumper[9].

(9) This richly-pigmented[10] concealer consists of 7 pieces in 7 different natural colors.

单词解析:

1. sumptuous [ˈsʌmptʃuəs] adj. 华丽的(近义词:gorgeous、magnificent)

2. shade [ʃeɪd] n. 色度

3. hydrating [ˈhaɪdreɪtɪŋ] adj. 使吸入水分的

4. dashing [ˈdæʃɪŋ] adj. 时髦的(近义词:fashionable、stylish、classy)

5. auburn [ˈɔːbən] adj. 红褐色的

6. saturated [ˈsætʃəreɪtɪd] adj. (溶液)饱和的

7. shiny [ˈʃaɪni] adj. 闪亮的

8. ounce [aʊns] n. 盎司

9. plumper [ˈplʌmpə] adj. 丰腴饱满的

10. pigmented [pɪgˈmentɪd] adj. 天然色的;本色的

产品质量与特色介绍：

(10) We use an adhesive[11] formula with a double layer elastomer[12] that fills in the fine curves of your lips.

(11) The contemporary packaging stands out with its black shiny finish with the MM logo embossed on the top.

(12) The concealer features a micro-corrector applicator for an easy and precise application.

(13) Multi-use contour stick now is available in 4 cruelty-free, gluten[13]-free, and fragrance-free shades.

(14) Super stay liquid lipstick, featuring micro flex technology, swipes[14] on effortlessly with the precision tip applicator.

(15) This mascara is made with pure and natural ingredients that are non-toxic[15] for sensitive eyes and contact-lens wearers.

(16) It is made with organic shea butter, organic argan oil, and Vitamin E for skin hydration[16] while plant pigments and minerals deliver gorgeous color.

(17) The silky creme formula[17] lasts up to 5 hours without drying, fading or settling into lines.

(18) Instead of using toxic chemicals to preserve, color or nourish, we substitute[18] them with high-quality, efficacious natural ingredients.

(19) Colour rich shine is formulated with 70 percent oils and a low wax[19] volume.

(20) Each glossy color delivers sheer[20] to medium coverage that melts onto your lips.

(21) This brilliant lip balm is made with high-shine emollients[21] that reflect light for a super glossy finish.

(22) Our light and fluffy lip mousse delivers luscious[22], full-coverage color with a non-drying feel.

(23) The built-in sharpener[23] of this award-winning matte[24] lipstick keeps the tip ultra-precise.

(24) Our cream foundation has supremely comfortable matte formula and soft

creamy texture.

(25) This long-lasting, no-transfer[25] eyebrow gel looks freshly and can be applied all day long.

(26) It is a liquid lipstick that provides a rush of pigment-soaked color in a velvety[26], matte finish.

(27) A lightweight[27] layer of color on your lips helps you get through the day without having your lips feel sticky or clumpy.

(28) The matte liquid lipstick has a high-intensity[28] pigment.

(29) The container[29] of this mascara has the magnetic closure.

(30) The hydrating, paraben-free lip color is infused[30] with hyaluronic acid, aloe, and rose quartz for intense moisture and a full, plump look.

(31) All of our makeup is certified[31] and acknowledged by PETA as a cruelty-free brand.

单词解析：

11. adhesive [əd'hiːsɪv] *n.* 胶黏剂；黏合剂

12. elastomer [ɪ'læstəmə(r)] *n.* 弹性体

13. gluten ['gluːtn] *n.* 谷蛋白

14. swipe [swaɪp] *v.* 刷

15. toxic ['tɒksɪk] *adj.* 有毒的

16. hydration [haɪ'dreɪʃən] *n.* 水化（合）作用

17. formula ['fɔːmjələ] *n.* 配方

18. substitute ['sʌbstɪtjuːt] *v.* 以……代替（近义词：replace、displace）

19. wax [wæks] *n.* 蜂蜡

20. sheer [ʃɪə(r)] *adj.* 又薄又轻几乎透明的

21. emollient [ɪ'mɒlɪənt] *n.* 润肤剂；润肤霜

22. luscious ['lʌʃəs] *adj.* 柔和的

23. sharpener ['ʃɑːpnə(r)] *n.* 磨具；削具

24. matte [mæt] *n.* 哑光

25. transfer [trænsˈfɜː(r)] *v.* 改变

> 26. velvety ['velvəti] adj. 光滑柔软的
> 27. lightweight ['laɪtweɪt] adj. 轻薄的
> 28. intensity [ɪn'tensəti] n. 强烈
> 29. container [kən'teɪnə(r)] n. 容器
> 30. infuse [ɪn'fjuːz] v. 使具有；注入（某特性）
> 31. certify ['sɜːtɪfaɪ] v.（尤指书面）证明；证实

产品功能介绍：

（32）These ingredients are beneficial[32] to the skin, making your lips look plumper.

（33）Our tints use a breakthrough formula with high intensity color pigments that naturally stain[33] your lips.

（34）6 lip liner pens makeup kits give your lip a full, sensuous[34] temptation.

（35）Turn back time with this anti-aging under eye treatment concealer infused with haloxy.

（36）Lightweight texture[35] and intense hydration offers a zero-gravity silky feel.

（37）Exclusive fanning mascara brush with ten layers of bristles[36] reveals layers of lashes for a sensational full-fan effect.

（38）Infused with Mediterranean algae extract[37], this lipstick balm moisturizes and smooths skin's appearance to create a perfect canvas[38] for optimum color laydown.

（39）The full coverage under-eye concealer instantly erases dark circles and fine lines to visibly diminish puffiness[39].

（40）In one swipe of a contour stick, you can get catwalk-ready cheekbones, naturally flushed cheeks or an insanely glowy complexion.

（41）This color has gone so viral recently and looks so stunning[40] on the lips.

（42）Color rose lipstick gives lips a light reddish color for a natural-looking flush[41].

（43）It feels so comfortable, weightless and ultra-creamy on face with a medium-to-full coverage.

(44) Specially designed brush wraps mascara evenly around every lash as it separates for a full, lush, high-volume look.

(45) The formula is infused with goji berry, an effective blood circulation booster, to create a radiant refreshed looking eye area.

> **单词解析：**
>
> 32. beneficial [ˌbenɪˈfɪʃl] adj. 有益的(近义词：constructive、helpful)
>
> 33. stain [steɪn] n. 染色剂
>
> 34. sensuous [ˈsenʃuəs] adj. 愉悦感官的；性感的
>
> 35. texture [ˈtekstʃə(r)] n. 质地
>
> 36. bristle [ˈbrɪsl] n. 刷子毛
>
> 37. extract [ɪkˈstrækt] n. 提取物
>
> 38. canvas [ˈkænvəs] n. 帆布；(帆布)画布
>
> 39. puffiness [ˈpʌfɪnəs] n. 膨胀；肿胀
>
> 40. stunning [ˈstʌnɪŋ] adj. 惊人的；极有魅力的 (近义词：amazing、dazzling、glorious)
>
> 41. flush [flʌʃ] n. 潮红；脸红(近义词：blush、flush)

产品服务与优势介绍：

(46) With a perfect package, it's ready for as a birthday gift to friends or families.

(47) Please notice that lipstick set may be damaged during shipment, if you receive a broken good, or you are not satisfied with our product, please feel free to contact us and we will spare no efforts to offer you a best solution.

(48) We're committed to celebrating beauty, self-expression and creativity with our full line of makeup, from foundations, BB creams, concealers and bronzers to mascaras, brow pencils, eyeliners and lipsticks.

(49) We combine technologically advanced formulations with on-trend expertise and Paris City edge.

(50) For everyone, whether you are a lady or you are a student, whether you are a make-up novice or a make-up artist. You can rely on our products.

直播模板 Template

_____ is the perfect lipstick that is comfortable to wear, with stunning colors that lasts for _____ hours. The lightweight lipstick leaves your pout looking _____ and _____ with instant-setting color payoff. Available in a range of _____ shades from beautiful everyday shades of _____ and _____ and _____ to bold shades of _____ and _____ and _____. Don't worry this highly pigmented lipstick will dry your lips out, because it is enriched with nourishing and skin-loving ingredients like _____ and _____, so it helps to provide _____ for your lips through the day. Plus, this product contains _____ to condition and soften lips, leaving you for a _____ feel. What's more, packaged in a _____ lipstick tube, it's perfect as a gift to send to _____ or _____ on festivals, such as _____ and _____.

5.2 粉类美妆 Powder Products

词汇积累 Vocabulary

序号	中文名称	英文名称
1	闪粉	shimmering powder/glitter
2	定妆粉	setting powder
3	蜜粉	loose powder
4	高光	highlighter
5	腮红	blush(er)/rouge

续表

序号	中文名称	英文名称
6	眉粉	eyebrow powder
7	粉饼	pressed powder
8	散粉	loose powder
9	矿物粉饼	mineral face powder
10	非矿物粉饼	non-mineral face powder
11	防晒粉饼	SPF powder
12	粉底	foundation
13	修容粉	shading powder
14	古铜粉	bronzer
15	眼影盘	eyeshadow palette
16	散粉眼影	loose eyeshadow
17	压粉眼影	pressed eyeshadow
18	烤粉眼影	baked eyeshadow
19	哑光眼影	matte eyeshadow
20	珠光眼影	shimmer eyeshadow
21	透亮眼影	sheer shimmer eyeshadow
22	高亮珠光眼影	bright shimmer eyeshadow
23	哑光微珠光眼影	matte with sparkle eyeshadow
24	丝绒眼影	velvet eyeshadow
25	闪耀眼影	sheen eyeshadow
26	贝母眼影	reflective eyeshadow
27	弹性眼影	bouncy eyeshadow
28	缎光眼影	satin eyeshadow
29	闪片眼影	glitter eyeshadow
30	金属眼影	metallic eyeshadow
31	偏光眼影	chrome eyeshadow
32	哑光质感	matte finish
33	轻薄质感	sheer finish

续表

序号	中文名称	英文名称
34	透亮质感	luminous finish
35	水润质感	dewy finish
36	无酒精	alcohol-free
37	无香精	fragrance-free
38	无味道	scentless
39	无刺激	no-irritating
40	持妆	long lasting
41	滋润	hydrating
42	防水	waterproof
43	抗老	anti-aging
44	防皱	anti-wrinkle
45	抗痘	anti-blemish
46	控油	oil control
47	提亮	brightening
48	紧致	tightening
49	防晒	sun-proof
50	细致毛孔	pore minimizing

话术演练 Language Skills

产品规格介绍：

（1）This travel-friendly mini highlighter is the perfect size to go everywhere with you.

（2）Available in matte, pearly[1], and sparkly[2] collections, so you can pick the right combination to suit your mood.

（3）A magically iridescent[3] eyeshadow palette[4] contains 20 professional cool-toned and warm-toned pigments[5] and shades[6].

（4）It offers different textures: soft smooth mattes[7], shimmery[8] pressed pearl and dazzling[9] metallic[10] glitters[11].

(5) This professional-level makeup palette features over 30 highly-pigmented shades from matte, shimmer, and metallic.

(6) Aromas palette includes 18 gorgeous shades which are smooth and velvety[12] texture powder.

(7) It consists of 10 highly-pigmented matte, 4 reflective shades, 2 glitters, 1 pressed pearl and 1 concealer[13] base shade.

(8) This eyebrow palette features in gorgeous neutral, brown and earthy tones with matte and shimmer finishes[14].

(9) This perfect powder eyebrow kit includes brow powder, brow pomade, flat brush and built-in mirror for on-the-go touch-ups.

(10) Our bite-size blush can be held in the palm of your hand, making them the perfect size for your purse and travel.

(11) These 6-pan cases are small compacts, and come in 6 color palettes that can be used solo or snapped together to mix and match as you please.

(12) Discover the ultra[15]-pigmented, multi-finish eye palette, including an eye primer, an eyeshadow, a highlighter and a liner.

单词解析：

1. pearly ['pɜːli] adj. 有珍珠光泽的（近义词：golden）

2. sparkly ['spɑːklɪ] adj. 耀眼的

3. iridescent [ˌɪrɪ'desnt] adj. 彩虹色的；色彩斑斓的（近义词：shot、irised）

4. palette ['pælət] n. 调色板；一组颜色

5. pigment ['pɪgmənt] n. 颜料；天然色素

6. shade [ʃeɪd] n. 浓淡深浅

7. matte [mæt] n. 哑光

8. shimmery ['ʃɪməri] adj. 闪烁的（近义词：glittery、scintillant）

9. dazzling ['dæzlɪŋ] adj. 耀眼的（近义词：glaring、sparkly）

10. metallic [mə'tælɪk] adj. 有金属光泽的

11. glitter ['glɪtə] n. 闪闪发光

12. velvety ['velvətɪ] *adj.* 天鹅绒般柔软的
13. concealer [kən'siːlə] *n.* 遮瑕膏
14. finish ['fɪnɪʃ] *n.* 抛光；质地
15. ultra ['ʌltrə] *adv.* 很；非常（近义词：extremely、excessively）

产品质量与特色介绍：

（13）It is a lightweight pressed powder with a demi-matte finish that lasts up to 24 hours.

（14）This reasonably-priced blusher is suitable for different occasions such as party, wedding or casual.

（15）The brand partnered with a famous artist on this palette which is filled with 20 deep and vibrant[16] shades of pink, blue, green, and more.

（16）This must-have eyeshadow palette is filled with a dozen majorly pigmented shades, ranging from super wearable nudes to bolder neons.

（17）The luxe highlighter formula is smooth, creamy, blendable, and ultra-luminous.

（18）These super-saturated[17] shades have uplifting names to match, like Lucky Charm, Kaleidoscope, and Fantasyland.

（19）It has the rainbow-inspired hues[18] and finishes, ranging from shine glitter topcoat[19] to entrancing[20] ultra-reflective metallic.

（20）The powder adheres[21] easily to the eyes, and blends smoothly and evenly.

（21）It has cruelty-free ingredient and lightweight formula, and provides creamy butter-like application[22].

（22）Our crease[23]-proof eyeshadows are baked from cream pigments for 24 hours, resulting in the smooth blendable texture and minimal fallout.

（23）Formulated with micro-fine pearls, this highlighter creates a multi-dimensional, light-catching effect.

（24）Use eyebrow powder for daily effortless brow look, or eyebrow pomade for dramatically defined brows.

（25）Rose blusher has rich shades with intense pigment payoff[24], which deliver striking[25] impact.

(26) Advanced artistry palette housed inside a cute, rectangle[26]-cut, lightweight, black packaging.

> **单词解析：**
> 16. vibrant [ˈvaɪbrənt] adj. 鲜亮的
> 17. saturated [ˈsætʃəreɪtɪd] adj. 饱和的（近义词：satd、penetrating）
> 18. hue [hjuː] n. 色调（近义词：tonality）
> 19. topcoat [ˈtɒpkəʊt] n. 外涂层
> 20. entrancing [ɪnˈtrɑːnsɪŋ] adj. 使人神魂颠倒的
> 21. adhere [ədˈhɪə] v. 使黏附
> 22. application [ˌæplɪˈkeɪʃn] n. 涂抹
> 23. crease [kriːs] n. 皱纹
> 24. payoff [ˈpeɪˌɒf] n. 结果（近义词：event）
> 25. striking [ˈstraɪkɪŋ] adj. 引人注目的；显著的（近义词：tremendous）
> 26. rectangle [ˈrektæŋgl] n. 长方形

产品功能与优势介绍：

(27) This richly toned palette features versatile[27] shades that can be blended and layered to create endless amounts of looks.

(28) It is a coveted[28] palette with pressed powder shadows that can be used for shading, highlighting, and defining eyes, brows, and the contours of the face.

(29) These silky eyeshadows from warm to cool can create a range of looks with smoky, neutral, gorgeous and luminous[29].

(30) These high-performance shadows in 6 futuristic[30] finishes are designed for infinite artistry[31].

(31) Eyeshadow stick set delivers uniform shimmer in every swipe[32], perfect for quick, easy eye looks on-the-go.

(32) The glittering highlighter palette with shimmering powder immediately gives the face a three-dimensional display effect when applied.

(33) This pressed powder effectively minimizes the appearance of red tones

within the skin.

(34) Beauty brick eyeshadow collection gives you the best of all colors to allow you to create stunning[33] looks!

(35) Translucent face powder helps to absorb excess oil, keeping your skin looking fresh.

(36) Mix and match shades to achieve everything from a natural look to high drama[34] eyes.

(37) This eyeshadow stick does double-duty, thanks to the hydrating[35], nourishing formula with Vitamin C & E.

(38) Each high-quality blusher features a highly pigmented mix of finishes from matte and satin[36] to shimmery and metallic.

(39) Use shimmery pretty pink blusher to contour your face and add a natural rosiness to your cheeks[37].

(40) Your eyes can be illuminated[38], defined and emboldened[39] according to each occasion.

(41) Mineral powder sunscreen protects skin from harmful sun rays[40].

(42) With autorotation[41] tube design, it's easily twist up for convenient use, so no need to sharpen.

(43) Regardless of whether you pick one that's neutral, bright pink, or subdued[42] purple, you'll get nothing but full pigment and zero fallout[43].

单词解析：

27. versatile [ˈvɜːsətaɪl] *adj.* 多功能的

28. coveted [ˈkʌvətɪd] *adj.* 梦寐以求的

29. luminous [ˈluːmɪnəs] *adj.* 有光泽的（近义词：bright）

30. futuristic [ˌfjuːtʃəˈrɪstɪk] *adj.* 极现代化的

31. artistry [ˈɑːtɪstri] *n.* 艺术创造技巧

32. swipe [swaɪp] *n.* 刷

33. stunning [ˈstʌnɪŋ] *adj.* 极吸引人的（近义词：wonderful、excellent）

34. drama [ˈdrɑːmə] *n.* 戏剧性（近义词：stage、theater）

> 35. hydrating ['haɪdreɪtɪŋ] *adj.* （使）水合的
> 36. satin ['sætɪn] *n.* 缎子般光滑（近义词：smooth、glossy、glabrous）
> 37. cheek [tʃiːk] *n.* 脸颊
> 38. illuminated [ɪ'luːmɪneɪtɪd] *adj.* 发光的
> 39. emboldened [em'bəʊldənd] *v.* 变粗；放大
> 40. ray [reɪ] *n.* （热或其他能量的）射线
> 41. autorotation [ˌɔːtə(ʊ)rə(ʊ)'teɪʃ(ə)n] *n.* 自转
> 42. subdued [səb'djuːd] *adj.* 柔和的
> 43. fallout ['fɔːlaʊt] *n.* 悬浮物

产品服务介绍：

(44) We offer a 10-day money back guarantee in case you are not satisfied (sales tax and shipping will not be refunded).

(45) Each luxurious glossy book has a double-ended brush and mirror inside.

(46) The product may will be damaged during the shipment, if you received the broken goods, or you not satisfied with our product. We will offer a solution to you.

(47) The outer pack of this palette is <u>FSC certified and recyclable</u>.

(48) Our mission is to offer innovative, accessible and effortless cosmetics for everyone.

(49) As the biggest beauty brand in the world, we have an unparalleled commitment to combining the latest in technology with the highest in quality for the ultimate in luxury beauty.

直播模板 Template

Discover this super-affordable eye shadow palette from _____ brand. It has gone viral on _____ (social media) recently! Believe me, it's the palette you'll be pulling out time and time again! Now let me open up the floral motif case, and you'll find _____ highly-pigmented shades in _____ and _____ tones. This versatile palette can be easily blended and layered to create a _____ look or _____ look. So, whether you go for a sparkly metallic, solid matte, or a mix of both, one thing's for sure: You'll look beyond stunning! Here, I am applying this product on my eyelids to show you the texture and finish. For usage, personally I love using the shades with a wet angle brush as a liner or a fluffy brush for a beautiful wash of color. As you can see, this eyeshadow palette is effortlessly buildable, and it applies evenly and consistently with _____ texture, leaving amazing _____ finish. Also, it is not patchy, and will not wear off quickly. Moreover, I bet you will be surprised with its skincare benefits! This product is uniquely infused with the extract of _____ and _____. These healthy skincare ingredients are well-known to effectively erases the look of _____ and _____. It helps to strengthen and restore our skin's moisture barrier, giving your eyes and surrounding area a _____ feeling.

5.3 个体护理 Personal Care

词汇积累 Vocabulary

序号	中文名称	英文名称
1	护手霜/乳	hand cream/lotion
2	身体霜/乳	body cream/lotion
3	卸妆水	makeup remover
4	洗面奶	cleanser/face wash
5	沐浴露	body wash
6	香皂	bar soap
7	面部磨砂膏	facial scrub
8	身体磨砂膏	body scrub

续表

序号	中文名称	英文名称
9	染发剂	hair coloring/dye
10	洗发水	shampoo
11	护发素	hair conditioner
12	护发油	hair treatment oil
13	免洗型护发素	leave-on conditioner
14	脱发护理剂	hair loss treatment
15	去屑洗发水	anti-dandruff shampoo
16	指甲油	nail polish
17	护甲液	nail saver
18	卸甲油	nail polish remover
19	眼霜	eye gel/cream
20	面膜	facial mask
21	手膜	hand mask
22	足膜	foot mask
23	睡眠面膜	sleep mask
24	保湿霜	moisturizer
25	精华液	essence/serum
26	乳液	emulsion/milk
27	喷雾	facial mist/spray
28	爽肤水	toner
29	牙齿美白	teeth whitening
30	漱口水	mouthwash
31	牙线	dental floss
32	剃须刀	razor/blade
33	上蜡除毛剂	waxing

续表

序号	中文名称	英文名称
34	激光脱毛器	laser electrolysis hair removal
35	睫毛夹	eyelash curler
36	修眉刀	eyebrow knife
37	吸油纸	oil-absorbing sheet
38	化妆棉	cotton pad
39	棉签	Q-tip/cotton swab
40	卷发棒	hair curler
41	吹风机	hairdryer
42	梳子	hair comb
43	洗脸仪	cleansing device
44	镊子	tweezers
45	扁平发夹	bobby pin
46	描眉卡	brow template
47	美妆蛋	beauty blender
48	粉扑	powder puff
49	眉刷	brow brush
50	眼影刷	eye shadow brush

话术演练 Language Skills

产品规格与优势介绍：

（1）Box contains 1 Garnier color sensation permeant[1] cream, luminous brown.

（2）Available in 40 shades[2], you'll find a fit for every skin tone.

（3）The product comes with 1 case, 2 refills and 2 puffs[3].

（4）It has the size of 1.5×1×3.5 inches, and a capacity of 1 ounce[4].

（5）You will have six 14.2-fluid ounce bottles of 2-in-1 dandruff[5] shampoo and conditioner.

(6) This is a gel nail kit with super multi-color gel nail polish, including 32 bottles of classic gel nail polish (7 ml each).

(7) It's a 18-fluid ounce bottle of daily moisturizing body lotion with prebiotic oat.

(8) Fragrance-free and fast absorbing, this body serum is enhanced by caffeine, botanical[6] firming complex and omega oil.

> 单词解析：
> 1. permeant ['pɜːmɪənt] n. 渗透物
> 2. shade [ʃeɪd] n. 色度
> 3. puff [pʌf] n. 粉扑
> 4. ounce [aʊns] n. 盎司（重量单位，1 盎司等于 28.35 克）
> 5. dandruff ['dændræf] n. 头皮屑
> 6. botanical [bə'tænɪkl] adj. 植物学的

产品质量与特色介绍：

(9) It's an ADA approved product and has become one of the United States' best-selling speciality oral hygiene[7] treatments.

(10) Being the number 1 deodorant brand by volume, Degree' best deodorant for men is known to give you the ultimate[8] freshness.

(11) This eye gel is known for its exceptional affinity[9] to skin.

(12) It is infused with multitasking serum[10] to care for your skin.

(13) It contains pro vitamin[11] B_5, a dermatologist[12]-recognized ingredient.

(14) Non-comedogenic[13] serum is free of fragrances, parabens[14], alcohol, and sulfates.

(15) Mint oral rinse is free of dyes, perfumes, detergents, and other harsh additives[15] that can dry or damage the mouth.

(16) This carefully formulated[16] body shower for mature skin is made with vitamin B_3 and hydrating serum.

(17) The sleep mask is infused[17] with 58% essence[18] for not sticky or greasy feeling.

（18）This teeth-whitening product is our flagship[19] product and has been dentist- and pharmacist-recommended for more than 10 years.

（19）This gentle, non-irritating[20] formula is ideal for sensitive skin.

（20）The creamy texture enriched[21] with camellia wraps[22] every hair without dripping.

（21）Queens Award Winning Company, made in the US for women & men, sulphate free, paraben free for your hair and scalp[23] health.

单词解析：

 7. hygiene ['haɪdʒiːn] n. 卫生

 8. ultimate ['ʌltɪmɪt] adj. 终极的；最好的

 9. affinity [ə'fɪnɪtɪ] n. 喜好；类同

 10. serum ['sɪərəm] n. 精华

 11. vitamin ['vaɪtəmɪn] n. 维生素

 12. dermatologist [ˌdɜːmə'tɔlədʒɪst] n. 皮肤病医生/专家

 13. comedogenic [ˌkɔmɪdə(ʊ)'dʒɛnɪk] adj. 易导致粉刺的

 14. paraben [pə'ræben] n. 对羟基苯甲酸酯

 15. additive ['ædətɪv] n. 添加剂

 16. formulate ['fɔːmjuleɪt] v. 制定

 17. infuse [ɪn'fjuːz] v. 灌输；注入

 18. essence ['esns] n. 要素（近义词：substance、texture）

 19. flagship ['flægʃɪp] n. 最重要产品；王牌

 20. irritating ['ɪrɪteɪtɪŋ] adj. 刺激

 21. enriched [ɪn'rɪtʃt] v. 使饱含（某物）

 22. wrap [ræp] v. 用……包裹

 23. scalp [skælp] n. 头皮

产品功能介绍：

（22）This hand cream helps to retain[24] skin's natural moisture[25], and provide long-lasting hydration.

（23）This refreshing antibacterial cleanser rinse is praised for its ability to attack and eliminate embarrassing breath odor[26] for up to 14 hours.

(24) Our popular eye gel visibly diminishes[27] the look of fine lines, wrinkles, dark circles and other blemishes[28].

(25) It's oil-free and supercharged[29] with glycerin[30] to hydrate and soften your skin.

(26) With SPF 20, this sunscreen protects against UV damage and future discoloration.

(27) Rose body scrub gently exfoliates[31] to reveal visibly radiant and smooth skin.

(28) This men's deodorant gives an energizing burst of crisp, arctic freshness in men's fragrance and 28 h odor protection.

(29) Intensive care nourishing moisture lotion provides a radiant look, color correction, and a buildable coverage all at once.

(30) 3D whitening toothpaste removes 85% more surface stains, protects against future stains, and leaves your smile bright and minty fresh.

(31) It will help stimulate your hair growth, strengthen hair follicles[32], improve scalp circulation and condition.

(32) Its friendly formula is clinically proven to remove dirt, makeup and impurities while preserving the skin's natural moisture barrier.

(33) This facial cream can refine pores[33] and they won't clog pores or cause additional breakouts[34].

(34) Silk-expert pro 6 IPL uses our unique SensoAdapt technology to provide safe and effective long-lasting reduction in hair regrowth.

(35) Hair treatment oil strengthens and repairs fibers, making hair more soft, shiny, and resistant to external aggressors.

(36) This antiperspirant for women is designed to be the best deodorant for sweat through any extreme sport, workout, and alternative forms of movement.

(37) The formula's three oil absorbers resist sweat, water, and transfer.

(38) High durability and intense pigmentation nail polish can bring you a brilliant shine finish without color-fading or peeling-off problems.

(39) Try herbal essences hair conditioner to deeply condition and de-frizz hair for a soft, sleek end-look.

(40) Foot peel mask is designed to remove the dead skin on your feet and allows you to have incredibly firm elastic[35] skin.

(41) Ultra daily moisturizer enhances radiance and light reflection and to help banish[36] unwanted shadows.

(42) It is proven to remove damaging environmental pollutants from skin and prevent the reoccurrence.

(43) This moisturizing conditioner features with argan oil to moisturize, soften, and add shine to dry hair.

(44) Proprietary self-foaming technology is more effective in removing free radicals for a better and deeper clean.

单词解析：

24. retain [rɪ'teɪn] v. 吸收并保留（近义词：keep up）

25. moisture ['mɔɪstʃə] n. 湿润（近义词：rainfall、humidity、content）

26. odor ['əʊdə] n. 气味

27. diminish [dɪ'mɪnɪʃ] v. 使削弱

28. blemish ['blemɪʃ] n. 瑕疵；污点

29. supercharged ['suːpətʃɑːdʒd] adj. 充满

30. glycerin ['ɡlɪsərɪn] n. 甘油

31. exfoliate [eks'fəʊlɪeɪt] v. 使死皮脱落

32. follicle ['fɔlɪkəl] n. 毛囊

33. pore ['pɔː] n. 毛孔

34. breakout ['breɪkaʊt] n. 爆痘

35. elastic [ɪ'læstɪk] adj. 有弹力的

36. banish ['bænɪʃ] v. 清除

产品服务介绍：

(45) Plus, our professional customer service team will help you solve any problem, please feel free to contact us.

(46) Our company is a professional makeup manufacturer with a professional design, production, quality inspection, and sales team.

(47) We combine high-performance pigments and dermatologist-created standards to create products intended for all skin types, tones and conditions.

(48) All our products are made from skin-loving ingredients you want, minus the toxins you don't need—all at good-for-you prices!

(49) For customers who purchase products from our store, we provide 7 days free return guarantee and 1 year warranty.

(50) We are the trusted beauty destination for beauty lovers of all ages, ethnicities, skin colors, and economic statuses. No matter who or where you are in life, we have a product for you.

直播模板 Template

Nourish and soothe your skin with moisturizing body lotion by _____. This product has a _____ texture that is absorbed quickly, leaving skin feeling smooth and hydrated. Clinically proven to provide immediate and long-lasting relief of _____ skin. Enriched with _____ and _____, this daily body lotion gets to work instantly to hydrate the skin and protect it from dryness for _____ hours, leaving it feeling soft, smooth and nourished. Besides, formulated with our new ingredient blend of _____ and _____, this improved formula helps to preserve the skin's moisture barrier, improve water retention, soothe the skin, and improve the overall quality of sensitive skin in _____ week. _____% of users agree that skin seems more hydrated over time. Also, lotion with _____-fluid ounce is non-_____ and non-_____, and gentle enough for daily use as part of a regular beauty and skincare routine. To use, apply _____ as often as needed.

5.4 实战脚本 Script

Live Streaming Script of Makeup and Personal Care

Hello, welcome to our live streaming, I am Betty. As we all know, a busy social life, lack of sleep or sun damage can wreak havoc on our face. Today, I am introducing you the iconic, fan favorite liquid foundation "True Match". So, it's time to say goodbye to the look of fine lines, redness, scars and dark circles, and hello to a flawless and natural-looking finish! Matching 90% of Chinese female skin tones, from ivory to mocha, our foundation is available in 26 true-to-skin shades, so I promise you would find your unique shade easily! Also, being fragrance-free and alcohol-free, it is suitable for all skin types, even sensitive. Now with an upgraded, breathable formula that provides up to 12-hour wear, this product controls oil all day. It allows you to look flawless, fresh and bright through heat, sweat and humidity. It's truly powerful and amazing, right? As you can see from my face, this liquid foundation applies, builds and blends easily. It unifies uneven skin tone and covers imperfections with buildable, medium-to-full coverage that feels lightweight and so comfortable. You will find no caking, no poring, no streaking, no settling into fine lines or pores. For everyone, whether you are a lady or you are a student, whether you are a make-up novice or a make-up artist, you can choose this product! Find your "True Match" today 100% satisfaction guaranteed as this best-selling foundation is produced by a worldwide leading beauty care company Beautycat. Based in Paris, Beautycat offers innovative and high-end products, and accessible luxury for all those who demand excellence in beauty. Personally, I am completely obsessed with this exceptional foundation! And we know how much you love this product, so we've decided to give you a little treat. The original price for each is 49.9 dollars, but 20% off on EVERYTHING only for the next 1 hour in our live streaming! We have only got 300 pieces for this special prize! Hurry before the sale ends! And the most exciting part for our live streaming is that, once you hit the first 5K likes, we will have a lucky draw and 10 lucky participants will get a custom design cosmetic bag for free! Hit it up! Start now on!

Beauty is power, "Let your lips do the talking". As long as with a bit of lipstick color, you open the doors to a brilliant day and a brilliant smile. I can't wait to present you with our next popular product, a new launching 4pcs liquid lipstick makeup set manufactured by world's number 1 makeup brand! This is an iconic product that everyone is talking about! This makeup set contains 4 sheer liquid lipsticks with different shades. Now, I am applying these 4 lipsticks on my hands together to show you the different shades. Wow, what luxuriously rich colors! As you can see, here we have got 1 bold red, 1 coral orange red, 1 natural nude and 1 dusty rose lipstick. These are the most popular and charming colors for you to choose on any occasion, such as dating, party, wedding, bar, and office. You can't go wrong with any of these colors honestly! Really love these outstanding colors myself, and I can't wait to give them a really fair shot. What shade do you like best? Type in the comment section and let me know!

Ok, I see Lisa just commented "LOVING coral orange". Me too! I just adore this vibrant orange red! It's such a highly pigmented shade that gives you a feeling of summer vibe! Well, to show you guys the color and texture, let me apply this gorgeous coral orange red on my lips. Wow, this lipstick glides on so smoothly and feels incredible on the lips, and it's very lightweight and hydrating. Also, the texture is so buttery and creamy, which delivers a medium-to-full coverage that easily melts onto my lips. Besides, if you hate having touch-ups all the time, then this long-lasting and waterproof lipstick is a must-have for you, as it's never sticky and tacky. It always leaves your lips soft, supple and kissable! Now, grab one set at only ＄29.9 and then you can try all of our 4 delicious shades! If you order up to ＄59, you can also get ＄10 coupons. Take advantage of our special offer! These are limited edition makeup sets, which means they go out of stock quickly! Act now before it's too late, this deal won't last forever.

All right sweeties, thanks for being with me all the time, we are about to end our live streaming very soon. Tomorrow, we will be in live at 10 a.m., see ya! Bye bye!

第六章
玩具产品英语直播

中国是世界第一大玩具出口国。从中国海关总署发布的贸易数据来看,中国玩具出口金额逐年增长,2022年上半年度,中国玩具出口金额214亿美元,全年玩具出口总额483.56亿美元,同比增长5.6%。从中国玩具细分产品出口地区来看,美国、日本和英国是我国玩具的主要出口国。中国玩具的制造工艺较为成熟,玩具生产企业众多,玩具品种繁多,包括益智玩具、模型玩具、科技智能玩具、运动健身玩具、户外玩具、社会性玩具等。

6.1 启蒙及益智类玩具 Educational Toys

词汇积累 Vocabulary

序号	中文名称	英文名称
1	视觉发育黑白卡	black and white flash cards
2	手摇铃	baby handbell/rattle
3	悬挂床铃	hanging rotating bell
4	牙胶	chewing toy
5	早教机	early education tablet
6	画板	writing and drawing tablet
7	配对类玩具	matching toy
8	婴儿健身架	baby gym rack
9	儿童手机	kids' cellphone toy
10	有声读物	audio book
11	鲁班锁	interlocking burr puzzle

续表

序号	中文名称	英文名称
12	儿童电子音乐琴	piano keyboard toy
13	有声玩偶	talking doll
14	拼图	jigsaw puzzle
15	早教挂图	educational poster
16	超轻黏土	air-dry clay
17	拨浪鼓	rattle-drum
18	水果切切乐	fruit cutting simulation toy set
19	儿童相机	kids' digital camera
20	数独游戏	sudoku puzzle
21	折纸	paper folding
22	九连环	9 linked ring puzzle
23	儿童望远镜	kids' microscope
24	电动磁性钓鱼玩具	magnetic fishing toy
25	数字华容道	klotski puzzle
26	打地鼠玩具	whack-a-mole toy
27	婴儿游戏毯/垫	baby play mat
28	太空沙	colorful magic sand
29	叠叠高/乐	stacking toy
30	七巧板智力拼图	tangram puzzle
31	木质积木	wooden building blocks
32	乐高	Lego building blocks
33	魔方	rubik's cube
34	磁力片	magnetic building tiles
35	拼插积木	interlocking building blocks
36	轨道比赛汽车	race track game
37	手工制作类玩具	DIY toy
38	3D立体迷宫	3D maze puzzle
39	摇摇木马	wooden rocking horse

续表

序号	中文名称	英文名称
40	棋盘游戏	board game
41	算数计算架	abacus wooden toy
42	有声卡片	talking flashcard
43	贴纸	sticker
44	万花筒	kaleidoscope
45	挖沙玩具	sand toy set
46	手敲琴	wooden xylophone toy
47	手鼓	hand drum
48	婴儿抚触球	sensory ball
49	绕珠/串珠	bead toy
50	科学实验玩具	science lab kit
51	空间想象	spatial imagination
52	感知能力	sensory ability
53	逻辑思维能力	logical thinking ability

话术演练 Language Skills

产品规格与特色介绍：

（1）The LCD[1] drawing pad[2] for kids provides 10 inches of space for kid's writing and drawing.

（2）The LCD drawing pad is thin and of lightweight.

（3）The talking toy uses 3 pieces of LR6 AA 1.5 V alkaline[3] batteries.

（4）The magnetic tiles[4] package includes 20 pcs of square, 12 pcs of equilateral[5] triangle, 2 pcs of right angled triangle, 4 pcs of acute angled triangle[6], 2 pcs of windows, 4 pcs of rectangle, 2 pcs of large square base, 1 pc of manual, and 1 pc of retail box.

（5）The recommended age is between 36 months to 6 years.

（6）Our construction toys include 200 pcs of flexible track components, 2 race cars, 4 mini construction trucks, 8 traffic signs, 2 trees, and a bridge.

（7）This toy will introduce more than <u>100 age-appropriate</u> words chosen by learning experts, which includes word categories like pets, animals, food, mealtime, colors, activities, opposites, outside, vehicles, clothes, the body and fruit.

（8）The sticker <u>bulk pack</u>[7] is of a great value, including 16 sheets with <u>over 200</u> stickers of fun designs, like <u>hearts, stars, rainbows, smiley faces, balloons, flowers, sweet treats and more</u>.

（9）<u>The sound book</u> is designed for children of <u>3 years old and up</u>.

（10）<u>This comprehensive ABC book</u> makes learning fun, includes 6 learning activities, 8 learning pages, and 100 + sounds, songs and melodies.

（11）This talking flashcard set contains <u>255 cards（510 sides）, 31 topics</u> in total, such as letters, numbers, animals, colors, shapes, family members, transportation, behavior, months, and more.

（12）The card reader weights <u>71 g</u>, which is easy for kids to hold.

（13）These cards are sized to fit <u>small hands（similar to ordinary playing cards）</u>.

（14）This set of <u>50</u> cards features images <u>silhouetted</u>[8] in <u>black-on-white</u> on one side, and in <u>white-on-black</u> on the opposite side.

（15）These cards are suitable learning toys for newborns <u>from 0－6 months</u>, infants from 6－12 months and toddlers <u>from 12－18 months</u>.

（16）Our play mat has an ideal <u>26 plus 20</u> inches size that is suitable for all baby girls or boys older than 3 months.

单词解析：

1. LCD *abbr.* 液晶显示

2. pad ［pæd］ *n.* 平板

3. alkaline ［ˈælkəlaɪn］ *adj.* 碱性的

4. tile ［taɪl］ *n.* 片状材料

5. equilateral ［ˌiːkwɪˈlætərəl］ *adj.* 等边的

6. acute angled triangle 锐角三角形

7. bulk pack 散装；大包装

8. silhouette ［ˌsɪluˈet］ *n.* 形状；轮廓

产品质量与优势介绍:

(17) Compared with other monochrome[9] tablets, our color screen tablets are brighter and clearer.

(18) The LCD writing tablet adopts pressure-sensitive flexible screen, with no blue light, no glare[10], no radiation[11], no harm to eyesight.

(19) The writing tablet toddler[12] drawing toy is drop-resistant, shock-proof and water proof.

(20) Magnetic building tiles are made of non-toxic and durable ABS plastic[13], food grade material.

(21) It has round edge design without sharpness, there is no need to worry about hurting your kid's little hands.

(22) This plush[14] toy uses non-toxic and harmless plush fabric which is soft and comfortable for kids to play with confidence.

(23) The bottom of the electronic Tik Tok cactus toy is plastic, so it can stand firmly on the table.

(24) Each construction track is in a unique design and perfectly fit in kids' hands, portable to carry in the pocket to play everywhere.

(25) Race car can cross the bridge, and the track pieces can be flexed[15], snapped[16] to form various different track shapes.

(26) This eco-friendly stationery[17] is made with paper from well-managed forests.

(27) Just insert the card into the reader slot[18], the reader will read the words and make a simulated sound automatically.

(28) The toddler toy comes with built-in rechargeable battery and can be used for up to 4.5 hours, no need to charge frequently.

(29) The toys are made of BPA-free[19], durable ABS plastic material that meets China/US toy safety requirements.

(30) Our baby water mats are made from durable, 100% BPA-free and non-toxic, heavy PVC materials. Each of our game mats has been rigorously[20] tested, is of superior quality and 100% leak-proof.

(31) The mat is made from safe and skin-friendly material.

(32) The arch bridge and keyboard are removed easily; and the floor mat can easily be folded up when it is taken outdoors or even for traveling.

> 单词解析:
>
> 9. monochrome ['mɑːnəkrəʊm] *adj.* 单色的;黑白的
>
> 10. glare [gleə] *n.* 强光
>
> 11. radiation [ˌreɪdɪ'eɪʃn] *n.* 辐射
>
> 12. toddler ['tɑːdlər] *n.* 学步的儿童
>
> 13. ABS plastic 丙烯腈-丁二烯-苯乙烯塑料(acrylonitrile butadiene styrene)
>
> 14. plush [plʌʃ] *n.* 长毛绒
>
> 15. flex [fleks] *v.* 弯曲;屈伸
>
> 16. snap [snæp] *n.* 摁扣
>
> 17. stationary ['steɪʃəneri] *adj.* 静止的;不可移动的
>
> 18. slot [slɑːt] *n.* 键槽
>
> 19. BPA-free 不含双酚基丙烷
>
> 20. rigorously ['rɪɡərəsli] *adv.* 严厉地

产品功能介绍:

(33) The drawing tablet is a good educational learning toys, which helps child free their imagination and creativity.

(34) The preschool toddlers can have all the pleasure, enjoy painting, count the numbers, spell phrases at any time and place (home, car, outside, airplane, school) with no longer making a mess on the ground or walls, especially the time they are at home.

(35) Your child can create with this magnetic building blocks and tiles 3D geometric[21] figures while they are playing, naturally recognizing the principles of magnets by feeling the magnetic power.

(36) The magnetic building tiles set includes different shapes so that kids can stretch their imagination to the next level by creating different styles, recognize basic

colors and foster an interest in construction.

(37) Baby cactus[22] toy can dance to the rhythm, can sing 120 English songs, can also imitate the baby's speech and attract the baby's attention.

(38) The toy can dance, sing, move, turn around.

(39) This construction toys helps your kids fly his/her imagination to build his/her own track world on their own, which help them overall develop, limit screen time, make time for healthy hands-on play.

(40) These racing cars for boys can not only satisfy children's obsession[23] with cars but also can be interesting decoration.

(41) 3 colorful push buttons are added to the toddler puppy toy to help promote fine motor skill development in infants and toddlers alike.

(42) The stickers are perfect for decorating notebooks, pencil cases, invitations, greeting cards, and more.

(43) Perfect for grading papers, handing out as party favors, or personalizing your gear for school or home, these fun stickers have a design for every style.

(44) This toddler toys can be used by parents and teachers to teach little ones learning talking, expand vocabulary and reinforce sight words in a much more interesting way, especially helpful for autistic[24] kids to develop speech capability.

(45) As your infant or toddler handles flashcards, they develop movement skills and dexterity[25].

(46) Your little one's vision and recognition skills will grow as they view the cards and encounter images of animals, shapes and common objects, as well as simple repeating patterns.

(47) During tummy[26] time play or as a high chair activity, black-and-white flash cards provide a beautiful opportunity for wee[27] ones to begin discovering the world.

(48) This set of cards uses black-and-white images to activate early brain and visual development.

(49) The soft, comfortable baby tummy time water mat is the perfect sensory toy for developing solid head, neck and shoulder muscles as well as refining[28] the hand-eye coordination, fine motor and social skills.

(50) The bright, colorful sea animals and eye-catching illustrations will keep your baby playing for hours.

(51) The baby gym provides a much interactive activity center for babies, with 5 detachable colorful hanging rattles[29] and graceful piano music can stimulate the baby's sensory and physical coordination skills with baby kicking the keyboards or catching the toys.

(52) The 3D maze[30] puzzle toy is the best office game for stimulating inspiration, relieve stress, and also good for parents-children interaction and parties in killing time.

(53) The rattle toy is light in weight and small in size, which is convenient for babies to grasp and exercise grasping ability.

(54) These sensory balls provide support for autistic children with ADHD[31], autism, fidgeting[32], or stress-related behaviors.

(55) It is Montessori[33] toys for 1 year old and also a great bath toys for infants from 6 to 12 months and silicone teether toys for infants.

单词解析：

21. geometric [ˌdʒiːəˈmetrɪk] adj. 几何图形的

22. cactus [ˈkæktəs] n. 仙人掌

23. obsession [əbˈseʃn] n. 痴迷；着魔

24. autistic [ɔːˈtɪstɪk] adj. 患自闭症的

25. dexterity [dekˈsterəti] n. 灵巧；敏捷

26. tummy [ˈtʌmi] n.（非正式）肚子

27. wee [wiː] adj. 很小的；极小的

28. refine [rɪˈfaɪn] v. 提炼

29. rattle [ˈrætl] n. 拨浪鼓

30. maze [meɪz] n. 迷宫

31. ADHD abbr. 注意缺陷障碍(伴多动)；多动症

32. fidget [ˈfɪdʒɪt] v. 坐立不安；烦躁

33. Montessori [ˌmɔntiˈsɔri] 蒙台梭利教育法

产品服务介绍：

(56) × × × is committed to providing consumers with the best product and service, your satisfaction is the most important.

(57) If you are not completely satisfied with our product, please feel free to contact us. we will give you a satisfactory solution.

(58) If you have some issues with our products, please contact our team, we offer 24 hours and 7 days service for you.

直播模板 Template

This classic creative kit of _____ building blocks comes with _____ different colored bricks, totaling _____ pieces. Each large building blocks set includes _____ (shape) bricks, _____ (shape) bricks and a baseplate for these bricks to create hours of creativity for kids.

This set contains different colors, including _____, _____, _____, making it possible to build different scales or projects, and giving children a wonderful visual experience while also improving their ability to recognize and match colors.

The _____ are made from _____, which is non-toxic and kid-friendly. The building blocks have built-in card slots. So we just need to insert it lightly and blocks can be connected tightly. They connect firmly together lasting for years. The baseplate in this set measure over _____ inches long and _____ inches wide. Every piece of brick is large enough to avoid any choking hazard. Mom's choice!

The bricks and plates are compatible with all construction sets of major brands. All models pictured can be built from this set simultaneously, like this _____.

Kids will become creative builders as they use these color toys to build a _____ or build a _____ while also engaging in kids' playtime. It is ideal for boys and girls between the ages of _____ and _____ years old. Actually, it is wonderful for all ages with varying interests.

Engage your kids in _____ by letting them build their own play toys. It's an educational toddler toy that makes a great holiday, birthday or any day gift for both boys and girls.

6.2 运动型体育及户外玩具 Sports and Outdoor Toys

词汇积累 Vocabulary

序号	中文名称	英文名称
1	婴儿学步车	toddler walker
2	电动平衡车	self-balancing electric scooter
3	滑板车	scooter
4	儿童可调节杠铃	adjustable barbell toy
5	三轮脚踏车	kids' tricycle
6	儿童滑梯	kids' slide
7	弹力球	bouncy ball
8	平衡板	wobble board
9	扭扭车	wiggle car
10	儿童自行车	kids' balance bike
11	碰碰车	electric bumper car
12	秋千	swing seat
13	感统旋转椅	sensory training swivel chair
14	蹦床	trampoline

续表

序号	中文名称	英文名称
15	攀登架	jungle gym
16	玩耍帐篷	play tent
17	玩具电瓶车	battery-powered ride-on vehicle
18	注水气球	water balloon
19	溜溜球	yo-yo
20	皮球	rubber ball
21	跷跷板	seesaw
22	沙包	beanbag
23	风车	pinwheel
24	弹射风筝	thumb ejection kite
25	陀螺	spinning top
26	飞盘	frisbee
27	接抛球	toss-and-catch ball
28	飞镖	dart toy
29	弹弓	slingshot
30	毽子	shuttlecock
31	跳绳	skipping rope
32	呼啦圈	hula hoop
33	射箭玩具	archery toy set
34	悬挂式乒乓球	hanging table tennis
35	跳跳杆	pogo stick
36	桌上足球	foosball/table football
37	竹蜻蜓飞碟	flying disc
38	婴儿游泳圈	baby swimming float
39	儿童羽毛球	kids' badminton set

续表

序号	中文名称	英文名称
40	跳房子地毯	hopscotch rug
41	袋鼠跳跳袋	sack-race bag
42	儿童篮球架	kids' basketball hoop
43	套脚甩圈球	ankle skip ball
44	套圈圈玩具	ring toss combo set
45	悬浮足球	hover soccer ball
46	回旋镖	boomerang
47	儿童保龄球	bowling set
48	儿童棒球	kids' baseball set
49	儿童拳击吊袋	kids' punching bag
50	爬行隧道	collapsible tunnel

话术演练 Language Skills

产品规格介绍：

(1) Swivel[1] chair has a load-bearing[2] of about 75 kg − 100 kg.

(2) The adjustable barbell set includes 8 weight plates, barbell bar, and 2 lock collars.

(3) ××× is compact[3], weighting just 28 lbs with a max load of 220 lbs.

(4) Thanks to the dual 400W motors, it can easily reach a max speed of 10 mph.

(5) A single fully charged battery can run up to 13.7 miles.

(6) The handlebar[4] also has 4 adjustable height options to accommodate kids of different ages.

(7) 12 nylon[5]-covered beanbags[6] for bean bag toss games are in a variety of colors: red, yellow, green, blue, orange & purple.

(8) This high performance pogo[7] stick is one of the best hopping toys for kids

aged 5 and up or who weigh 18 kg to 36 kg.

(9) Each table soccer ball weighs 0.85 oz and measures 1.42 inches diameter, fits mostly all tables.

(10) Helicopter spin toy includes 2 launchers[8] with 4 colorful flying discs.

> 单词解析：
> 1. swivel ['swɪvl] n. 旋转；转环
> 2. load-bearing [ləʊd 'berɪŋ] n. 承重
> 3. compact [kəm'pækt] n. 紧凑的；体积小的
> 4. handlebar ['hændlbɑːr] n. (自行车或摩托车)把手
> 5. nylon ['naɪlɑːn] n. 尼龙
> 6. beanbag ['biːnbæg] n. 豆子袋（内填豆粒或碎塑料的小布袋，可以当球玩）
> 7. pogo ['pəʊgəʊ] n. 弹簧单高跷
> 8. launcher ['lɔːntʃər] n. 发射装置

产品质量与特色介绍：

(11) The ankle skip ball is made of eco-friendly PP[9] material, odor-less and non-toxic, and is safe to use.

(12) The thickened foam[10] ring does not grind the feet and effectively protects the bare feet of users.

(13) The flashing lights work by electromagnetic[11] induction[12] when you skip it, and the rotating wheel automatically produces multi-color light.

(14) The hopscotch[13] rug features a classic hopscotch design and 2 colorful beanbags for hours of jumping and counting entertainment.

(15) Our hopscotch rug is made from high-quality woven materials that can be used indoors or outdoors.

(16) The rug is machine-washable for easy cleanup.

(17) Hide and seek collapsible tunnels are made with the highest quality soft polyester[14] fabric and thick steel wiring.

(18) Designed with safety in mind, the tunnel features round corners, durable

stitching[15] and safe material.

(19) Weight plates can be filled with sand or water to increase weight.

(20) The smart battery management system provides reliable battery performance.

(21) Pneumatic[16] tires provide a comfortable and smoother ride on bumpy roads.

(22) The 3 wheels are equipped with multi-colored LED lights, and as your child scoots[17], the wheels light up in a variety of twinkling colors.

(23) Trikes for toddler has safety carbon steel frame, soft handle grips and seat, durable widen silent wheels, strong enough for riding indoor or outdoor.

(24) The sturdy structure and strong load-bearing capacity ensure the stability and safety, the penguin pattern is also loved by toddlers.

(25) The professional designed 24.5° section angle keeps the board an unbalanced status, which can make more fun from doing exercise with it.

(26) Our wobble[18] board is made of high-quality environmentally friendly PP&TPE[19] material, which is completely non-toxic.

(27) Dirty can be easily washed off comparing to the surface of the wooden balance boards.

(28) The ××× yo-yo is made from a high-impact[20] plastic with a fixed metal axle[21] that cannot be screwed apart, designed to withstand plenty of use.

(29) The design of external net is different from that of other trampoline, so the trampoline has more space and more beautiful and durable and comfortable.

(30) We adopt a seamless[22] design between the enclosure and the mat, never need to worry that your kids will get stuck in the gap.

(31) The customized robust safety net is manufactured from high density, tight weave, UV treated, PE thread.

(32) These bean bags are made of high-quality materials so they can be enjoyed for years without tearing[23] open.

(33) The pogo stick for kids is made to rigorous safety standards and comes complete with non-slip pedals[24] and a safety foam handle.

(34) The string-powered design keeps this helicopter toy easy-to-use and

uncomplicated without any need for batteries.

(35) This inflatable[25] bag is made of PU leather and takes everything a kid can dish out!

> 单词解析：
>
> 9. PP *abbr.* 聚丙烯
>
> 10. foam ［fəʊm］ *n.* 泡沫
>
> 11. electromagnetic ［ɪˌlektrəʊmæɡˈnetɪk］ *adj.* 电磁的
>
> 12. induction ［ɪnˈdʌkʃn］ *n.* 电磁感应
>
> 13. hopscotch ［ˈhɑːpskɑːtʃ］ *n.* 跳房子
>
> 14. polyester ［ˈpɑːlɪestər］ *n.* 聚酯纤维
>
> 15. stitch ［stɪtʃ］ *n.* 缝
>
> 16. pneumatic ［nuːˈmætɪk］ *adj.* 充气的
>
> 17. scoot ［skuːt］ *v.* 疾行
>
> 18. wobble ［ˈwɑːbl］ *n.* 摇晃
>
> 19. TPE（triphenyl phosphate） *abbr.* 磷酸三苯酯
>
> 20. high-impact ［haɪ ˈɪmpækt］ *adj.*（材料）高强度的
>
> 21. axle ［ˈæksl］ *n.* 车轴
>
> 22. seamless ［ˈsiːmləs］ *adj.* 无缝的
>
> 23. tear ［teə］ *v.* 撕裂；扯破
>
> 24. pedal ［ˈpedl］ *n.* 踏板
>
> 25. inflatable ［ɪnˈfleɪtəbl］ *adj.* 充气的

产品功能介绍：

(36) Swivel chairs focus on the targeted balance adjustment, exercise children's muscle endurance, stimulate vestibular sense to develop a sense of balance.

(37) The rotational movement makes the child strong.

(38) The toy can improve motor skills, burn excess energy, and provide fun aerobic[26] exercise for kids with friends.

(39) It is educational and playful, and will not only contribute to a fun time but will also help kids learn letters and numbers with creative pictures.

(40) This baby tunnel helps develop arm and leg muscles and gross[27] motor skills.

(41) Not only is this toy barbell a fun way to introduce your child to proper exercise and weightlifting forms and routines, it also teaches them how muscles move and how the body works as they pretend to bench-press or power lift.

(42) With 3 wheels for extra stability, your child will be able to balance with ease.

(43) This plastic slide promotes fitness, balance and coordination.

(44) By throwing and catching, your child will polish up his or her hand-eye coordination skills.

(45) Pogo stick helps build leg and core muscle, is brilliant in helping with balance and looks awesome too.

(46) Our light-up archery[28] set gives your children fun while practicing their accuracy skills, fine motor skills, hand-eye coordination and collaboration skills!

> 单词解析：
>   26. aerobic [eəˈrəʊbɪk] adj. 有氧的
>   27. gross [ɡrəʊs] adj. 总的
>   28. archery [ˈɑːtʃəri] n. 射箭运动

产品服务介绍：

(47) If you are not satisfied with our bike, please feel free to contact us, we will be happy to work out a replacement or a refund.

(48) The workout board/core trainer is backed by unbeatable quality and customer support, which come with 12-month warranty[29] and lifetime after-service.

(49) We accept comparisons with other brands, and if the quality is not better than them, we receive a full unconditional refund.

(50) If there is any problem with our table footballs, please contact our customer service, we will treat it sincerely.

> 单词解析：
>   29. warranty [ˈwɒrənti] n. 担保；(商品)保用单

直播模板 Template

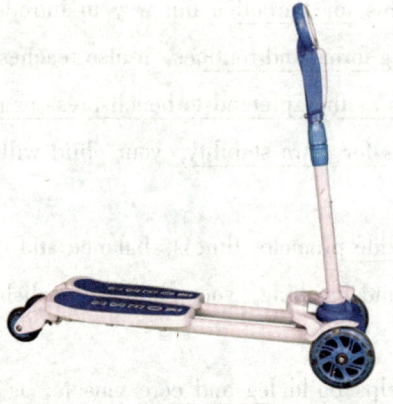

This scooter for toddlers is equipped with a unique _____ capacity. It has _____ seat which kids can use while cruising along with the built-in foot pad. The pad can be detached when they feel more confident standing up. The lightweight and compact kids scooter features an adjustable handlebar with _____ height options—_____, _____, _____, and _____ inches. It works with kids of all ages. It is ideal for little ones aged _____ years old and up with a weight capacity of _____ lbs.

The scooter is equipped with anti-slip and wide deck that is large enough to fit both feet. _____ scooter is built with _____ pipe and _____ inches deck with _____ base design, strong enough to carry out the weight of your child.

It also has smooth _____ gliding roller wheels that run smoothly even on surfaces that are uneven or bumpy. The _____ scooters for kids feature colorful LED turning wheel lights that light up in a variety of flashing colors as you scoot, adding a fun twist to the ride, and making children safe in dark. It is also easy to carry and for storage, just remove the handlebar from the deck.

It features _____ technology, which means the scooter is controlled by _____ rather than _____. This design helps your child develop balance skills and coordination.

6.3 观赏收藏类玩具 Collectible Toys

词汇积累 Vocabulary

序号	中文名称	英文名称
1	模型玩具	model toy
2	船类模型	ship model
3	飞机模型	aero-plane model
4	航天模型	aviation model
5	火车模型	train model
6	汽车模型	car model
7	军事模型	military model
8	武器模型	weapon model
9	人物模型	figure model
10	动漫模型	anime figure model
11	建筑模型	architectural model
12	动物模型	animal model
13	卡通模型	cartoon model
14	木制模型	wooden model
15	玩偶模型	doll model
16	手办	garage kits
17	坦克模型	tank model
18	火箭模型	rocket model
19	机器人	robot
20	变形玩具	transformer
21	拼装模型	assembled model
22	航空母舰模型	aircraft carrier model

续表

序号	中文名称	英文名称
23	时钟模型	clock model
24	宇航员模型	astronaut model
25	地球仪模型	globe model
26	赛车模型	racing car model
27	角色模型	character model
28	机械传动模型	mechanical transmission model
29	仿真模型	simulation model
30	花束模型	flower model
31	蜡像模型	wax figure model
32	芭比娃娃	Barbie doll
33	布娃娃	rag doll
34	陶瓷娃娃	porcelain doll
35	墙壁挂画模型	wall painting model
36	永生花	preserved fresh flower
37	扭蛋	capsule toy
38	搪胶娃娃	vinyl doll
39	毛绒玩具	plush toy
40	雕塑摆件	sculpture ornament
41	积木	building blocks
42	潮流玩具	designer toy
43	盲盒	mystery box
44	街景模型	street scene model
45	黏土玩偶	clay doll
46	人偶定制	doll customization
47	落地摆件	floor ornament

续表

序号	中文名称	英文名称
48	八音盒模型	music box
49	模型展示盒	model display box
50	动态模型	kinematic model
51	静态模型	static model

话术演练 Language Skills

产品规格介绍：

（1）This ×××building toy consists of 307 parts, including nuts[1], bolts, small screwdriver[2] and spanner[3].

（2）When finished assembling, the dimension is 15.4 cm in length, 13.6 cm in width and 4.3 cm in height.

（3）This DIY craft kit contains 13 pre-cut plywood sheets (assemble parts and spare[4] parts), 1 illustrated instruction with graphics, accessory[5] tool.

（4）The toy comes secured in a velvet pouch within a luxury gift ready box.

（5）Not recommended for kids below 3 years old.

> **单词解析：**
> 1. nut [nʌt] n. 螺母
> 2. screwdriver ['skruˌdraɪvər] n. 螺丝刀
> 3. spanner ['spænər] n. 扳手
> 4. spare [sper] adj. 外加的；备用的
> 5. accessory [əkˈsɛsəri] adj. 辅助的；附属的

产品质量与优势介绍：

（6）This aircraft building set is a highly detailed reproduction[6] of the harrier jet[7], well-made and perfect for model aircraft collectors and DIY craft enthusiasts.

（7）Compared to similar models on the market, our aircraft model is larger in size and more suitable for children to play.

(8) With clear and concise color-printed instructions, each step is clearly marked, and thus easy to follow.

(9) The metal material is extremely durable and will stand up to rough play without the fear of collapsing easily.

(10) Each part is polished[8] and smooth, safe and non-toxic.

(11) The box contains 739 blocks that can be assembled into a large battleship or individually into 12 smaller models.

(12) The materials included in this engineering kit for boys and girls are super tough and durable, not flimsy[9] and breakable like with other models.

(13) Safe and non-toxic ABS plastic bricks are used, compatible[10] with Lego and the hand feel is smooth, and it is matched with electroplating[11] and spray paint materials to make the whole cool.

(14) The hatch[12] cover fin[13] and the solar panel[14] of the satellite can be moved, and it is equipped with a bracket[15] to adjust the angle flexibly.

(15) Black-grey appearance combined with metal silk-printed technology retain the wood grain while giving it a metallic texture.

(16) All parts are made of high-quality, non-toxic, tasteless and recyclable safety materials.

(17) This Big Ben building block set contains 3600 pcs to build models with incredible detail and unparalleled realism, which you can follow the detailed instructions to build the different colored and sized parts into the Big Ben step by step.

(18) Parents can rest assured that every building block is tightly connected without sharp edges and corners, ensuring the safety and allowing kids have fun with the block set.

(19) More than 20 movable details increase the playability of building blocks.

(20) Each particle of our astronaut building sets is made by multiple processes, which can be firmly spliced[16] and not easy to fade[17], and the texture is excellent.

(21) The astronaut can quickly fix on the matching base or remove from the

base, and can still stand stably after being removed.

(22) High-quality anime figure requires no assembly, which will be friendly for those who have never built a model kit before!

(23) From design and production to inspection to sales, every link is strictly controlled, and every customer is satisfied with high quality and reasonable price.

(24) Each bobblehead will come in a colorful printed collector's box with molded[18] styrofoam inserts for easy and safe storage.

(25) It is crafted with quality materials like 24K gold and studded with precision cut crystals.

(26) Each doll is a soft and realistic design with elastic skin and delicate facial features!

单词解析:

6. reproduction [ˌrɪprə'dʌkʃ(ə)n] n. 复制品
7. harrier jet 鹞式喷气式飞机
8. polish ['pɔlɪʃ] v. 磨光;抛光
9. flimsy ['flɪmzɪ] adj. 劣质的;不结实的
10. compatible [kəm'pætəb(ə)l] adj. 兼容的;可共存的
11. electroplate [ɪ'lektrəˌpleɪt] v. 电镀
12. hatch [hætʃ] n. 舱口
13. fin [fɪn] n. 鳍板
14. solar panel 太阳能电池板
15. bracket ['brækət] n. 支架
16. splice [splaɪs] v. 胶接
17. fade [feɪd] v. 褪色;逐渐消失
18. mold [məʊld] v. 用模子塑造

产品功能介绍:

(27) The screwdriver and spanner included let kids learn to use tools and assemble more effectively.

(28) During the 5 to 6 hours assembly process, they are learning exercising

brain and developing patience.

(29) This military block toy set is the perfect gift for little military fans and has all kids need for a fun and rewarding play experience!

(30) The aircraft model can serve as a beautiful decoration and educational toy.

(31) This challenging but doable educational building kit will entertain your kids for hours.

(32) This wood mechanical model kit will bring you highly satisfying and educational user experience.

(33) Every accidental or doomed choice of path will create dozens of fun to watch.

(34) This ××× micro building block set with LED lights is especially suitable for all those who are interested in travel, architecture, culture, history or design, as this mini Clock Tower is a wonderful collection and can be unique decoration for offices, rooms etc..

(35) The assembly of this wooden marble run 3D wooden puzzle-model building kit is favorable to learn the fundamentals of engineering, improve kids' hand-eye coordination.

(36) Just rotate the handle, you will witness incredible and amazing mechanical engineering designs.

(37) This model for adults to build is not only a 3D wooden puzzle, but also a classically sophisticated desk decor[19] and a night light with a warm glow.

(38) The puzzle for adults can be used as a beautiful decoration when displayed on the office desk, dressing table or shelf, perfect for home and aesthetic office decor, as a stylish modern look.

(39) You can enjoy the fun of assembling while experiencing the great structure of the world famous architectural.

(40) These micro building blocks allow you to feel the great spirit of craftsmanship[20] and the weight of history in the process of assembly.

(41) This block set has a certain degree of difficulty, it is a good chance to do a team work with your friends and family, learning collaboration and teamwork while

promoting communication.

(42) This figure can be placed in many places you can imagine, such as <u>car, bedside table, desk, living room, shop window, etc.</u>.

(43) The size ensures it is perfect for any interior design motif, home decor or collection!

> 单词解析：
> 19. decor [deɪˈkɔr] n. 装饰风格
> 20. craftsmanship [ˈkræftsmənʃɪp] n. 手艺；工艺

产品服务介绍：

(44) If there are missing <u>parts</u>, contact us and they will be resent unconditionally.

(45) A paper <u>manual</u>[21] is included with the product, if you would like to assemble the 12 <u>miniatures</u>[22], please contact us via ×××to download the eBook.

(46) We have gone through <u>3</u> inspections when the product leaves the factory. If you are still missing accessories, please contact us as soon as possible, and we will send them to you for free.

(47) If you have any problems during the assembly, we are willing to offer assistance.

(48) We wish every good toy will bring happiness, if you have any problem please contact us freely, we will provide 100% satisfied service within 24 hours.

(49) All products are covered by a 100% money-back satisfaction guarantee and <u>a 2-year</u> warranty.

> 单词解析：
> 21. manual [ˈmænjuəl] n. 手册；指南
> 22. miniature [ˈmɪnɪtʃər] n. 微缩模型

直播模板 Template

Every child has a _____ dream, to have their own _____ and build their own _____. This is a perfect gift for them. It is a _____ technology _____ building set. It packed with realistic details and fun features. Our _____ toy contains _____ parts, _____ pieces, _____ motors, _____ remote controller, _____ battery box and _____ instruction manual. _____ model size is _____ cm.

The _____ are all made of environmentally friendly materials and _____ molding. The _____ model itself is very stable and constructively very attractive. All _____ fit perfectly and are neatly machined. The clamping thickness/accuracy of the _____ is very good and compatible with _____ brands. The precise _____ technology controls the error of the parts within _____ microns, making the assembling process smooth. All parts have no sharp edge and are safe for children.

The instruction booklet is professional and detailed with pictures, making it easy to identify the parts, and making the construction steps clear. It is easy to install and disassemble.

This collectible _____ is a great display project and a great model. A unique _____, making it a great addition to your _____ collection of _____. It's definitely a great valuation collection and souvenir for _____ lovers, and a great gift for _____ who loves challenge.

If you encounter _____ problem during the assembly process, please feel free to contact us.

6.4 实战脚本 Script

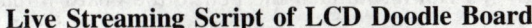

Live Streaming Script of LCD Doodle Board

Hi guys, welcome to our livestream. I'm your host Joyce. If this is your first time to join us, please follow our channel and hit the subscription button.

Today, we will introduce you toys with high performance and value. This first item is one of our best-selling products, a writing board for kids. Let me show you more details. It comes in green and pink. The drawing board provides 10 inches of space for kid's writing and drawing. It has a replaceable battery, which supports 100,000 times of writing. So, it avoids paper wasting, and can be replaced and used continuously. It's very economical and reusable. Unlike the other writing board on the market out there, our writing boards come with a protective case so that we can put them in the case. It protects the screen from getting scratches, and dents and it is made of leather. On the top there is a button. You can button up and keep the board inside.

Compared with other monochrome tablets in stores, our color screen tablets are brighter and clearer, more eye-catching. This LCD writing tablet adopts pressure-sensitive flexible screen, it creates lines of different thickness based on how hard you push. It has no blue light, no glare, no radiation, no harm to eyesight. So, you don't have to worry too much about your kids using this for too long. No chalk dust, no harmful chemicals, no mess at home. It's safe for your kids to doodle.

The writing board is really easy to use. Let me show you. It provides a pen and a little string. You wear the string around your wrist so you don't have to worry about dropping the board. We can also attach the pen to the board through the pen holder and take it off easily. The pen cannot write on the walls or tables so they are not going to ruin your furniture. What's great about these boards is that they are mess-free. Down here is the button to erase. You can erase anything you write on it. If you are writing something and want to save it, you can just slide this little lock button down here and it will lock the screen. So, in this way, it won't erase the board. It's also water-proof, so if you or your kids splash some water on the tablet, it still works.

The drawing tablet is a perfect gift for girls and boys for back to school, birthday, Thanksgiving Day, Christmas and any occasion. It can be kids' learning toys. They can draw or write down their great ideas. They can play teacher and quiz each other. They can write equations on the board. It also can be a travel toy for long drives and road trips. It's a great gift to keep your kids busy.

The board has a 10 inches of writing area, 0.26-inch ultra-thin design, 6 ounces weight. It is thin and lightweight. Kids can hardly feel the weight of the LCD writing tablet. They can take it anywhere, like put it in school bags, handbags, travel bags etc..

Doodle board is an ideal choice of drawing tablets for little kids who are just starting to explore the world. The colorful screen provides a better preschool experience, cultivates children's ability to distinguish colors, free their imagination, release creativity. We highly recommend you to buy now. Just check our yellow shopping cart below and get one for your kid now. Our stocks are running short now.

Ok, so now let's go for the next item...

Thank you guys for supporting and joining us. So if you guys like my livestream and our products, please follow us. Our next livestream will be at 9 p.m. tomorrow, see you next time.

第七章
首饰和饰品类产品英语直播

中国海关总署的统计数据显示,2022 年 9 月,中国贵金属或包贵金属的首饰出口数量为 77 吨,同比增长 18.7%；出口金额为 17.85 亿美元,同比增长 65.5%。2022 年 1—9 月,中国贵金属或包贵金属的首饰出口数量为 758 吨,出口金额为 96.27 亿美元。

7.1 金属类首饰和饰品 Metal Jewelry and Accessories

词汇积累 Vocabulary

序号	中文名称	英文名称
1	手链/脚链	bracelet
2	手镯/脚镯	bangle
3	项链	necklace
4	耳饰	earring
5	戒指	ring
6	脚链	anklet
7	吊坠	pendant
8	胸针	brooch
9	颈链	choker
10	头饰	hair accessory
11	链条(或镯子)上的小饰物	charm
12	耳夹	clip-on

续表

序号	中文名称	英文名称
13	耳圈	earring jacket/hoop
14	耳钉	stud
15	纯银	sterling
16	999 纯银	fine silver
17	925 银	sterling silver
18	925 银镀金	gold vermeil
19	纯金	gold
20	镀金黄铜	gold-plated brass
21	镀金	gold-plated
22	包金	gold-filled
23	美国 14K 包金	14K US gold filled
24	K 金	14karat gold
25	铂金	platinum
26	铜	copper
27	黄铜	brass
28	合金	alloy
29	钛钢	titanium steel
30	不锈钢	stainless steel
31	首饰盒	jewelry box
32	龙虾扣	lobster claw/clasp
33	延长链/尾链	extender
34	单圈	jump ring
35	法国耳钩	lever back hook
36	米珠	seed bead
37	定位珠	crimped section bead
38	鱼丝线	fishing wire/string
39	链条	chain

续表

序号	中文名称	英文名称
40	蜡绳	cotton cord
41	弹力线	stretch string
42	卵状的/椭圆形的	oval
43	水滴形的	teardrop
44	圆的	round
45	正方形的	square
46	长方形的	rectangle
47	叶状的	leaf-shaped
48	翅状的	wing-shaped
49	心形的	heart-shaped
50	线形的	linear
51	曲线形的	curved
52	特殊形状的	graphic
53	极简风格	minimalist style
54	复古风格	vintage style
55	最好的	finest
56	有光泽的	glossy
57	不规则的	irregular
58	优雅的	elegant
59	新娘的	bridal
60	抗氧化的	antioxidant
61	厚电镀工艺	plating thickness
62	不过敏的	hypoallergenic
63	甜美的	sweet
64	韩风/lns 风的	Korean/lns style
65	清新的	fresh
66	复古的	vintage

续表

序号	中文名称	英文名称
67	冷淡的	cool
68	欧式的	European style
69	夸张的	exaggerated
70	简约的	simple
71	异国风情的	exotic
72	精美的	exquisite
73	闪闪发光的	sparkling
74	时髦的	stylish
75	拇指	thumb
76	食指	forefinger
77	中指	middle finger
78	无名指	ring finger
79	小指	little finger
80	磨光/擦光	polish
81	重量	weight
82	两	tael
83	克	gram
84	盎司	ounce/oz
85	公斤	kilogram
86	克拉	carat
87	长度	length
88	英尺	foot/feet
89	英寸	inch
90	米	meter
91	厘米	centimeter
92	毫米	millimeter

话术演练 Language Skills

产品材质与特色介绍：

(1) The pendant and the chain are made of 925 sterling silver with rose gold plating.

(2) These safe materials are hypoallergenic and antioxidant and won't rust, fade[1], corrode[2], tarnish[3] or turn your skin green.

(3) The elegant and beautiful bracelet has an upgraded[4] clasp that is super secure.

(4) Crafted[5] in 925 sterling silver and plated in 14K gold, this X-ring exudes[6] understated[7] style and elegance.

(5) With a simple and dainty[8] twisted[9] rope design, this elegant eternity[10] ring offers premium quality fashion and is available in rose gold, white gold and yellow gold.

(6) Gold-layered paperclip chain letter initial[11] necklaces set with hexagon[12] charm, engraved[13] with initial and heart in back and front.

(7) The initial brooch is nicely made, no sharp edges on the letter itself, the clasp is sturdy[14].

(8) This necklace is made of handpicked brass, and plated in 14K gold to ensure a long lasting finish that is tarnish-resistant, lead-free[15], and hypoallergenic.

(9) The necklace is 14K gold plated over high quality brass plated to ensure a long without faded.

(10) This chunky[16] gold heart layered necklace is perfect for anyone that wants a little sparkle. It is made from brass, and it has then been gold plated for even longer lifespan.

(11) This necklace is made of silver plated, you can rest assured to wear it to your child.

(12) This gold chunky hoop earring is made of 14K gold plated. We use only high-quality metals which means our pieces are 100% hypoallergenic.

(13) You will received earrings like our pictures. These earrings are made from

sterling silver, and have then either been gold plated, or left in sterling silver, which means they'll be sparkling for years.

(14) A simple and dainty design that swivels[17] as an eye-catching modern fashionable ring that is available in rose gold, white gold and yellow gold.

(15) This bangle are hidden clasp. First, use your thumb to push the bottom part. Then insert your index finger and pull the top part. Last, squeezing the pieces in the opposite direction to release.

(16) Full polishing can bring the most comfortable wearing feeling. 3 mm thin round bracelet can be stacked[18] or worn individually.

(17) 14K gold-filled is a thick layer of 14K over titanium—it doesn't flake[19] or wear thin and is made to last decades.

单词解析：

1. fade [feɪd] *v.* 褪色；凋谢；逐渐消失

2. corrode [kəˈrəʊd] *v.* 腐蚀；侵蚀

3. tarnish [ˈtɑːnɪʃ] *v.* 玷污；(使)失去光泽；暗淡
   n. (金属表面上的)锈

4. upgraded [ˌʌpˈɡreɪdɪd] *adj.* 升级的；提升的

5. craft [krɑːft] *v.* (尤指用手工)精心制作

6. exude [ɪɡˈzjuːd] *v.* 流露；显露(感觉或品质)；(感觉或品质)显现；流出

7. understated [ˌʌndəˈsteɪtɪd] *adj.* 低调的；淡雅的；素雅的；柔和的

8. dainty [ˈdeɪnti] *adj.* 娇小的；精致的；优雅的

9. twisted [ˈtwɪstɪd] *adj.* 扭曲的；弯曲的

10. eternity [ɪˈtɜːnəti] *n.* 永恒；永生

11. initial [ɪˈnɪʃl] *adj.* 最初的；开始的
    n. (名字的)首字母

12. hexagon [ˈheksəɡən] *n.* 六角形；六边形

13. engrave [ɪnˈɡreɪv] *v.* 雕刻；在……上刻(字或图案)

14. sturdy [ˈstɜːdi] *adj.* 结实的；坚固的

> 15. lead [led] *n.* 铅（lead-free 无铅的）
> 16. chunky ['tʃʌŋki] *adj.* 厚实的；结实的
> 17. swivel ['swɪvl] *v.* 旋转；转动
> 18. stack [stæk] *v.* （使）放成整齐的一叠（或一摞、一堆）（在饰品话题中一般指饰品的叠戴）
> 19. flake [fleɪk] *v.* 脱落

产品规格介绍：

（18）Pendant size for the sterling silver birthstone necklace women: 0.83″ × 1.02″ | Zircon size: 0.3″×0.3″, Chain length: 17.72″+1.97″.

（19）Small bead size is approx 4 mm in diameter. Large bead size is approx 6 mm in diameter.

（20）This bracelet is adjustable and will fit most wrist[20] sizes.

（21）This stylish earring set includes 3 pairs of huggie hoops[21] with an inner diameter of 8 mm, 10 mm, and 12 mm.

（22）They are rhodium[22] plated and designed with an 18-inch chain plus 2-inch extender, and a lobster claw clasp.

（23）Size of the gold paperclip chain initial necklaces is 18″+2″ extension, and the layering paperclip chain necklace is 14″+2″ extension.

（24）The love choker is 15.7″×0.67″×0.08″（L×W×H）, which suits for neck size from about 12.5 inches to 15 inches, fit most necks. There are 4 size settings, could choose looser or tighter depend on yourself.

（25）The total weight of our necklaces and pendants is only 0.14 oz（4 grams）, which is very light and comfortable.

（26）Our heart choker necklace size is 30 cm + 18 cm extended chain, width 1 cm. The total length reaches 48 cm. This goth choker necklace uses adjustable lobster clasp, suitable for most people's size.

（27）Inner necklace size: 3 mm/14″+2″ extension. Outer necklace size: 1.5 mm/16.5″+2″ extension. This length works on practically anyone.

（28）The flat snake chain can be worn alone or with other favorite chains. If you like, you can choose to add a charm to the chain.

(29) Chunky hoops' outer dimensions are approx 23 mm in diameter and inner diameter is approx 17 mm.

(30) This elegant finger ring is 3 mm wide, lightweight but sturdy, never out of shape.

> 单词解析：
> 20. wrist [rɪst] *adj.* 手腕；腕关节
> 21. hoop [huːp] *n.* 箍；环；圈
> 22. rhodium [ˈrəʊdɪəm] *n.* 铑

产品功能与特色介绍：

(31) The double-heart design symbolizes love for each other, and no words are needed between the two hearts.

(32) This bead bracelets set is suitable for daily wear, ball, party, anniversary, graduation, birthday or any special occasions.

(33) These deltas make the perfect minimalist[23] earrings for everyday wear.

(34) Presented by Miss ABC this heart necklace is a regal[24], symbolic statement piece that unveils[25] your feminine[26] spirit.

(35) Bridal jewelry set for wedding will add more eye-catching and charm for your outfit.

(36) This beautiful design is suitable for wearing with everyday outfits or as a formal accessory; keep as an addition to your own collection or give as a gift to someone special.

(37) This simple necklace looks very fashionable whether worn alone or superimposed[27] with other necklaces.

(38) These hoops have an architectural and dimensional three hollow[28] hoop elements to make the earring more lightweight for everyday wear.

(39) These unique hoop earrings add a strong edgy[29] twist to your look. Shape like croissants[30], they will become your must-have for an elegant night out.

(40) Pure gold color, eye-catching charm design, adding shine glamour to

women or men at any age wear it every day.

(41) Find a special gift for a loved one or a beautiful piece that complements[31] your personal style with jewelry from the ABC.

> **单词解析：**
>
> 23. minimalist ['mɪnɪməlɪst] n. 极简主义者
>   adj. 极简艺术的；极简风格的
> 24. regal ['riːɡl] adj. 帝王的；豪华的
> 25. unveil [ˌʌn'veɪl] v. 揭幕；拉开……的帷幕
> 26. feminine ['femənɪn] adj. 女性化的；阴性的；女性特有的（气质或外貌）
> 27. superimpose [ˌsuːpərɪm'pəuz] v. 使重叠；使叠加
> 28. hollow ['hɔləu] adj. 中空的；空心的
> 29. edgy ['edʒɪ] adj. 激动人心的
> 30. croissant ['krwæsɔ] n. 牛角面包；羊角面包
> 31. complement ['kɔmplɪmənt] v. 补充；使完美
>   n. 补充物

产品服务介绍：

(42) ABC is an enterprise of jewellery that pursues product quality and customer satisfaction.

(43) To ensure your complete satisfaction, we offer a hassle-free 90-day money-back guarantee.

(44) This girls' ring was packaged in a beautiful jewelry pouch and ready for giving.

(45) Every accessory set is delicately placed in a stylish classic jewelry box.

(46) We have changed the carton packaging to the current plastic packaging box, which not only looks more refined[32] but also more waterproof[33], it is the best box for daily jewelry storage.

(47) Our specialism is in personalized jewellery but we also have a wide collection of earrings, bracelets, chains, rings and necklaces to choose from.

(48) We have made several different types of love necklaces for you to choose, suitable for women and children.

(49) You will received heart necklace like our pictures. All our jewelry is enthusiastically designed with a classic artisan[34] style and minimalist style to ensure a stylish and personalized quality piece.

(50) We're all about making quality, sustainable jewelry that you can wear every day. Loved by millions of customers worldwide we commit to bring you stylish, on-trend jewelry that you can trust.

> 单词解析：
> 32. refined [rɪˈfaɪnd] *adj.* 精制的；精炼的
> 33. waterproof [ˈwɔːtərpruːf] *adj.* 不透水的；防水的
> 34. artisan [ˈɑːtɪˌzæn] *n.* 工匠；手艺人

直播模板 Template

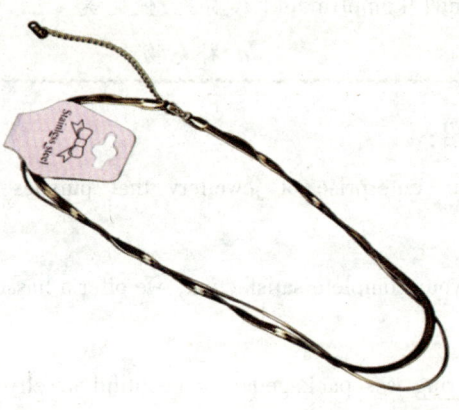

This _____ is made of _____, and plated in _____ to ensure a long lasting finish that is tarnish-resistant, lead-free, and hypoallergenic. That reduces concerns about sensitive skin and product quality issues.

The inner _____ size is _____ extension. Outer _____ size is _____ extension. This length works on practically anyone!

The _____ can be worn alone or with other favorite _____. If you like, you can choose to add a charm to the _____. This _____ is a must-have in any jewellery collection. It makes the perfect base for layering with other _____ and adds a touch of sophistication to any look.

Those _____ can be sent to your friends and relatives in festival, it's an ideal gift for women and teen girls. It is also perfect for all dressup and any occasions, for example, a wedding, Mother's Day, a party, a date, or whenever you feel like making a statement.

7.2 宝石类首饰和饰品 Gemstone Jewelry and Accessories

词汇积累 Vocabulary

序号	中文名称	英文名称
1	宝石	gemstone
2	钻石	diamond
3	红宝石	ruby
4	蓝宝石	sapphire
5	绿柱石	beryl
6	锆石	zircon
7	橄榄石	olivine
8	翡翠	jadeite
9	绿松石	turquoise
10	托帕石	topaz
11	珊瑚	coral
12	琥珀	amber
13	象牙	ivory
14	祖母绿	emerald
15	坦桑石	tanzanite
16	碧玺	tourmaline
17	石榴石	garnet
18	石英	quartz

续表

序号	中文名称	英文名称
19	水晶	crystal
20	粉晶	rose quartz
21	孔雀石	malachite
22	大理石	marble
23	贝壳	shell
24	猫眼石	opal
25	缟玛瑙	onyx
26	葡萄石	prehnite
27	玛瑙	agate
28	珍珠	pearl
29	天然珍珠	natural pearl
30	养殖珍珠	cultured pearl
31	淡水珍珠	freshwater pearl
32	人造珍珠	artificial pearl
33	紫晶	amethyst
34	黄晶	citrine
35	紫黄晶	ametrine
36	月光石/月亮石	moonstone
37	黑曜石	obsidian
38	萤石	fluorite
39	针板镶座/棒镶	bar setting
40	包镶	bezel setting
41	夹镶	channel setting
42	群镶	cluster setting
43	珍珠光泽	luster
44	串链	strand
45	锥形	taper
46	梨形	pear

续表

序号	中文名称	英文名称
47	八角形	octagon
48	半圆形	semicircle
49	马眼形	marquise

话术演练 Language Skills

产品材质与特色介绍：

（1）A gem-quality cubic[1] stone is embellished in the middle of the pendant, with high precision[2] and fine cutting, it reflects extraordinary brilliance[3].

（2）Our infinity love heart necklace for women is an original design from our studio in Boston and features a precious Austrian birthstone crystal. All of our jewelry products are polished[4] by hand.

（3）This woman's necklace is adorned[5] with a 0.75×0.88-inch amber brown birthstone crystal for November.

（4）These birthstone charms and love gifts meet rigid safety standards.

（5）The ××× ring combines the precision and quality of sparkling crystals with a timeless design to showcase the beauty of the gleaming[6], drop-shaped faceted[7] stones.

（6）The ××× ring is embellished with white, drop-shaped stones that reflect and refract[8] light, for an accessory that sparkles alone or when paired with other rings.

（7）In the center of the pendant, it is inlaid[9] with a gem-quality 5A cubic zirconia.

（8）Fine diamond-inlaid technology and high-quality environmental protection plating are applied to ensure rhinestones[10] keep shiny for a long time.

（9）Pearls on the pins are manually[11] connected by durable fishing lines, free of glue[12].

（10）The sparkling round-cut stones all around each of the stones are set in a square box style mounting all joined together to create a stunning[13] box link bracelet.

(11) ABC's heart lock necklace collection is made entirely of first-class crystals imported from Austria.

(12) Good crystals are pure in color and show a very distinct iridescence[14] in light or sunlight.

(13) The translucency[15] of Austrian crystal is incomparable to other ordinary or natural crystals.

(14) The natural properties[16] and composition of mined[17] gemstones define the unique beauty of each piece.

(15) The fox pendant necklace amulet[18] is crafted from 100% natural and genuine rose quartz/obsidian gemstone.

(16) The 18K gold created gemstones 7 × 10 mm teardrop earrings adopt contrast color design, which looks simple and elegant.

(17) Give your formal wear an elegant upgrade when you slip on this dazzling ring encrusted[19] with a beautiful 14K white gold and natural white round-cut diamonds.

(18) These earrings are crafted from the highest quality cultured freshwater pearls, each pair is as lustrous[20] and stunning as the next.

(19) Each pair is meticulously[21] hand selected and matched from thousands of top-grade AAA pearls, the best on the market.

(20) This freshwater pearl bracelet set grades AAA, which represents the top 5%-10% of a pearl harvest with an 85% flawless[22] pearl.

(21) Encrusted with stunning crystals of various sizes, this necklace set shines bright like diamond which is unparalleled[23] in flawlessness and clarity.

(22) This necklace uses the heart crystal as an eye-catching centerpiece to make romantic pieces dazzle[24] as much as sleek[25] designs.

(23) Pendant crystals were embellished[26] with Austrian crystals, but the design belongs to ABC.

(24) ABC purchased genuine ××× crystals as raw material and skillfully applied on our own products.

单词解析：

1. cubic ['kju:bɪk] *adj.* 立方体的；立方的
2. precision [prɪ'sɪʒn] *n.* 精确；细致
3. brilliance ['brɪljəns] *n.* 透明（洁净）度；亮（明）度；光彩（缩写词为 bril 或 BRIL）
4. polish ['pɔlɪʃ] *v.* 磨光；润色；擦光
5. adorn [ə'dɔ:n] *v.* 装饰；使更美观
6. gleaming ['gli:mɪŋ] *adj.* 闪耀的；明亮的
7. faceted ['fæsɪtɪd] *adj.* 多面的
8. refract [rɪ'frækt] *v.* 使（光线）折射；使产生折射
9. inlay [,ɪn'leɪ] *v.* 镶嵌；把（图案等）嵌入
10. rhinestone ['raɪnstəʊn] *n.* 水钻；莱茵石（用于仿钻石首饰）
11. manually ['mænjʊəli] *adv.* 用手地；手动地；人工地
12. glue [glu:] *n.* 胶；胶水
13. stunning ['stʌnɪŋ] *adj.* 惊人的；极有魅力的；给人以深刻印象的
14. iridescence [,ɪrɪ'desns] *n.* 彩虹色
15. translucency [træns'lu:sənsi] *n.* 半透明
16. property ['prɔpəti] *n.* 性质
17. mine [maɪn] *v.* 开采
18. amulet ['æmjʊlət] *n.* 护身符
19. encrust [ɪn'krʌst] *v.* 包上外壳
20. lustrous ['lʌstrəs] *adj.* 有光泽的；柔软光亮的
21. meticulously [mə'tɪkjələsli] *adv.* 极仔细地；一丝不苟地
22. flawless ['flɔ:ləs] *adj.* 完美的；无瑕的
23. unparalleled [ʌn'pærəleld] *adj.* 无与伦比的；空前的
24. dazzle ['dæzl] *v.* 使目眩；使赞叹不已
    n. 耀眼；炫目；令人眼花缭乱的东西（或特性）
25. sleek [sli:k] *adj.* 光滑的；时髦的；造型优美的
26. embellish [ɪm'belɪʃ] *v.* 修饰；美化

产品规格介绍：

(25) Pendant size for the sterling silver birthstone necklace is $0.83'' \times 1.02''$. The zircon size is $0.3'' \times 0.3''$, and the chain length is $17.72'' + 1.97''$.

(26) The special twisted band shank[27] measures 2.5 mm in width. There are 22 stones in total set in sides.

(27) The ABC heart lock collection necklace is paired with a 0.8 mm diameter length of 18 inches box chain with an additional 3 inches extension chain.

(28) The bracelet includes about 22pcs 8 mm round beads, you will receive the similar item as picture.

(29) The round bead size is 7.5 mm to 8.5 mm, and the bracelet length is about 7 inches.

(30) Our bespoke[28] pearls are mounted on 14K yellow or white gold posts. With sizes ranging from 5 – 10 mm, we tailor to all of our clients' needs.

(31) The smaller 5 – 6 mm pearls are perfect for women who enjoy a delicate, understated look.

(32) Our 7 mm pearls are the most popular size, perfect for day-to-day style.

(33) For women who like to make a statement with their jewelry, the 8.5 mm pearls and above are ideal.

(34) This real elegant pearl set comes with an 18 inches necklace, 7.5 inches bracelet, and earrings with matching clasps and backings.

单词解析：

27. shank [ʃæŋk] n. 长柄；杆

28. bespoke [bɪˈspəʊk] adj. 定做的；专做订货的

产品功能介绍：

(35) The wearing of rose gold birthstone jewelry necklace can also bring good luck, health, and protection.

(36) The jewelry will maintain its brilliance over time when simple care practices are observed; remove before contact with water, lotions or perfumes to extend your jewelry's life.

(37) There are 12 different colors of gemstones, corresponding to the birthstone of each month. You can choose the color according to the birth month. Ruby in July means passion, kindness and dignity. Olivine in August means happiness. Sapphire in September means love, honesty, virtue. Tourmaline in October means joy and peace. Topaz in November means friendship and hope. Tanzanite in December means victory, good luck and success.

(38) Silver diamond chain necklace not only has a unique design, but also easy to match with different outfits. Every girl deserves to have her beautiful rhinestone necklace to bring out their beauty and charm.

(39) It is an excellent healing stone with a positive energy around it. Fluorite also can balance the energy around you.

(40) Fluorite promotes spiritual and psychic wholeness and development, truth, protection, and brings peace. It can help get rid of mental blocks and similar mental issues.

(41) Amethyst in 7 chakra[29] corresponding to the eyebrow wheel which can promote the activity of brain cells, helping to think and concentrate.

(42) The opal is the October birthstone, so it could be given as a gift to any stylish woman who has an October birthday.

(43) Our freshwater pearls feature a bright, rich luster with distinctive warmth.

(44) Conveying unmatched craftsmanship and timeless elegance, our genuine pearl necklace set will radiate[30] the essence of beauty.

(45) Wearing a dinner dress or formal gown with this crystal necklace earrings set, which radiates elegance and luxury in ceremony, show, ball, dancing party, banquet and other events.

单词解析：

29. chakra ['tʃʌkrə] n. 轮（人体精神集中点之一）

30. radiate ['reɪdieɪt] v. 显出；流露

产品服务介绍：

(46) The pendant birthstone necklace for women with no artificial damage is

eligible for a full refund or free replacement within 12 months.

(47) The ABC crystal necklace comes in a black gift box with an LED spotlight on the lid[31] that will illuminate[32] the moment the box is opened.

(48) Our jewelry passes extensive quality checkpoints before being shipped to you.

(49) Every single ethically-sourced[33] natural diamond has been hand-picked by our experts and comes with a certification by Independent Gemological Lab.

(50) We create all pearl earrings for women in house to ensure that every order adheres[34] to the highest standards of pearl quality available.

> 单词解析：
> 31. lid [lɪd] *n.* 盖子
> 32. illuminate [ɪˈluːmɪneɪt] *v.* 照明；照射
> 33. ethically-sourced [ˈeθɪk(ə)lɪ sɔːst] *adj.* 符合道德标准的（采购）
> 34. adhere [ədˈhɪə] *v.* 遵守；附着

直播模板 Template

Our _____ is an original design from our studio in _____ and features a precious _____. All of our jewelry products are polished by hand.

This _____ is adorned with a _____-inch _____ for _____. They are _____ plated and designed with an _____-inch chain plus _____-inch extender, and a lobster claw clasp.

These _____ charms and love gifts meet rigid safety standards. Our jewelry collections pass _____ regulation, and are lead-free, nickel-free, and allergy-free.

Honor your inner royalty with this unique _____. Presented by _____, this _____ is a regal, symbolic statement piece that unveils your feminine spirit.

Looking for exceptional birthday, anniversary, holiday, Christmas, Valentine's Day, and Mother's Day gifts for your wife, mom, sister, daughter, or girlfriend? Each _____ is stored in an _____ gift box and gift bag, making it an ideal _____ for the special women or girl in your life.

7.3 其他种类的饰品 Other Kinds of Accessories

词汇积累 Vocabulary

序号	中文名称	英文名称
1	塑料	plastic
2	树脂	resin
3	亚克力	acrylic
4	流苏	tassel
5	夹子	clip
6	发夹	hair clip/pin
7	发箍	hair hoop
8	抓夹	hair claw clip
9	发箍	hairband/headband（hairband 指的是硬的头箍，headband 用于指发箍发带皆可）

续表

序号	中文名称	英文名称
10	发绳	hair tie
11	大肠圈	scrunchies
12	发饰	hair accessory
13	真人假发	human hair wig
14	化纤假发	synthetic wig
15	夹式假发	clip in/on hair extension
16	发帘	hair weft
17	发髻	bun
18	刘海	clip in hair fringe
19	男士假发	toupee
20	短发	short wig
21	中发	medium wig
22	长发	long wig
23	马尾	pony tail
24	大波浪	deep wave
25	卷的	curly
26	微卷的	wavy
27	发尾	nail tip
28	自然黑	natural black
29	棕黑色	brownish black
30	双扣	double knots
31	漂底	bleached knots
32	手钩	hand implanted/hand knotted
33	接发环	micro ring
34	钥匙扣	key holder

续表

序号	中文名称	英文名称
35	袖口纽	cufflink
36	雕刻品	carving
37	捕梦器	dream catcher
38	棉绳	cotton cord
39	节日饰品	holiday decoration
40	贝壳	cowry
41	丝绒	velvet
42	蕾丝	lace
43	皮革	leather
44	丝	silk
45	瓷	porcelain
46	黑玉	jet
47	珊瑚	coral
48	玉石	jade
49	修剪	trim

话术演练 Language Skills

产品材质与特色介绍：

（1）The high-quality velvet material is comfortable to wear, anti-allergy, and can also be worn by people with sensitive skin.

（2）This double-layered love red necklace is a whole piece, not easily tangled[1].

（3）This black choker necklace is made with soft slightly stretchy[2] nice velvet and silver-plated base accessories.

（4）The black choker necklace for women is made of environmentally friendly lace and high-quality alloy. It does not cause itch[3] and redness on the skin of your neck.

(5) These choker necklaces are made of high-quality soft synthetic[4] leather materials, they are durable and safe to wear.

(6) These chokers are made of soft stretchy but sturdy plastic, which is non-toxic and odor-free[5].

(7) The ABC imitation[6] clay earrings are made of clay-touch acrylic, which combines the tactile[7] feel of polymer[8] clay with the lightness and strength of acrylic for a more refined and better textured[9] look than either material.

(8) The trendy rattan[10] dangle[11] earrings are very lightweight and durable, which won't burden your ears.

(9) This long wavy wig is made of 100% heat-resistant high-quality synthetic fiber.

(10) These latest resin earrings are made of the season's most popular acrylic material, with mottled[12] flower decorated.

(11) Bring out your inner temperament[13] with these acrylic drops earrings—crafted from colorful resin.

(12) The flower earrings are made of quality chain and acrylic. The brightly colored petals use advanced painting and sanding techniques to make them look more textured and realistic.

(13) U-shape resin texture embellished with floral pattern, which is chic[14] and stylish. These earrings can fully show your personal temperature and sense.

(14) Each pattern is made with acrylic and resin while the main frame is crafted with zinc[15].

(15) This ring set is made of high-quality acrylic and rhinestones. It is smooth, comfortable, lightweight, durable and non-toxic[16].

(16) Our statement open cuff[17] bracelet features mottled resin wide bangle with high polished gold-tone metal edge.

(17) Each one is made using high-quality textured fabric to ensure optimal[18] comfort and hold-soft to the touch, gentle on hair and extremely comfortable to wear all day long without damaging your hair.

(18) These headbands are made with 100% pure mulberry[19] silk (not satin[20])

on the outside. Silk is an anti-friction[21] natural fabric[22] with 18 amino acids[23]. Unlike cotton, it does not absorb moisture[24].

(19) These claw hair clips are made of durable plastics, which secure your hair all day long with the double teeth claw clips by non-slip[25] materials and strong spring[26].

(20) This bracelet is made of blue and white glazed porcelain beads with high polished smooth surface and long-lasting color retention[27].

(21) The pendant is adorned with soft pink roses, which are made of genuine porcelain for a vintage-inspired look that is charming and sweet.

单词解析：

1. tangle ['tæŋgl] *v.* 使缠结；纠结；乱作一团

2. stretchy ['stretʃi] *adj.* 有弹性的

3. itch [ɪtʃ] *v.* 发痒

    n. 痒

4. synthetic [sɪn'θetɪk] *adj.* （人工）合成的；人造的

5. odor ['əʊdər] *n.* 气味；臭味（odor-free 无味的）

6. imitation [ˌɪmɪ'teɪʃn] *n.* 仿制品；仿造品

    adj. 人造的；仿制的

7. tactile ['tæktl] *adj.* 触觉的

8. polymer ['pɒlɪmər] *n.* 聚合物；多聚体

9. texture ['tekstʃər] *n.* 纹理；质地

10. rattan [ræ'tæn] *n.* 藤（东南亚蔓生植物）

11. dangle ['dæŋgl] *v.* （使）悬垂；（使）悬挂

    n. 悬荡；悬垂

12. mottled ['mɒtld] *adj.* 斑驳的；杂色的

13. temperament ['temprəmənt] *n.* 性情；（人或动物的）气质；性格

14. chic [ʃiːk] *adj.* 时髦的；雅致的

15. zinc [zɪŋk] *n.* 锌

16. toxic ['tɒksɪk] *adj.* 有毒的；引起中毒的（non-toxic 无毒的）

17. cuff [kʌf] n. 袖口

18. optimal [ˈɔptɪməl] adj. 最优的;最佳的

19. mulberry [ˈmʌlberi] n. 桑树（mulberry silk 桑蚕丝）

20. satin [ˈsætn] n. 缎子

21. friction [ˈfrɪkʃn] n. 摩擦;摩擦力（anti-friction 耐磨）

22. fabric [ˈfæbrɪk] n. 织物;布料

23. amino acid 氨基酸

24. moisture [ˈmɔɪstʃər] n. 潮湿;水分

25. slip [slɪp] v. 滑落（non-slip 防滑的）

26. spring [sprɪŋ] n. 弹簧;弹性

27. retention [rɪˈtenʃn] n. 保持;保留

产品规格介绍：

(22) These hairbands measure approx 5 inches in diameter, which has a certain elasticity[28], suitable for people with different head circumferences[29] to wear.

(23) It can be trimmed and shaped. There are different facial shapes and head circumferences, please rest assured that you can trim it to the length you like.

(24) There are 4 claws at each side of hair grip. The strong claws and interlocking teeth can hold your hair in place well and non-slip.

(25) The length of the hair clip is 3.5 inches. These hair clamps have strong, durable spring, which can be opened to 180°, hold all hair well.

(26) The ponytail[30] holder can stretch easily from 4 cm to 30 cm and it would not deform[31] or tear[32].

单词解析：

28. elasticity [ˌiːlæˈstɪsəti] n. 弹性;弹力

29. circumference [səˈkʌmfərəns] n. 圆周;圆周长

30. ponytail [ˈpəʊniteɪl] n. 马尾辫

31. deform [dɪˈfɔːrm] v. 改变……的外形;损毁……的形状

32. tear [teə] v. 撕碎;扯破

产品功能与特色介绍：

（27）This velvet red heart choker adopts a classic love pattern, which represents elegance, beauty, love, playful and cute personal temperament.

（28）The big scrunchie is premium, shiny and soft which causes minimal pulling on the hair.

（29）The elastic band inside the scrunchies for girls has an excellent stretch, not too tight or too loose, the hair scrunchies for women's hair can grip into your hair really well without loosening or falling down. They can stay in place well and are suitable for all hair types.

（30）Our premium stain hair scrunchie set is a must-have hair accessory for women and girls. They can be used on all different types of hair ranging from curly, wavy to straight hair and other hair textures as well. They are suitable for both thick and thin hair.

（31）The velvet hair band in different colors can be stretched easily for its good elasticity to fit your head size and bring out your charm.

（32）The chokers inspired by the 90s are a must-have piece of the season.

（33）Versatile[33] and easy to wear, the choker can be an eye-catching feminine accessory for day and night.

（34）These styles enhance your neckline and add the perfect touch to any outfit.

（35）These geometric[34] earrings are distinctive pieces that add a contemporary finish to any outfit, whether you're going to work or going out.

（36）The wig with bangs is a popular style at present, which helps to create a sweet look.

（37）At the same time, brown with highlight hair color can brighten up your skin tone, and the highlight adds more vitality. It must be on your wish list and your first choice as a gift.

（38）Easter acrylic earrings with rich patterns can not only add vitality to your makeup, but also can be matched with various styles of clothing.

（39）ABC soft, ultra-textured scrunchies for women are ideal for thick, fine, curly or straight hair.

(40) The perfect additions for your ponytail or wrist, these adorable scrunchies provide fast, easy and effortless styling.

(41) These scrunchies stretch easily and generously to hold up all your hair in a ponytail, messy bun[35] or braid[36] with ease, and comfortably stretch to be worn as a bracelet on your wrist when not in use. So they are ready for ponytail or messy bun duty at any time.

(42) Using a silk headband and pillowcase helps improve overall hair health, keeps your hair calm and hydrated[37].

(43) ABC original jewelry & accessories focus on classic vintage, mass pop, street fashion and sub-cultures.

> 单词解析：
> 33. versatile ['vɜːrsətl] *adj.* 多功能的；多用途的
> 34. geometric [ˌdʒiːə'metrɪk] *adj.* 几何的；(似)几何图形的
> 35. bun [bʌn] *n.* 圆发髻
> 36. braid [breɪd] *v.* 编织；把(头发)编成辫子
> 37. hydrate ['haɪdreɪt] *v.* 使吸入水分；使水合

产品服务介绍：

(44) Each black velvet choker collar will be carefully checked before packaging, so don't worry about quality issues.

(45) We have our own factory. We also have multi-layer process to control the product quality, and ensure that your favorite jewelry reach your hand to get a perfect display.

(46) We strive to bring you the highest quality jewelry at unbeatable prices. This is why we are sure you will be more than satisfied with our services.

(47) Our mission is to provide accessible luxury to all by offering high-quality jewelry, good service and provide a beautiful, fashion line that every woman and girl can wear and be confident as she walks out the door.

(48) We are specialized in fashion jewelry and committed to create freedom,

elegant, distinctive style for you.

(49) We are committed to providing the best wigs and the best service for all customers. If you have any questions about wigs, please contact us. We will give you a satisfactory reply within 24 hours.

(50) We handwoven this cuff bangle with superior crafts and unbelievable attention to detail so you can get a unique yet chic fashion piece.

直播模板 Template

This _____ wig was made by _____ high quality _____ hair, can be styled with heat tools up to _____ ℃ (_____ ℉). In the strong sunlight, it can be a _____ wig highlighted at the hair ends, soft and smooth, more natural and good texture just like your own hair.

Unlike other glueless wigs for women, we add one procedure to brush the residual hair after production process, and this high-quality hair replacement wigs hair is really sturdy enough, even with constant brushing.

This glueless wig is made by _____ Mesh for the inner cap with _____ clips added, breathable, no tightness, much more comfortable when wearing, and couldn't see the wefts no matter how the hair lays. _____ adjustment straps and _____ buckles at the back of the wig, fit most head circumferences and shapes. Its adjustable range is _____ inches.

This wig is _____ inch wig, designed for daily use, you also can use it for Halloween, bachelorette parties, weddings, dating, or just for those days when you don't want to style your own hair. With this _____ wig, bad hair days, eliminated.

7.4　实战脚本 Script

Live Streaming Script of Necklaces

Hello, everyone! This is Lexie, from ABC, a professional jewelry brand. We have over 10 years of experience in jewelry design and sales.

Today is our happy Friday day, so we prepare a lot of beautiful jewelries and follower benefits only for you guys. So please stay tuned to check out what's going on.

All of our fancy jewelries are made with high quality and professional design. The original price are all above 30 pounds, but today all the jewelries will be sold for the biggest promotion.

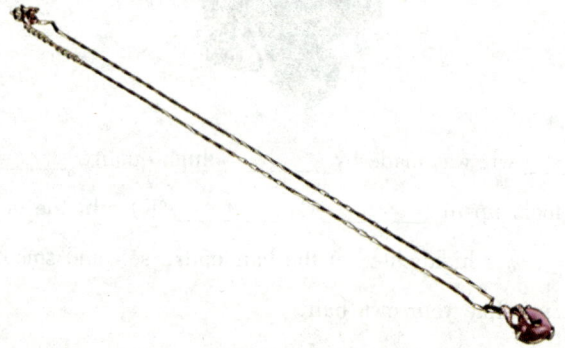

First of all, let's come to the necklace in link No. 1. This pendant is really beautiful! I really love silver and purple stones together like amethyst. I think they work beautifully together. And this pendant heart shape is timeless. Heart shape design has always been the first choice for gift giving. Especially with the colorful stones like this will definitely bring a good mood to the people who receive them. This classic pendant sells well every year. I think it's perfect for spring and summer. This is like more of a choker style which I love. The length of this necklace is adjustable. I have it on the loosest setting here. And this is as loose as it will go. You can have it to be more of a layering piece.

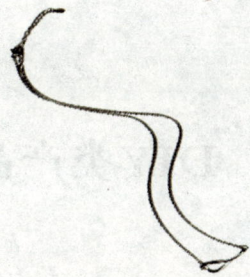

  Then let me show you our best sellers and this classic infinite necklace is so gorgeous and it's a bargain. It's very easy to match with all your outfits for every season. This is the popular style for any occasions. And this one can be a perfect gift to your wife or girlfriend. Or you can even buy it as a special gift to yourself, because you deserve it! This silver infinity shape can symbolize your love. What's more, this necklace has a great polishing and looks so shiny and sparkly. We also have matching earrings and rings, so I just suggest choosing a whole set if you are going to prepare something for friends and family. Because it's beautiful and high-quality. If you buy it, you won't regret it! I promise.

  Ok and that's all for today. Big thanks to everyone, and don't forget to follow Lexie, follow ABC. Ok, so have a nice day, bye bye, see ya.

第八章
DIY类产品英语直播

中国海关总署的统计数据显示,2022 年上半年,我国五金制品行业外贸进出口总额 955.99 亿美元,同比增长 6.96%。其中:出口总额 826.62 亿美元,同比增长 10.39%;进口总额 129.37 亿美元,同比减少 10.73%。五金制品中,主要出口种类为手动工具、专业电动工具、电动工具配件等。在国外,人们热衷于 DIY 文化,几乎每个家庭都有一个工具箱。一到周末,他们就会自己动手制作、修理物品。这极大地带动了 DIY 相关工具类产品需求的迅猛增长。随着网上零售的兴起及各种电商渠道的逐渐普及,消费者获得手工艺品的方式更加便利。这不仅促进了全球手工 DIY 制品的销售,也方便手工爱好者们在线上进行分享,借此学习、分享、获取灵感。

8.1 DIY 工具 DIY Tools

词汇积累 Vocabulary

序号	中文名称	英文名称
1	凿子	chisel
2	钉锤	hammer
3	钻子	drill
4	锉刀	file
5	梯子	ladder
6	油漆刷	paint brush
7	钳子	pliers

续表

序号	中文名称	英文名称
8	尺子	ruler
9	锯子	saw
10	螺丝刀	screwdriver
11	螺丝钳	spanner
12	水平仪	spirit level
13	卷尺	tape measure
14	剪刀	scissors
15	缝纫机	sewing machine
16	针	needle
17	别针/大头针	pin
18	针垫	pincushion
19	线	thread
20	扣子	button
21	毛线	wool
22	拉链	zipper
23	螺栓	bolt
24	钉	nail
25	螺母	nut
26	螺丝	screw
27	垫圈/垫片	washer
28	管子	pipe
29	剪钳	combination pliers
30	圆口钳	round mouth pliers
31	尖嘴钳	needle nose pliers
32	透明带	transparent belt
33	胶水	glue
34	热熔胶枪	hot melt glue gun

续表

序号	中文名称	英文名称
35	镊子	tweezers
36	打火机	lighter
37	工具箱	toolbox
38	扳手	wrench
39	滚筒/滚轴	roller
40	回形针/夹子	clip
41	电池	battery
42	刀片/刀刃	blade
43	弹簧	spring
44	金属丝	wire
45	工具刀/美工刀	utility knife
46	折叠/对折	fold up
47	捏	pinch
48	塑造	mold
49	揉	knead
50	擦/摩擦	rub
51	拍打	beat/pat
52	把……弄平/涂抹	smooth
53	戳/捅	poke
54	按/压/挤	press
55	扭转/扭弯/旋转/绞	twist
56	把……打结/捆扎	knot
57	裱糊/涂	paste
58	扣住/扣紧/钩住	clasp
59	抓/握	grip
60	成套工具	kit

话术演练 Language Skills

产品材质介绍：

(1) The claw hammer has high-frequency quenched[1] head, which is sturdy and durable. TRP coated handle is non-slip and comfortable to use.

(2) The long nose pliers are constructed from forged[2] carbon steel with heat treatment for durability.

(3) The adjustable wrench is constructed of high-quality carbon steel for strength and chrome[3] plated for durability.

(4) The combination wrench set is made of premium chrome vanadium[4] steel with a mirror chrome finish.

(5) Ratcheting[5] bit driver and bit set comes with 1-piece 1/4″ ratcheting bit driver and 50 pieces different tip Cr-V steel bits for around house DIY applications. The bit holder is easy to organize.

(6) The hack saw comes with heat treatment steel blade for durability. 2pcs replacement saw blades are included.

(7) The 72-tooth ratchet is a quick-release ratchet with reversible[6] 72-tooth gearing[7] and a soft grip to reduce hand fatigue[8]. The chrome plating prevents it from rust and corrosion.

(8) A complete range of chrome vanadium 1/4 inch and 3/8 inch metric[9] sockets[10] can be used for small engine repair as well as other fasteners[11] found on bikes, cars, etc..

(9) The utility knife has compact and comfortable grip utility cutter with retractable SK-5 blade for cutting and shaping material, and it is perfect for various hobby and craft applications. 10pcs replacement blades are included.

(10) The tape measure is designed with 2 measurement scales (inch & metric) for multi-purpose reading. The thumb locking is easy to operate. Its hand strap[12] is easy for carrying.

(11) The magnetic[13] level has high-visibility green bubbles at 3 angles: 45°, 90°, 180°. Strong magnetic base attached to metal surface is easy to use.

(12) The rust-proof and flexible stainless[14] steel ruler comes with laser-engraving scales (one side is centimeter scale, another side is inch scale).

(13) Package includes all the furniture and accessories in the pictures, including the dust-proof cover and music movement. And also including the toolkit, such as scissor, ruler, tweezers.

(14) High quality and excellent design match its price: materials are of good quality, the furniture and other wooden pieces are precisely cut so that they fit together correctly.

(15) All pieces are packed in the rugged[15], compact pink carry pouch[16] (size: 13 × 8.1 × 2.8 inches) for storage and portability. Each tool fits snugly[17] into its respective place to prevent moving around and scraping.

(16) Our tools come with a soft grip handle that makes them more comfortable and secure than others.

(17) It is made of high-temperature forged high-carbon steel material and not easy to fall out hammer and durable head.

(18) They are made of high-quality steel and finished in heat-treated chrome, durable and corrosion resistance. Handles are made of TPR material, which is comfortable for grip.

(19) The lightweight and multi-functional pen comes with a longer cord[18] and works at adjustable heat setting from 200℃ to 450℃.

(20) The bend assist tools are made of quality stainless steel, can resist to most acids[19] and corrosive[20] agents.

(21) Amazingly compact size and rubber wrapped around the body make the tool easy to grip and control.

单词解析：

1. quenched [kwentʃt] *adj.* 淬火的
2. forge [fɔːdʒ] *v.* 锻造；伪造（forged steel 锻钢）
3. chrome [krəʊm] *n.* 铬；铬合金
4. vanadium [vəˈneɪdiəm] *n.* 钒
5. ratchet [ˈrætʃɪt] *n.* （防止倒转的）棘轮；棘齿

6. reversible [rɪ'vɜːsəbl] adj. 可逆的;可翻转的;正反两用的

7. gearing ['ɡɪərɪŋ] n. 齿轮装置;传动装置

8. fatigue [fə'tiːɡ] n. 劳累;厌倦

9. metric ['metrɪk] adj. 按公制制作的;用公制测量的

      n. 度量标准

10. socket ['sɔkɪt] n. (电源)插座;窝;(电器上的)插孔

11. fastener ['fɑːsnə(r)] n. 纽扣;拉链;扣件

12. strap [stræp] n. 带子

13. magnetic [mæɡ'netɪk] adj. 有磁性的;磁的

14. stainless ['steɪnləs] adj. 不锈钢的;不生锈的 (stainless steel 不锈钢)

15. rugged ['rʌɡɪd] adj. 坚毅的;结实的

16. pouch [paʊtʃ] n. 小袋;邮袋

17. snugly [snʌɡli] adv. 紧贴地;贴身地

18. cord [kɔːd] n. (细)绳;(结实的)粗线;电源线

19. acid ['æsɪd] n. 酸

    adj. 酸的;酸性的

20. corrosive [kə'rəʊsɪv] adj. 腐蚀性的;侵蚀性的

产品规格介绍:

(22) This toolbox includes comprehensive assortment[21] of professional-grade wrenches, magnetic level, a complete range of 1/4 inch and 3/8 inch metric-sized sockets and precision screwdrivers, hammer, tape measure, pliers etc..

(23) ABC super gauge[22] duplicator[23] goes with a metal locking mechanism, it can keep the shape without moving out of form, help you duplicate and transfer the shape accurately to anywhere you need.

(24) The high-quality aluminum[24] core will keep the master outline tool working well for years.

(25) Smooth 12,000 RPM single-speed for precise control, this cordless[25] rotary tool makes light-duty DIY and home-crafting projects easy.

单词解析：

21. assortment [əˈsɔːrtmənt] n. 各种各样
22. gauge [ɡeɪdʒ] n. 测量仪器(或仪表)；计量器
    v. (用仪器)测量；判定
23. duplicator [ˈdjuːplɪkeɪtər] n. 复制器
24. aluminum [əˈlumənəm] n. 铝
25. cordless [ˈkɔːdləs] adj. 无电线的；不用电线与电源相连的

产品功能介绍：

(26) The claw hammer is easy to bang nails into, or extract nails from wood and other materials.

(27) The long nose pliers can get into hard-to-reach areas for cutting, bending, twisting and gripping wire.

(28) This wrench can be used to grip and turn nuts and bolts of various sizes.

(29) The combination wrench set is suitable for automotive and mechanic repairs. Metric sizes: 8 mm, 10 mm, 12 mm, 13 mm, 14 mm, 15 mm.

(30) This saw can be used with wood, plastic and general DIY tasks.

(31) The ruler is easy to be used as drawing straight edge or measuring device.

(32) The 210-pc tool set is perfect for most small repairs and DIY projects around the house.

(33) You can use this multi-functional wood-burning tools to do fabric embossing[26], carving, soldering[27], image transferring, paper crafting, hot stamping and stencil[28] cutting.

(34) This pen comes with high-quality 60 W heated ceramic technology can quickly heat wood burning kit in 60 seconds.

(35) ABC contour[29] gauge is designed for winding[30] pipes, circular frames, ducts[31] and many objects.

(36) The contour gauge is ideal for fitting tiles, laminate[32], carpet, checking dimensions, moulding, etc..

(37) The contour gauge is a useful tool for operations on car bodies, carpentry[33]

and for all kinds of modelling.

(38) The plastic ruler with inches and centimeters on the body of the gauge makes it easy to measure the length of irregular graphics.

(39) Cover shield[34] provides better protection for cutting and grinding.

(40) Drill locator helps for precision work on wood.

(41) Diamond cutting wheel is the best tips for glass, ceramic, floor tile etc..

(42) Versatile accessories include a pair of extra carbon brush, rescue you from searching new set and saving money.

(43) The variable speed adjustment knob[35] showing 5 step speeds from 8,000 to 30,000 RPM. By adjusting the speed you can make delicate engravings on wood, glass, metals, plastics, tiles and other materials with control easily.

(44) Its ergonomic[36] compact[37] rotary[38] tool design makes it handhold size and lightweight. Moreover, it does not make the loud noise.

(45) Whether you are repairing home tasks or lighting your creations, this is really a worth value investment.

(46) Clipper is great for cutting pieces from the metal sheet, you don't need to remove each piece by bending[39] back and forth.

(47) This 3 jaw keyless chuck[40] allows you to change accessories on ABC rotary tools quickly and easily without using collets[41] and wrench.

(48) Detailer's grip allows you to focus on your precise carving, grinding, and engraving and gives more stability.

(49) Cutting guide is suitable for different depth cutting, and keeps good perspective and stability.

单词解析:

26. emboss [ɪmˈbɒs] v. 浮雕;压印浮凸字体(或图案);凹凸印

27. solder [ˈsəʊldə(r)] v. 焊接;焊合

28. stencil [ˈstensl] n. (印文字或图案用的)模板;(用模板印的)文字或图案

29. contour [ˈkɒntʊr] n. 外形;轮廓

30. wind [wɪnd] v. 缠绕;绕成团

31. duct ［dʌkt］ n. 管道；管子
32. laminate ［ˈlæmɪnət］ n. 薄片制成的材料；层压（或黏合）材料
33. carpentry ［ˈkɑːrpəntrɪ］ n. 木工工艺；木匠活
34. shield ［ʃiːld］ n.（保护机器和操作者的）护罩
35. knob ［nɔb］ n. 旋钮
36. ergonomic ［ˌɜːɡəˈnɔmɪk］ adj. 工效学的；人类工程学的
37. compact ［kəmˈpækt］ adj. 紧凑的；小型的
38. rotary ［ˈrəʊtərɪ］ adj. 旋转的；转动的
39. bend ［bend］ v.（使）倾斜；把……弄弯（或折起）
40. chuck ［tʃʌk］ n.（固定钻头等用的）夹盘；卡盘
41. collet ［ˈkɔlɪt］ n.（弹簧）筒夹；（弹性）夹头

产品服务介绍：

(50) Assortment of necessary tools are in one box, <u>durable plastic case with internal molded compartments[42]</u> to keep each component protected and easily accessible.

单词解析：

42. compartment ［kəmˈpɑːtmənt］ n.（家具或设备等的）隔层

直播模板 Template

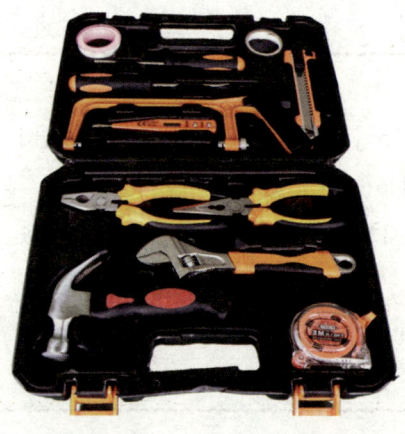

This _____ is made of _____ and finished in _____. The _____ is durable and corrosion resistance. Handle is made of _____, which is comfortable for grip.

This _____ can be used for most small repairs and DIY projects around the house. This _____ is easy to carry and stock. It is perfect for handyman, construction workers, mechanics, work shops etc.. _____ is also a good gift choice for family members, friends, partners, etc..

Comprehensive assortment of professional-grade _____, _____, a complete range of _____ and _____, _____, _____ etc.. The _____ can be easily shifted to change direction by _____. Variety of _____: _____, _____, _____, and _____. Soft-grip handle on _____, _____, _____ and _____ provides excellent comfort and control.

Assortment of necessary tools are in one box, durable plastic case with _____ compartments to keep each component protected and easily accessible. Here is a kindly tip: when opening the toolbox, please place the side with _____ logo on the top to prevent the tools falling out from the box.

8.2　DIY 玩具 DIY Toys

词汇积累 Vocabulary

序号	中文名称	英文名称
1	装配/集会	assembly
2	微缩模型	miniature
3	手册/指南	manual
4	家具	furniture
5	配件	accessory
6	装饰品	ornament
7	缝	stitch

续表

序号	中文名称	英文名称
8	粘贴	stick
9	积木	block
10	片	plate
11	梁	beam
12	轮子	wheel
13	轮胎	tyre
14	齿轮	gear
15	轴	axis
16	手绘	handprint
17	刮画	scratch painting
18	聚合黏土	polymer clay
19	星形切割工具	star-shaped cutter
20	擀面杖	rolling pin
21	羊皮纸	parchment paper
22	无毒的	non-toxic
23	纸板框	chipboard frame
24	书签	bookmark
25	贴纸	sticker
26	回形针	paper clip
27	发光胶带	glittery tape
28	固体胶	glue stick
29	描画针	stylus
30	画笔/画刷	paintbrush
31	泡沫刷	foam brush
32	毯子	blanket

续表

序号	中文名称	英文名称
33	流苏	fringe
34	珠子	bead
35	图案	pattern
36	磁性积木	magnetic building blocks
37	科学实验套装	science kit
38	护目镜	goggles
39	试管	test tube
40	量勺	measuring spoon
41	量杯	measuring cup
42	漏斗	funnel
43	滴管	dropper
44	木头拼图	wooden puzzles
45	原木	virgin wood
46	风铃套装	wind chime kit
47	木盆	wooden pot
48	铃杆	chime rod
49	玩具屋套装	dollhouse kit
50	黏胶套装	slime kit

话术演练 Language Skills

产品材质与特色介绍：

（1）This tiny house kit included a variety of materials like paper, wood, metal and plastic, which could be used for making up a variety of furniture, plants, and decorations.

（2）You could choose silicone[1] liquid glue. It needs 2pcs of AA batteries.

（3）Our DIY mini dollhouse is very well made, using a miniature scale of about

1∶24. It includes printed paper, cloth, wooden parts, LED lights as well as glue, paint and a brush.

(4) A lot of effort has been spent on little things such as drawer handles, picture frames and accessories. Turn on the LED lights and you'll have a realistic-looking room.

(5) The DIY model kit includes wood, fabric, thread, wire, and other accessories.

(6) The product also includes delicate details such as porcelain, desserts, magic brooms and other decorations to make the scene more rich and interesting.

(7) LED light, plants, ornament, furniture are quite realistic and cleverly designed.

(8) The furniture and other wooden pieces are precisely cut so that they fit together correctly.

(9) All the furniture and accessories are almost the same as real house with similar material.

(10) This miniature house mimics a well-designed transparent[2] glass greenhouse, like a dream garden house in real.

(11) Each kit comes with everything included: paint, glue, cloth, and an instruction book with illustrations to give you an idea of the possibilities.

(12) These truck play vehicles are made of high-quality plastic, which complies with toy standards.

(13) These miniature holiday duck figures are made of sturdy resin material that is waterproof[3] and resistant to fade.

(14) The 3D puzzle Eiffel Tower is made of high-quality and non-toxic wood with grooved[4] edges which makes it safe for children.

(15) All the furniture and accessories shown in the picture need DIY making. The process includes cutting, stitching and sticking, which will take 20 to 30 hours to finish for the whole process.

(16) This coffee & flower shop DIY miniature dollhouse is made from non-toxic materials including wood kits, paper kits, fabric kits, plastic kits, metal kits, and

so on.

(17) ABC rose flower toy building set is made of high-quality ABS plastic mini bricks, with unicorn[5], pedestal[6], transparent glass cover and detailed colorful graphic instructions.

(18) Our miniature accessories are hand-crafted with high-quality resin with great details, which is not easy to fade or deform.

> 单词解析:
> 1. silicone ['sɪlɪkəʊn] n. 硅酮;聚硅氧烷
> 2. transparent [træns'pærənt] adj. 透明的
> 3. waterproof ['wɔːtərpruːf] adj. 防水的;耐水的
> 4. grooved [gruːvd] adj. 有沟的;有槽的
> 5. unicorn ['juːnɪkɔːrn] n. (传说中的)独角兽
> 6. pedestal ['pedɪstl] n. 底座

产品规格介绍:

(19) The assembly is suitable for people older than 14 years and needs about 30 hours. Finished assembly product size is 7.87×7.75×7.08 inches.

(20) The house kits are the furniture and accessories which you need to DIY, such as grinding, bonding, assembling, modelling to finish building your own house.

(21) This flower shop miniature kit is approximately 1/24 scale with assembled size: 8.7×7.5×8.3 inches.

(22) The dimension of the mini house is 7.7″×6.9″×6.9″ after assembled, recommended age is 14+.

(23) Our DIY mini dollhouse is very well made, using a miniature scale of about 1∶24.

产品功能介绍:

(24) It grows your kid's mind feature and leads towards the nature to create their own imaginations with colorful painting reflections.

(25) Making miniature dollhouse could be a fun project to do with friends;

completion time is estimated at 20 – 24 hours (plus glue drying time), but extra hands would make it go much faster.

(26) This set includes tools carefully chosen for their usefulness in everyday household and DIY tasks so you will always have the right tool for the job.

(27) The assembling process is about 10 – 12 hours. You will be immersed[7] in this inspiring, stress-relieving and enjoyable process.

(28) This wood model kits will make you fall in love with arts and crafts and become fulfilled.

(29) Although it may take up your time and effort to assemble, but after completed, you will get a lot of happiness.

(30) After completed, you will accomplish the sense of achievement and very satisfying to see all these little bits of nothing turn into your perfect little greenhouse.

(31) Completing DIY miniature dollhouse with family or friends will not only exercise logic and sensory coordination[8], but also give you the opportunity to build closer relationships and create a joyful atmosphere.

(32) Our DIY miniature dollhouse is good for home decoration.

(33) The DIY miniature dollhouse looks great to show on your table, bookshelf, add it in your collections or hang on the window. Wherever you put it, it makes your home more cozy and cute.

(34) The hollow[9] design not only enhances the sense of detail, but also allows light to penetrate better inside.

(35) Book nook[10] is more than just a DIY book corner project, also an exquisite[11] collection and decoration.

(36) This not only makes children's hands more coordinated, but also cultivates their creativity.

(37) This is a perfectly designed DIY kit that requires your hands-on work to complete.

(38) This wooden drum kit is very suitable for beginners. It only takes 2 hours to complete it.

(39) Our 3D wooden puzzles are excellent brain teasers[12]—it provides a fun,

yet complex task that would takes a good amount of critical thinking, focusing, and problem solving skills to complete.

(40) Flower building toy set comes with understand-friendly instructions. You can easily complete the exquisite flower building set while exercising hand-eye coordination and enjoying relaxing building time.

(41) It also has an LED lamp, so you can turn on the light at night to decorate the finished product in your favorite place and watch it at any time.

(42) It comes with original materials, and needs to be patience, which is challenging for people who first build such miniatures. However, if you can calm down, focus, and finally make it, you will find that all your efforts are worth it.

> 单词解析:
>
> 7. immerse [ɪˈmɜːs] v. 沉浸在;(使)深陷于
> 8. coordination [kəʊˌɔːdɪˈneɪʃn] n. 协作;协调动作的能力
> 9. hollow [ˈhɒləʊ] adj. 中空的;空心的
> 10. nook [nʊk] n. 僻静处;幽静的角落
> 11. exquisite [ɪkˈskwɪzɪt] adj. 精致的;精美的
> 12. teaser [ˈtiːzə] n. 难题;棘手的问题

产品服务介绍:

(43) If you have any questions such as steps of assembly or missing parts, please contact us for help. We will be right here waiting for you to solve your problems.

(44) If you find the instruction manual is not in English, please download it according our tip or contact us directly. Each step has been clearly showed in the instruction manual with pictures to guide you to assemble the house.

(45) The video can teach you how to assemble the entire miniature, just search "DIY dollhouse".

(46) A multi-page pictorial instruction booklet leads you through the process, but of course, you can add your own custom touches.

(47) There are many color photos to show you how to assemble each part and

where to place everything.

(48) The DIY book nook kit has been 100% carefully checked before delivery to ensure that the accessories are complete and not missing.

(49) If you meet any problem during the assemble, such as parts missing or damaged, we will provide you with unconditional replacement.

(50) It comes with dust cover, which makes it easy to decorate the finished product and is also convenient as a dust countermeasure[13].

> 单词解析:
> 13. countermeasure [ˈkaʊntərmeʒər] n. 对策;对抗手段

直播模板 Template

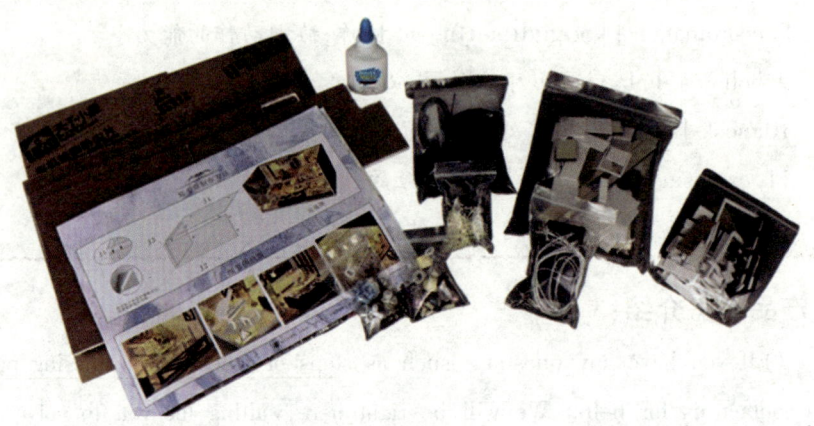

Our _____ is very well made, using a miniature scale of about _____. This _____ is made from non-toxic materials including _____, _____, _____ and _____. Package includes all the furniture and accessories in the pictures, such as _____, _____ and _____. And it also includes the toolkit, such as _____, _____ and _____. A lot of effort has been spent on little things such as _____, _____ and _____. Turn on the LED lights and you'll have a realistic-looking room.

You need to _____, _____, _____, _____ and _____ to finish the _____. In addition, you can use your imagination to customize some accessories to add decoration.

Completing _____ with family or friends will not only exercise logic and sensory coordination, but also give you the opportunity to build closer relationships and create a joyful atmosphere. After completed, you will accomplish the sense of achievement and very satisfying to see all these little bits of nothing turn into your perfect _____. Get one or more kits from our miniature model series and collect them all for yourself or a loved one for their birthday, Christmas, Valentine's Day, or other special occasion.

8.3 DIY 工艺品 DIY Arts and Crafts

词汇积累 Vocabulary

序号	中文名称	英文名称
1	蜡烛	candle
2	蜡	wax
3	蜡烛芯	wick
4	罐/瓶/壶	pot
5	香味	scent
6	雕塑	sculpture
7	编织	weave
8	毛毡	felt
9	丙烯酸的/(画家用的)丙烯酸颜料	acrylic
10	刺绣	embroidery
11	染料/染(色)	dye
12	染色底子	grounding
13	线	thread
14	编织	knit
15	针脚	stitch
16	外部的	exterior
17	美化/装饰	embellish

续表

序号	中文名称	英文名称
18	修补	patch
19	口罩	mask
20	手套	glove
21	画布	canvas
22	颜料	pigment
23	石膏彩绘	gupse colored drawing/pattern
24	浮雕	relieve
25	泥土	clay
26	组装	fabricate
27	不变形的	ametabolic
28	手模套装	hand casting kit
29	模具桶	molding bucket
30	石膏粉	plaster powder
31	砂纸	sand paper
32	马赛克	mosaic
33	杯垫	coaster
34	钻石画	diamond painting
35	树脂	resin
36	调色板	palette
37	油布	oil canvas
38	手工艺品	handcraft
39	艺术的/唯美的	artistic
40	柱脚/(雕像等的)垫座/台座	pedestal
41	精美的/精致的/制作精良的	exquisite
42	不同的/多种多样的	diverse
43	培养	cultivate
44	想象力	imagination
45	创造力	creativity

续表

序号	中文名称	英文名称
46	印/章	stamp
47	涂鸦	graffiti
48	（用于捆绑或装饰的）带子/丝带	ribbon
49	装饰物	ornament
50	彩色的/着色的	chromatic

话术演练 Language Skills

产品材质介绍：

（1）Safety is our priority. That's why this hand sculpture kit is non-toxic and skin safe and includes a protective mask and gloves.

（2）Some of the other cool things this kit features are a translucent[1] molding bucket that easily fits two to three hands as well as unique color-changing alginate[2] molding powder so you know when it's set.

（3）All paints are high-gloss acrylic paints that can be air-dried naturally in 48 hours, or can be heated to air-dry to speed up.

（4）The main moon light ball is made with high-quality opaque[3] plastic, which is not fragile, lightweight and portable.

（5）The paint tools in the kid's art and craft kit are safe and non-toxic, which is safe for your little kids to play with.

（6）The adult paint by number uses high-quality and safe acrylic paint and pure cotton canvas.

（7）The fabric has good water absorption and breathability and is easy to store for a long time.

（8）ABC DIY paint-by-number kits comes with eco-environment pigment set, waterproof canvas, nylon brush kit.

（9）Our candle-making supplies are made with high-quality, non-toxic beeswax that will make beautifully scented candles.

(10) Our unique beeswax pellets have a long burning time and no black smoke.

(11) No need to worry about the unhealthy chemicals found in traditional paraffin[4] wax, we only use plant-based additives that naturally exist in the environment.

(12) The cord of this dream catcher is made of pure cotton. It is soft and easy to weave, with no smell. It will not have any effect on your hands, please feel free to touch.

(13) Macrame[5] cotton cord is 100% natural cotton, no chemical or bleach[6] is used.

(14) This violent bear white embryo[7] is made of polyvinyl chloride[8] material, which is non-toxic and easy to clean.

(15) Our DIY wool rolls are made from natural wool, which is malleable[9], durable, soft and smooth, biodegradable[10] and safe for nature.

(16) DIY diamond painting full drill with high clear printing oil canvas is waterproof and has even texture. The pattern itself has a sticky background and plastic overtop to keep the picture sticky and then the gems will hold.

(17) Embroidery hoops are designed with an adjustment screw that you can tighten easily to keep the fabric tight and in place. They are made using only durable bamboo wood to make sure they are sturdy enough to handle daily use.

单词解析：

1. translucent [trænz'luːsnt] adj. 半透明的

2. alginate ['ældʒɪneɪt] n. 海藻酸盐

3. opaque [əʊ'peɪk] adj. 不透明的；不透光的

4. paraffin ['pærəfɪn] n. 石蜡

5. macrame ['mækrəˌmeɪ] n. 装饰编结艺术；编结艺术

6. bleach [bliːtʃ] n. 漂白剂

7. embryo ['embrɪəʊ] n. 胚

8. polyvinyl chloride [pɒlɪvaɪnl 'klɔːraɪd] 聚氯乙烯

9. malleable ['mælɪəbl] adj. 有延展性的；可塑的

10. biodegradable [ˌbaɪəʊdɪ'greɪdəbl] adj. 可生物降解的

产品规格介绍：

(18) This painting kits for kids aged 8 – 12 come with textured moon lamp—5.11″, support base, 12 paint pots, 2 paint brushes and batteries.

(19) The beads range in diameter from 0.22″ to 0.29″ and have holes from 0.06″ to 0.1″, making them versatile for necklaces, bracelets, and other DIY projects.

(20) This bead kit includes 9200pcs polymer[11] clay beads in 92 colors. The bead is 6 mm with a 2 mm hole and thickness is 1 mm.

(21) The paint brushes come as a kit of 3 different sizes separately for big or small areas to do the super fine lines and details easily. ABC's nylon brush is easy to clean.

(22) Paint your own masterpiece with our DIY acrylic painting kit, which includes a 16″×20″ canvas, 3 brushes and 1 set of high-quality colors.

(23) The candle making kit features 8 high-quality soy wax, 8 different scents to choose from, and 20 brightly colored candle dye blocks for quick coloring.

(24) 6 different essential oils and 6 color dyes meet your needs for candles of different scents and colors. You can even mix and match to create your own customized color.

(25) This cross stitch kit for adults is equipped with instructions, embroidery hoops, thread, needles and cotton fabric embroidery cloth, which is soft, strong and easy to stitch.

(26) This wind chime[12] craft kit includes 3 sets of unassembled fish bone wind chime with 12 acrylic paints of different colors, 12 chime rods[13], 16 strings, 2 brushes and a detailed instruction booklet.

单词解析：

11. polymer [ˈpɔːlɪmər] n. 聚合物；多聚体

12. chime [tʃaɪm] n. (尤指) 钟声；铃声

13. rod [rɔːd] n. (木质、金属或塑料) 杆；棒条

产品功能介绍：

(27) You can customize your hand mold kit using the carefully selected detailing tools, bronzing paint, and clear finishes.

(28) This hand casting kit is an innovative DIY way to celebrate special life's events such as weddings, anniversaries and Valentine's Day.

(29) Not only do you make your own instrument, you can customize your DIY ukulele with whatever design you want.

(30) Our unique molding formula makes sure to capture each fine line and fingerprint so that the final product is a truly one of a kind creation that perfectly reflects you.

(31) This moon kids' art and craft set can stimulate kids' fine motor skills, creativity, imagination, independent ability and build self-confidence.

(32) Not only the painting process is simple and delightful, but parents can also make with their children and enhance their relationships.

(33) These beads are believed to have therapeutic[14] benefits, such as reducing anxiety, relieving stress, and enhancing focus by accelerating metabolism[15] and neutralizing[16] negative energy.

(34) Premium paints glide[17] on smoothly, dry quickly and stay as beautiful as the day they were painted.

(35) Whether you're new to acrylic painting or a seasoned[18] artist, the paint kit will set fire to your imagination.

(36) We source only top-quality ingredients and sturdy tools. It is safe and easy to make your own candles and is suitable for family craft time.

(37) Delicate woven shapes and patterns will add a mysterious atmosphere to the dream catcher.

(38) Our DIY macrame cord kit will bring you charming dream catcher ornaments, then to decorate your home, garden, office, shop and more scenes as you want.

(39) Our DIY wool rolls can be easily moulded into any shape you want and are friendly to beginners in DIY crafting.

（40）Our wool is super soft and luxurious[19] to make the various projects like Christmas dolls, cute animal wool felt sets and more, and will help your projects look more beautiful and professional.

（41）This embroidery kit could be taken as great alternative[20] to TV or social media. Just give yourself a chance to relax with a hand-sewing craft.

（42）For DIY embroidery kits, you can enjoy the embroidery process. Moreover, sending your completed cross stitch as a gift to your family or friends will be a special and meaningful gift for them.

（43）The repetitive nature of embroidery lets busy workers to relax, clear and restore their minds (similar to meditation[21]).

（44）This hands-on DIY felt wallet activity will keep your children entertained for a couple of hours having fun while helping to develop their long attention of span, fine motor skills, problem-solving, and to gain self-confidence.

（45）The wind chime kit combines the science of wind power with art and craft materials to create and personalize a pair of beautiful terracotta[22] flower pot wind chimes, making it a great addition to any porch[23] or backyard.

单词解析：

14. therapeutic [ˌθerəˈpjuːtɪk] adj. 有助治疗的；有疗效的

15. metabolism [məˈtæbəlɪzəm] n. 新陈代谢

16. neutralize [ˈnuːtrəlaɪz] v. 中和

17. glide [ɡlaɪd] v. 滑动；掠过

18. seasoned [ˈsiːznd] adj. 老练的；富有经验的

19. luxurious [lʌɡˈʒʊriəs] adj. 十分舒适的；奢侈的

20. alternative [ɔːlˈtɜːrnətɪv] n. 可供选择的事物

    adj. 可供替代的

21. meditation [ˌmedɪˈteɪʃn] n. 冥想；沉思

22. terracotta [ˌterəˈkɒtə] n.（无釉的）赤陶土；赤褐色

23. porch [pɔːrtʃ] n. 门廊；门厅

产品服务介绍：

(46) Unlike other ukulele kits available on the market, we offer not only all the necessary parts for DIY ukulele construction but also assembly instructions.

(47) We've included a small practice kit to use before you create your final masterpiece.

(48) We have include all macrame supplies. We are proud to offer the most all inclusive and premium-quality starter macrame kits for adults.

(49) We carry out sealed packaging of felt, to prevent the felt from getting loose or damp during the process of transportation.

(50) High-quality needle felting kit, it may be just the best treasure you are looking for. In addition to providing wool suits, there are also felting needles. We will provide sincere service, waiting for your visit.

直播模板 Template

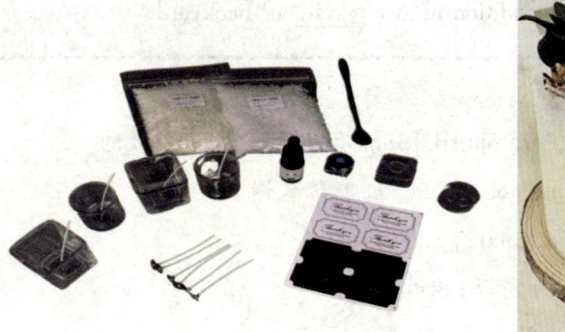

Our _____ kit is made of 100% _____, the candle will not be easily deformed, cracked or melted, it can burn cleanly for a long time and effectively release the smell. The _____ is suitable for all levels and contains everything needed to make scented homemade candles: _____, _____, _____, _____ and _____.

To top off the candle making experience, we also provide _____ scents of _____, _____, _____, _____, and _____, you can fill every room in your house with the amazing scents of own candles. This set is very suitable for family art project, you can make _____ cans of _____ oz candles.

This kit is suitable for various holiday gifts. You can also use your DIY candles as a more meaningful gift for your loved ones, and write your wishes on the label.

8.4　实战脚本 Script

Live Streaming Script of DIY Tools

Hello, everyone! Welcome to my live show. This is Lexie. If you love DIY, you have come to the right place. We want all the DIY lovers enjoy the best DIY products at the cheapest prices.

Today the first product I would like to introduce is the ABC 210-piece tool kit, which is a great back-up set to stash in your house or vehicle for emergency repairs. Ideal for auto repair or home maintenance, this durable tool set with chrome plating has just about everything you need. For example, the claw hammer, which has high-frequency quenched head, is sturdy and durable. TRP coated handle is non-slip and comfortable to use. It is easy to bang nails into, or extract nails from wood and other materials. The long nose pliers are constructed from forged carbon steel with heat treatment for durability. It can get into hard-to-reach areas for cutting, bending, twisting and gripping wire. The adjustable wrench is constructed of high-quality carbon steel for strength and chrome plated for durability. This wrench can be used to grip and turn nuts and bolts of various sizes. Compact and comfortable grip utility cutter with retractable SK-5 blade can be used for cutting and shaping material, and it is perfect for various hobby and craft applications. 10pcs replacement blades are included. Tape measure is designed with two measurement scales (inch & metric) for multi-purpose reading. Thumb locking is easy to operate. A hand strap is easy to carry.

This tool set is organized in a sturdy blow-molded toolbox with a convenient handle for easy transport. This handy tool set features chrome vanadium steel sockets and wrenches for long service life. ABC is a trusted brand specialized on professional-quality power tools, hands tools, hardware tools that provide great selections and values for over 10 years experience. Over the years we have dedicated ourselves to assisting our customers with comprehensive range of superior products and best possible service to satisfy customers' needs. We believe in the power of tools, better tools, better life. You can just always follow Lexie, follow ABC. Ok, so have a nice day, bye bye, see ya.

第九章
家居产品英语直播

中国海关总署的统计数据显示,2022 年 1—6 月,中国家具及其零件累计出口额达 352.49 亿美元,同比增长 1.2%。2022 年 6 月,中国家具及其零件出口额为 61.63 亿美元。近年来,家具用品保持着较快速的增长,家居产品市场呈现出供需两旺的态势。

9.1 家具用品 Furniture

词汇积累 Vocabulary

序号	中文名称	英文名称
1	躺椅	recliner
2	摇椅	rocking chair
3	办公椅	office chair
4	按摩椅	massage chair
5	藤椅	cane chair
6	温莎椅	windsor chair
7	长凳	bench
8	蛋椅	egg chair
9	转椅	swivel chair
10	扶手椅	armchair
11	儿童椅	children's chair
12	长沙发椅	couch
13	帆布折叠躺椅	deckchair

续表

序号	中文名称	英文名称
14	实木椅	wood chair
15	办公椅	executive chair
16	来宾椅	guest chair
17	低背接待椅	low-back visitor chair
18	中背经理椅	managerial medium back chair
19	人体工程学椅	ergonomic chair
20	沙发边桌	sofa arm clip table
21	办公桌	bureau
22	独腿桌	pedestal table
23	边桌	side table
24	咖啡桌	coffee table
25	电话桌	telephone table
26	茶几桌	end table
27	玄关桌	console table
28	书桌	study desk
29	餐桌	dining table
30	方桌	square table
31	长桌	rectangular table
32	鸟巢桌	nesting table
33	饮食柜台	buffet
34	餐边柜	sideboard
35	酒水柜	glass display cabinet
36	鞋柜	shoe cabinet
37	储物柜	storage cabinet
38	书柜	bookcase
39	壁柜	wall cabinet
40	文件柜	file cabinet
41	电视柜	TV stand

续表

序号	中文名称	英文名称
42	衣帽架	coat rack
43	衣柜	wardrobe
44	折叠沙发	folding sofa
45	单人沙发	club sofa
46	组合沙发	sectional sofa
47	双人沙发	loveseat
48	真皮沙发	leather sofa
49	布艺沙发	cloth art sofa
50	沙发床	sofa bed

话术演练 Language Skills

产品规格介绍：

（1）The tea table weighs 13 pounds and measured 25″ by 25″ by 40″.

（2）This chair offers 90°–125° arbitrary[1] backrest[2] adjustment for multiple work positions.

（3）The smooth class-4 gas lift of the chair gives a seat-to-floor range of 18–22 inches.

（4）The storage cart includes 2 cups and 5 hooks[3] to hang on the side of storage cart for quick access.

（5）With a 270 lbs weight capacity, this heavy duty executive[4] office table will support gamers of all sizes big and small.

（6）Our folding sofa can recline[5] at 44 degrees and adjust up and down at a range of 4 inches.

（7）This rolling storage cart can withstand a maximum[6] capacity of up to 105 pounds.

（8）The armrest[7] spacing of the seat is 22″, which is suitable for people with a height of 5″–6″ and weight under 255 lbs.

单词解析：

1. arbitrary ['ɑːbɪtrəri] adj. 任意的；随心所欲的

2. backrest ['bækrest] n. 靠背

3. hook [hʊk] n. 挂钩

4. executive [ɪɡˈzekjətɪv] n. 总经理；主管领导

5. recline [rɪˈklaɪn] v. 斜倚；斜躺

6. maximum ['mæksɪməm] n. 最大限度；最大值（近义词：biggest、greatest、highest、most）

7. armrest ['ɑːmrest] n. （飞机、汽车等座位的）扶手

产品质量与特色介绍：

（9）Our TV stand aluminum[8] base is stable and durable, and the bearing quality is good.

（10）This PU leather chair has a heavy-duty nylon[9] wheelbase, reinforced with ribs and gussets[10].

（11）Sideboard has premium nylon casters[11], smoothly and silently rolling on any kind of floor.

（12）The ergonomic[12] design of the gaming chair is based on the human body dynamic digital model.

（13）The integrally molded[13] seat and backrest are made of natural wood.

（14）This managerial medium back chair features a durable plush upholstered[14] black faux[15] leather[16] with a variety of subtle colors.

（15）The shoe storage is made of healthy and non-toxic environmentally friendly plastic.

（16）The heavy-duty steel frame and rust-resistant powder coating makes this rolling cart durable[17] and higher quality.

（17）The soft premium microfiber[18] leather feature of this low-back guest chair is an additional advantage.

（18）The high-end manufacturing process of the sofa keeps it from not getting stained, scratched, corroded[19], or faded.

(19) High-strength carbon[20] steel[21] linkage foot rest, which is wear-resistant and silent, passed 10000 + of telescopic[22] tests.

(20) Integrally mold backrest and seat are made of natural eucalyptus[23] board, ensuring stability and durability of the massage chair.

(21) This sofa is equipped with thickened[24] 3D soft bags.

(22) This executive office desk applies double-layer[25] design, built-in premium 3D doll cotton and memory foam[26].

单词解析：

8. aluminum [ə'ljumɪnəm] n. 铝

9. nylon ['naɪlɔn] n. 尼龙

10. gusset ['gʌsɪt] n. 角板；角撑板

11. caster ['kɑːstə] n. （安装在家具底部的）脚轮；滚轮

12. ergonomic [ˌɜːgə'nɔmɪk] adj. 工效学的；人体工程学的

13. mold ['məʊld] v. 浇铸；塑造

14. upholstered [ʌp'həʊlstəd] adj. （椅子、座位等）铺软垫的；软面的

15. faux [fəʊ] adj. 人造的；仿制的

16. leather ['leðə(r)] n. 皮革

17. durable ['djʊərəbl] adj. 耐用的；持久的（近义词：lasting）

18. microfiber [maɪk'rəʊfɪbər] n. 微纤维

19. corrode [kə'rəʊd] v. 腐蚀

20. carbon ['kɑːbən] n. 碳

21. steel [stiːl] n. 钢

22. telescopic [ˌtelɪ'skɔpɪk] adj. 可伸缩的；套叠的

23. eucalyptus [ˌjuːkə'lɪptəs] n. 桉树

24. thicken ['θɪkən] v. （使）变厚

25. layer ['leɪə(r)] n. 表层

26. foam [fəʊm] n. 泡沫橡胶

产品功能介绍：

(23) This coffee table is easy to put together and comes with tools and

instructions.

(24) Our 5-point base with dual[27] castors gives greater stability[28] and strength.

(25) This work chair will suit different types of sizes and body structures.

(26) This sofa bed is made of quality materials, offering a sleek[29] and elegant design.

(27) In aesthetic terms, this tea table will easily fit into any work environment.

(28) Thanks to the ability to rotate 360 degrees, desk users are able to move in any desired direction and to have absolute freedom of movement.

(29) The dotted[30] mesh on the back is airy, making the seat a bit colder in this summer heat.

(30) These stackable shoe storage bins can be arranged to suit various spaces, e. g. entryway, closet, under the bed, cabinet.

(31) The upholstered armrests of the chair with built-in high-density sponges[31], provide strong support to your arms whenever working or relaxing.

(32) This ergonomic office chair can be adjusted electrically[32] between 90°– 160° by one button.

(33) Waterproof paint on the cabinet surface with natural rattan decorated door can effectively prevent moisture.

(34) The lumbar[33] part of this leather sofa maintains the natural curve[34] in the lower back.

(35) Swivel chair promotes an effortless upper-back posture[35], helping eliminate[36] back pain.

(36) This club sofa is made from premium-quality polyester and has a solid hardwood frame construction.

(37) Our breathable mesh of the folding chair provides optimal[37] airflow to avoid sweating and sticking.

(38) In terms of construction, this metal structure of the bookcase is sturdy[38] and can take a good weight load.

(39) Thanks to rotating[39] base, the wheel system is built for greater fluidity of movement.

(40) This ergonomic chair with adjustable headrest can make neck tilt[40] easily and comfortably.

> **单词解析：**
>
> 27. dual ['djuːəl] adj. 二重的；双重的
> 28. stability [stə'bɪləti] n. 稳定性（近义词：balance、equilibrium）
> 29. sleek [sliːk] adj. 时髦的；线条流畅的；造型优美的
> 30. dotted ['dɒtɪd] adj. 点状的
> 31. sponge ['spʌndʒ] n. 海绵
> 32. electrically [ɪ'lektrɪkəli] adv. 用电力；用电气；电动地
> 33. lumbar ['lʌmbə(r)] n. 腰椎
> 34. curve [kɜːv] n. 曲面；弯曲
> 35. posture ['pɒstʃə(r)] n. （坐立的）姿势
> 36. eliminate [ɪ'lɪmɪneɪt] v. 排除；清除（近义词：abolish、annihilate）
> 37. optimal ['ɒptɪməl] adj. 最优的；最佳的
> 38. sturdy ['stɜːdi] adj. 结实的；坚固的（近义词：strong）
> 39. rotating [rəʊ'teɪtɪŋ] adj. 旋转的；转动的
> 40. tilt [tɪlt] v. 倾斜（近义词：incline、lean、slant、slope）

产品服务介绍：

(41) If there is any quality problem, please contact us. After confirming, we will change the accessory for you.

(42) We promise to provide you with zero profit product accessories within 3 years of the warranty period.

(43) We love what we do because we want to help you feel and perform at your very best every day, and to bring a touch of joy through our designs.

(44) For your convenience, all accessories have extra backups.

(45) You are a lucky customer if you buy a chair from this store because you will get 90 days free return guarantee and 2 years warranty.

(46) We make sure that all materials used are for maximum comfort and affordable price.

(47) We provide all the tools and accessories with the package, and also the detailed instructions.

(48) If you have any problems, you can check the installation video for help.

(49) Our philosophy is that "Better design create better work and life experience", and try to change the boring work and life by using modern technology.

(50) If you have any questions when you receive the items or during use, please feel free to contact us here at "contact seller". We will provide the best solution in 24 hours. Your satisfaction is always our top priority.

直播模板 Template

Bring functional style and affordable comfort to any living space with the _____ sofa. This _____-seater sofa has a weight limit of _____ lbs and measures _____" W × _____" D × _____" H. Easy to provide entertainment and leisure places for _____ or _____ people. Made of _____ material with a _____ design, this sofa can easily fit into any living spaces, like _____ and _____. It features _____ arms and tailored _____ cushions that add a _____ style to your room. Besides, the couch is constructed with reinforced _____ materials, individually wrapped coils surrounded by _____ foam and _____ fibers, and pillowed back cushions that deliver both durability and supportive comfort. Now available in _____ and _____ colors, this sofa delivers premium coziness while making small spaces lively! All parts and instructions are cleverly packed into one box for easy assembly in less than _____ minutes. What's more, we promise to provide you with zero profit product accessories within _____ years of the warranty period. Anyway, this sofa is best described in just three words: simple, smart and durable, and all we can do is recommend it!

9.2 电器用品 Household Appliances

词汇积累 Vocabulary

序号	中文名称	英文名称
1	吹风机	dryer
2	烫衣板	ironing board
3	蒸汽电熨斗	steam and dry iron
4	电熨斗	electric iron
5	烘干机	laundry drier
6	旋转式脱水机	spin-drier
7	洗衣机	washing machine
8	暖气片	radiator
9	电扇	electric fan
10	落地电扇	stand fan
11	摇头电扇	oscillating fan
12	床头灯	bed light/bed lamp
13	日光灯	fluorescent lamp
14	吊灯	ceiling lamp/pendant lamp
15	台灯	desk/table lamp
16	壁灯	wall light
17	落地灯	floor lamp
18	枝状吊灯	chandelier
19	冰箱	refrigerator
20	电饭锅	automatic rice cooker

续表

序号	中文名称	英文名称
21	蒸锅	steamer
22	烤箱	oven
23	面包机	toaster
24	打蛋器	egg beater
25	刨冰机	ice crusher
26	料理机	food processor
27	高压锅	pressure cooker
28	微波炉	microwave
29	空气炸锅	air fryer
30	冷冻柜	freezer
31	洗碗机	dish washer
32	烧水壶	kettle
33	咖啡机	coffee maker
34	电磁炉	induction hob
35	榨汁机	juicer
36	搅拌机	blender
37	电视	TV
38	空调	air conditioner
39	除湿机	dehumidifier
40	投影仪	projector
41	智能音响	smart speaker
42	机器人吸尘器	robotic vacuum cleaner
43	立式吸尘器	upright vacuum cleaner
44	清扫吸尘器	sweeper vacuum cleaner
45	罐式吸尘器	canister vacuum cleaner

续表

序号	中文名称	英文名称
46	地毯吸尘器	carpet vacuum cleaner
47	中央吸尘器	central vacuum cleaner
48	无线电吸尘器	cordless vacuum cleaner
49	无袋吸尘器	bagless vacuum cleaner
50	干湿吸尘器	wet and dry vacuum cleaner

话术演练 Language Skills

产品规格介绍：

（1）Refrigerator product dimensions are 19″W × 51″H × 22″D with temperature range (refrigerator) from 30 ℉ to 45 ℉.

（2）Featuring a power-saving automatic shut-off function, the 120 Volt /55 Watt fan can be programmed to run in half-hour increments from 0.5 to 6.5 hours.

（3）Robot vacuum powered by a strong digital motor generates a maximum suction[1] power of 5000 Pa.

（4）Our combo robot vacuum and mop adopt a 300 ml water tank[2] and 300 ml dust box, which can clean up to 400 square feet.

（5）WHAT'S INCLUDED: 1000 Watt motor base professional blender & 70 oz total crushing pitcher with lid.

（6）A 1000 W bulky juicer machine has smooth modern stainless steel with 10 rows of saw-tip blades evenly distributed.

（7）The dimensions of the actual microwave are 12″H × 18″W × 13″D. The cutout dimensions of the cabinet should be 14″ H × 22″ W × 16″ D.

（8）Grounds and pods coffee system with 8 grounds brew sizes (small cup, cup, XL cup, travel mug, XL travel mug, 1/4 carafe, 1/2 carafe, 3/4 carafe, or full carafe) in addition to 4 traditional pod brew sizes (6, 8, 10, or 12 oz).

（9）This is all premium[3] stuff, delivering 30% wider double rubber rollers in a specially designed corner brush.

（10）2.6″ slim⁴ design allows the vacuum to glide under more furniture, picking up plenty of hidden debris.

（11）The battery holds a charge for 100 minutes of run time which is long enough for most sizes of room.

（12）1300 W high power system of the bread toaster quickly toasts the surface of the bread to crispy while retaining the moisture inside the bread.

> 单词解析：
> 1. suction [ˈsʌkʃn] n. 吸；抽吸
> 2. tank [tæŋk] n. 箱；槽；罐
> 3. premium [ˈpriːmiəm] adj. 高昂的；优质的
> 4. slim [slɪm] adj. 纤细的

产品质量与特色介绍：

（13）These smart robotics are produced by a high-tech company, a direct competitor of all the leading brands in the field.

（14）The provided 7x bonded granite nonstick inner pot that is more durable than ceramic and traditional pots, has a completely toxic-free makeup and is dishwasher safe.

（15）This portable washing machine features a durable, rust and corrosion-resistant steel tub with top loading transparent quiet close lid.

（16）The robot vacuum has advanced 3D precise obstacle⁵ avoidance function, and a full set of infrared⁶ sensors.

（17）We use food-grade stainless steel, a tri-ply bottom for more even cooking and perfect for sauteing.

（18）Pitcher is BPA free and dishwasher safe, making cleanup just as simple and easy as using the blender.

（19）The professional blender pitcher is excellent for making frozen drinks and creamy smoothies for the entire family.

（20）This coffee maker features an easy-to-grab stainless steel handle and body with fully automatic features.

（21）Its award-winning design and modern white finish help your air purifier fit anywhere in your home.

（22）Electric pressure cooker is equipped with finger-print resistant, stainless-steel sides and dishwasher-safe lid.

> 单词解析：
> 5. obstacle ['ɔbstəkl] n. 障碍物（近义词：bar、barrier、obstruction）
> 6. infrared [ˌɪnfrə'red] adj. 红外线的

产品功能介绍：

（23）The product comes with 3 different cleaning modes: auto spot, edge and single room.

（24）You control the rate of water flow through the app to reach a balance of moistness[7] and quick-drying.

（25）This vacuum robot features visual navigation to map your room and plan an efficient cleaning route.

（26）Modern and polished, the sleek curved design of TV fills the contours[8] of your space with an immersive viewing experience.

（27）Our coffee maker has a body with fully automatic features: 24-hour brew start, self-clean, adjustable auto-off, and ready alert system.

（28）This cooker not only includes all your favorite cooking options like cooking rice and grains, but also possesses the slow cook function that allows meals to simmer low and slow.

（29）The bagless, self-emptying base holds up to 60 days of dirt and debris[9].

（30）360° LiDAR vision quickly and accurately maps your home so your robot can methodically detect[10] and avoid objects in its path.

（31）Inverter technology delivers microwave energy in a way that allows delicate foods to simmer without overcooking.

（32）Blast ice into snow in seconds and blend your favorite ingredients into delicious resort-style frozen drinks.

（33）This vacuum cleaner is suitable for tile[11], wood floor, carpet, marble[12] and other different floors.

(34) With the toasting modes of 7 kinds of bread, it is easier to toast the corresponding bread scientifically and accurately.

(35) Our microwave helps foods retain more color, texture and nutrients for fast, easy and delicious results.

(36) With obstacle avoidance technology, it can navigate around common domestic[13] hazards[14] using its RGB camera.

(37) Motion rate 120 image processing technology allows you to enjoy fast-paced sports, movies, and 4K gaming without the lag.

(38) The robot vacuum has a unique air inlet[15] design, which will not be blocked by hair.

(39) Patented dirt finding technology helps your robot detect dirtier areas of your home, like high-traffic spots, and cleans them more thoroughly[16].

(40) Our 12-cup coffee brewer allows you to control your brew strength so you can boast light to strong coffee flavor as well as adjust your carafe water temperature.

(41) The robot cleaner runs for up to 100 minutes and will automatically back to the charging base and recharge when in low battery or finished cleaning.

(42) The auto vacuum cleaner robot is also compatible[17] with Alexa and Google Assistant, allowing users make the robot start and stop the clean by voice commands.

(43) The unique air outlet design improves the life of the juicer machine while ventilating and dissipating heat.

(44) Total crushing technology delivers unbeatable power with blades that pulverize[18] and crush through ice, whole fruits and vegetables in seconds.

(45) Expert coffee-making technology will allow you to ensure your coffee temperature is perfect without sacrificing flavor or quality.

单词解析：

7. moistness [ˈmɔɪstnɪs] n. 湿气

8. contour [ˈkɔːntʊr] n. 外形；轮廓

9. debris [ˈdebriː] n. 碎片；残渣；垃圾（近义词：garbage、junk、rubbish）

10. detect [dɪˈtekt] v. 发现（近义词：discern）

11. tile [taɪl] *n.* (贴墙或铺地用的)瓷砖;地砖
12. marble ['mɑːbl] *n.* 大理石
13. domestic [dəˈmestɪk] *adj.* 家务的
14. hazard [ˈhæzəd] *n.* 危险;危害
15. inlet [ˈɪnlet] *n.* (空气或气体进入机器的)入口
16. thoroughly [ˈθʌrəli] *adv.* 非常;彻底
17. compatible [kəmˈpætəbl] *adj.* 兼容的
18. pulverize [ˈpʌlvəraɪz] *v.* 粉碎

产品服务介绍：

(46) The product is refurbished[19], fully functional, and in excellent condition. Backed by the 90-day Amazon renewed guarantee.

(47) Combining our expertise in smart cleaning technology and our pursuit of excellence, iRobot Clean is committed to protecting the health of you and your family.

(48) We strive to provide you with the highest quality product and the best customer experience. Each product is strictly inspected when it leaves the factory.

(49) Please feel free to buy our juicer machine, we will guarantee our quality, not only provide a 1-year warranty, but also enjoy a lifetime after-sales consultation.

(50) Your privacy is our priority as we use the highest standards of data encryption[20] to make sure your cleaning data stays private and secure.

单词解析：

19. refurbish [ˌriːˈfɜːbɪʃ] *v.* 再装修;刷新
20. encryption [ɪnˈkrɪpʃ(ə)n] *n.* 加密;加密(技)术

直播模板 Template

This _____ vacuum cleaner is equipped with a _____ W brushless motor that reaches strong suction power over _____ Pa. So, it can effectively capture _____% of particulate particles as small as _____ microns. In addition, the vacuum body weighs only _____ kg with _____ liters dust cup capacity, so it is lightweight enough to be used with one hand, and greatly reduces the burden on household tasks. Meanwhile, _____ dB low noise reduction design reduces annoying driving noise. Also, depending on your cleaning location and application, you can easily switch among _____ suction modes, including _____ mode, _____ mode, and _____ mode... Besides, the motor head comes with _____ lamp, which can be rotated _____ degrees forward, _____ degrees left and right, so you can easily clean the table under and every corner. What's pretty cool about this versatile vacuum cleaner is that it comes with a _____ nozzle and _____ nozzle, so it can be switched between sofas, cars, ceilings, curtains, gaps, and more. _____ type battery has a large capacity of _____ mAh and can be used continuously for up to _____ minutes. Full charging only takes about _____ hours. Perfect for everyday cleaning!

9.3 床上用品 Bedding and Lines

词汇积累 Vocabulary

序号	中文名称	英文名称
1	弹簧床垫	innerspring mattress
2	海绵床垫	foam mattress
3	混合床垫	hybrid mattress
4	乳胶床垫	latex mattress
5	注水床垫	waterbed mattress
6	智能床垫	smart mattress
7	低过敏性床垫	hypoallergenic mattress
8	可翻面床垫	flipping mattress
9	可调节床垫	adjustable bed mattress
10	充气床垫	airbed mattress
11	床弹簧架	box spring
12	床框	bed frame
13	床垫芯	mattress core
14	床垫防尘套	mattress cover
15	床垫包装	mattress encasement
16	床垫保护套	mattress protector
17	床围	bed rail
18	床罩	bedspread
19	床单	sheet
20	床笠	fitted sheet
21	床裙	dust ruffle
22	被套	duvet cover
23	被单	quilt

续表

序号	中文名称	英文名称
24	床单套装	sheet set
25	三件套/四件套	quilt cover set
26	棉被	comforter/duvet
27	毛巾被	cotton terry blanket
28	羽绒被	feather quilt
29	蚕丝被	silk quilt
30	大豆纤维被	soybean fiber quilt
31	棉被芯	cotton filler
32	羽绒被芯	down filler
33	双层床	bunk bed
34	双人床	queen bed
35	单人大床	king bed
36	子母床	trundle bed
37	婴儿床	crib bed
38	床头柜	nightstands
39	梳妆台	dressing table
40	荞麦枕	buckwheat pillow
41	圆抱枕	bolster pillow
42	身体枕	body pillow
43	乳胶枕	latex pillow
44	背部靠枕	cushion
45	记忆海绵枕	memory foam pillow
46	枕套	pillow case
47	地毯	carpet/rug
48	毛毯	blanket
49	沙发盖毯	throw
50	电热毯	heated blanket

话术演练 Language Skills

产品规格介绍：

（1）Shipping dimensions[1] of full bed mattress: 32″L × 15″W × 15″H.

（2）This 8-inch[2] twin mattress is designed for sleepers of all ages, and the 10-inch mattress and 12-inch mattress offer even more comfort.

（3）This 11-inch memory foam[3] mattress features ventilated[4] 100% memory foam, a soft knit cover, and a durable[5] base layer[6].

（4）A queen size bed (60″ × 80″) is the most popular option, but plenty of people opt to go smaller with full size bed (54″ × 75″) or larger kings (76″ × 80″).

（5）California king size feather down comforter is 104″ × 96″ and 57 oz fill weights.

（6）The queen size pillow has a size of 25″ L × 15″ W × (4″–5″) H.

（7）We have two pillow heights designed for back & side sleeping: size 64 cm × (12.5/10) cm × 38 cm and 25.2 cm × (4.1/4.8) cm × 15 cm.

（8）Beige comforter set measured by 102″ × 95″ is perfect for any home.

（9）California king bed sets (4-piece): 1 fitted sheet 70″ × 85″ × 17″ (W × L × H), 1 flat sheet 110″ × 103″, 2 pillowcases (shams) 20″ × 35″.

单词解析：

1. dimension [dɪˈmenʃən] *n.* 维度；尺寸
2. inch [ɪntʃ] *n.* 英寸
3. foam [fəʊm] *n.* 泡沫材料
4. ventilated [ˈventɪleɪtɪd] *adj.* 通风的；空气流通的（近义词：draughty、airy）
5. durable [ˈdjʊərəbl] *adj.* 耐用的
6. layer [ˈleɪə] *n.* 覆盖层；涂层

产品质量与特色介绍：

（10）Our pillows are all hypoallergenic[7] and CertiPUR-US certified.

（11）This medium firm mattress is a gel memory foam mattress that features excellent weight and heat distribution[8].

(12) These foams have been tested for low VOC emissions[9], making this mattress of a safer choice for indoor air quality than some competitors.

(13) Pure beige quilt is soft and comfortable, bringing you warmth and spring vitality.

(14) Each blanket is hand sewn[10], assembled[11], compressed[12] and packaged in recyclable paper.

(15) Memory foam pillow is made with the brand's patented[13] adaptive foam which boasts several benefits over standard polyurethane[14] foam.

(16) Made with cotton and filled with whole-piece superior microfiber, so this comforter is soft, lightweight, yet durable.

(17) OCS standard 100% organic cotton fabric cover is unbleached, undyed, soft plush, breathable, durable and comfy.

(18) Revel the royale combination of luxury and softness every night with our authentic 1000 thread count range.

(19) The trundle bed is GOT's global organic textile[15] standard.

(20) These lavish bedding sets are made with 100% natural supima cotton yarns, giving them superior softness and smoothness.

(21) Premium white goose duck feathers & down is filled with 55% down fiber, 25% down, 15% feather fiber and 5% feathers.

(22) This fabric of the duvet cover is breathable, soft, and skin-friendly.

(23) Elviros ergonomic sleeping pillow core is made of high-density slow rebound memory foam.

(24) The responsive[16] design and durable materials of this pillow make it ideal for any bedroom.

(25) This quilt is made of high-end[17] knit fabric with a comfortable and breathable surface.

(26) Our products have the certification of standard 100 by OEKO-TEX, which is safe, healthy and skin-friendly.

单词解析:

7. hypoallergenic [ˌhaɪpəʊˌæləˈdʒenɪk] *adj.* 低致敏性的

8. distribution [ˌdɪstrɪˈbjuːʃn] *n.* 分发；分配

9. emission [ɪˈmɪʃn] *n.* 散发物

10. sewn [səʊn] *v.* 缝纫

11. assemble [əˈsembl] *v.* 组装

12. compressed [kəmˈprest] *adj.* 压缩

13. patented [ˈpætntɪd] *adj.* 获得专利(权)的

14. polyurethane [ˌpɒlɪˈjʊərɪθeɪn] *n.* 聚氨酯

15. textile [ˈtekstaɪl] *n.* 纺织

16. responsive [rɪˈspɒnsɪv] *adj.* 积极响应的；敏感的

17. high-end [ˌhaɪ ˈend] *adj.* 高端的(近义词:upper-scale、slap-up)

产品功能介绍:

(27) The high-quality carbon steel spring coil has high flexibility[18] and provides excellent customized support for your skeletal[19] system.

(28) Latex mattresses rebound more quickly and lessen the sensation of sinking into the mattress.

(29) Our duvet is incomparably soft and comfortable, with excellent moisture absorption and breathability.

(30) Proven contour design perfectly supports and aligns[20] your head, neck, shoulder, and back.

(31) Use the knitted blanket as a baby blanket in the nursery, as a sofa blanket in the living room or as a bed throw blanket in the bedroom.

(32) The slope of the pillow keeps your head from rolling out of a stable position.

(33) The fabric is delicate and makes less noise, suitable for light sleepers and users who have difficulty in falling asleep.

(34) This pillow can improve sleep and relieve neck and shoulder pain, and rejuvenate body.

(35) With beautiful flower & plant printed pattern design and high-quality printed technology, our luxury bedding sets show you high-quality life taste.

(36) Unlike other decorative cable knit throw blankets, this chunky thick spun cotton accent blanket is machine-washable for your convenience.

(37) The air-flow foam layer has millions of open cells, increasing airflow and reducing heat and humidity.

(38) This mattress is topped with natural latex to give unbeatable temperature regulation.

(39) A breathable surface lets air circulate to keep the pillow cool.

(40) This crib bed offers cloud-like comfort for all baby's sleep positions.

(41) Cushioning[21] memory foam minimizes pressure and conforms to your body.

(42) The premium bamboo material enables your queen sleeping pillow to be ultra-soft.

(43) Gel memory foam cradles[22] your body and relieves pressure.

(44) Whether you're a side sleeper, back sleeper, stomach sleeper, it offers optimal level of firmness, coolness and comfort.

(45) The zero-pressure foam provides you a weightless sleep by absorbing and dispersing your body pressure.

单词解析：
18. flexibility [ˌfleksəˈbɪləti] n. 弹性
19. skeletal [ˈskelətl] adj. 骨骼的
20. align [əˈlaɪn] v. 排成直线；正确排放
21. cushion [ˈkʊʃən] n. 软垫
22. cradle [ˈkreɪdl] v. 轻轻抱着

产品服务介绍：

(46) Each product comes with a 100-night NO-RISK trial and a 1-year warranty.

(47) We are one well-known American home textile brand. We promise that 30 days refund and 7×24 hours customer service. If you have any questions, contact us when you are free, we will provide the best solution in the shortest time.

第九章 家居产品英语直播

(48) This mattress comes compressed and shipped in a box for easier setup and please allow 24 – 72 hours for your mattress to regain its full shape.

(49) We've been manufacturing comforters since 2000 and work on the belief that you deserve to sleep with a comforter that's made for you. Just the way you need it: A Good Night, A Better Morning.

(50) Neatly folded & tied with ribbon, our chunky knit blanket is ready to give as a hostess gift, Christmas holiday gift, birthday gift, housewarming gift, get well soon gift, self-care gift or just because gift.

直播模板 Template

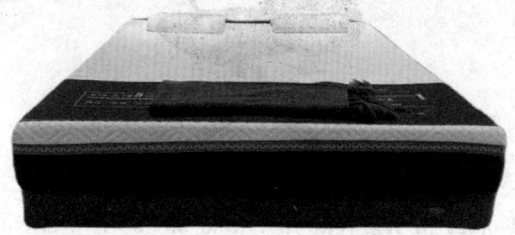

Have you ever bothered by a poor sleep? A bad night's sleep can cause you to have frequent headaches or trouble concentrating, and make you feel more anxious and depressed. Well, maybe it's time to pick the right memory foam mattress! Now, I am presenting you an affordable _____ mattress from a reputable brand _____. This _____ × _____ × _____ inches mattress supports a maximum weight of _____ pounds. It is available in _____ different thickness options, including _____, _____, _____ and _____ inches. Therefore, it is suitable for all types of sleepers. Whether you lie on your back, stomach or side, this mattress will give you incredible cradling comfort for more pressure relief. Additionally, this is a medium firm mattress which features _____ layers. A _____ base layer of pressure relieving, a _____ layer and a _____ layer of responsive but breathable foam. This _____-density memory foam helps to mold to your body, keeping your spine aligned and your joints supported. What's more, this mattress can absorb motion of restless sleepers. So, if you sleep with a partner who tosses and turns at night, you will have absolutely no problem here. Also, we promise you a worry-free _____ warranty year. Here, it also should be noted that all our highest quality foam is made with _____ certified and _____ material, and provides a fresh environment. Simply put, this mattress is a proof that sweet dreams really do come true!

9.4 实战脚本 Script

Live Streaming of Home and Furniture

Hi, guys, welcome! If it's your first time on my live streaming, my name is Jack. Are you tired of high chairs that make you hunch and cause you discomfort? I am presenting you an elite ergonomic chair by ABC company! Made of heavy-duty mesh with a sleek design, this chair is your go-to for durability, comfort and style. In terms of the size, this product weighs 30 pounds and measured 44 by 38 by 90 inches, and has an exceptional weight capacity to support users up to 290 pounds! One-touch height adjustment allows you to easily modify the chair's height from "16.5" to "22.5". Given this, this desk chair perfectly suits different types of sizes and body structures, and it is ideal for all types of work environments. Besides, boasting an adjustable lumbar support, this chair allows you to customize the sitting positions. And the idea is to naturally fit your spine, and therefore significantly eases the fatigue and pain of your back caused by sitting at a desk for hours. With this guy, you'll be able to work for hours and hours without a hitch! As you can see, padded armrests can fold up and down to better suit your sitting preferences while adding comfort to your arms and elbows. Thanks to the flexible edge of the seat, users will feel reduced pressure on the legs, which contributes to much better blood circulation. So, you will be more productive and energized! Also, set on a sturdy 5-point base, this chair allows you to enjoy smooth mobility with durable rolling caster wheels. Moreover, it comes with rich colors, including white, grey, orange and red. Therefore, this product will definitely elevate your room decoration. What's pretty awesome about this product is that it comes with a 5-year warranty. We've also included all the tools and instructions you need for assembly. And it only takes 10 minutes! Overall, this model delivers premium performance, classy looks and exceptional durability, all at the best possible price quality ratio. You want it the best you got it! And now is the time to upgrade your home or workplace with our best-selling piece in the biggest sale of the year! Only costs ＄269! And we will send another 20% discount voucher to people who follow our channel! So, if you like our live, please hit the subscribe button and to turn on the notifications, then you don't miss our latest contents. Here comes another big benefit—Lucky draw! You will have a chance to get "Gel Memory Foam Pillow—1 Pack Standard Size". You can only use ＄1.99 to win it and the price for this is over ＄29.99! We will only pick up 10 lucky participants. Go get it!

  Are you tired of cleaning your messy room all by yourself? Now it's time to treat yourself with clean, freshly wiped floors every day with our powerful robotic vacuum! It is taken a step forward in the search for perfection when cleaning the floor of your home and maintaining it in perfect hygienic conditions. It's designed to offer you that greatest comfort!

  Thanks to its innovative modern design, it fits perfectly into any home and is quite aesthetically pleasing. This robot vacuum comes in white with an outstanding suction power of 1,200 Pa. Provided with a 0.6-liter dust tank inside, it has the size of 13.8 by 13.8 by 2.8 inches, as well as a weight of 5.64 pounds. So, the device's thin and slim profile will ensure that it can easily slide over thresholds less than 3 cm without worrying about getting stuck. Besides, powered by 2,500 mAh battery capacity, it can continuously work 110 minutes in a 100 m^2 house before automatically docking and recharging. What's more, it has four-stage different cleaning modes (Auto/Spot/Edge/Zig-zag cleaning) to meet the different cleaning needs of users with high coverage, less missed scanning and high efficiency. All you have to do is scheduling it to clean up through its smart app or voice commands. Equipped with both dual multi-surface brushes and edge-sweeping brushes, this device can not only grab large debris from carpets or hard floors, but also take care of hidden corners and edges. Very cool! At the same time, this device is supported by a 3D obstacle-avoidance system to intelligently detect stairs or cliffs, and avoid walls, chairs or sofa. Keeping this gizmo safe and sound! What's the most amazing thing about this device is that it can learn the layout of your home with a laser rangefinder that rotates at 300 RPM. Using this data, this robot vacuum will generate a floor plan with an accuracy of 97%, allowing it to automatically recognize rooms. This means it can calculate the most efficient cleaning path for each room, and design the best way to avoid obstacles.

All in all, combined with precise laser mapping, advanced technology and powerful vacuuming, you get a top-level product! So far, we have received more than one million positive reviews averaging a 5-star rating from our shopping website. The original price for this product is $198. Get 25% off your purchase from now until 11pm at our live! Only 100 left in stock, order soon, my friends! Believe me, it has the best price quality ratio on the market in 2023! If you kindly share my livestream to 3 friends and then you can also get 1 extra lithium ion battery ($26) for free! Only for today! For such an affordable price, this guy cannot be beaten! Don't overthink it! Don't wait-shop now while it's on sale!

Thank you to all the great people at live for having us here. Tomorrow, we will be in live at 8 p.m., and you will see a bunch of new arrivals here! Byebye!

第十章

宠物用品英语直播

如今,"吸猫撸狗"已逐渐成为越来越多人的放松方式,宠物数量及养宠物的人群的规模均在不断增加,宠物相关产业和市场规模在蓬勃发展,"宠物经济"在资本市场也越来越受青睐。2019年,我国宠物行业进出口总额为195.42亿元,进出口产品均以宠物粮为主。中国海关总署的数据显示,2022年1—6月,我国宠物食品罐头产品累计出口额为2405万美元,出口量为1.25万吨,累计平均单价为1930.70美元每吨。与上年同期相比,数量增加39.30%,金额上升39.48%。宠物用品是指宠物生活所需的消费品类,主要包括宠物食品、宠物日用、宠物清洁、宠物服饰、宠物玩具等细分门类。

10.1 宠物食品 Pet Food

词汇积累 Vocabulary

序号	中文名称	英文名称
1	主食	main meal
2	宠物干粮	dried pet food
3	宠物湿粮	moist pet food
4	半湿粮	semi-moist pet food
5	风干粮	air-dried pet food
6	膨化粮	puffed pet food
7	烘焙粮	baked pet food
8	冻干粮	freeze-dried food

续表

序号	中文名称	英文名称
9	处方粮	prescription food
10	幼犬粮	puppy food
11	成犬粮	adult food
12	干狗/猫粮颗粒	kibble
13	全价饲料	complete feed
14	宠物罐头	canned pet food
15	适口性	palatability
16	配料表	ingredients list
17	高温杀菌	high temperature sterilization
18	热风干燥	hot-air drying
19	冷冻干燥	freeze drying
20	宠物奶粉	pet milk powder
21	宠物零食	pet treats
22	鸡肉干	chicken strip
23	肉干	jerky
24	肉汁	gravy
25	宠物饼干	pet biscuit
26	磨牙零食	chewy treats
27	家禽肉	poultry
28	冻干肉	freeze-dried meat
29	冻干蛋黄	freeze-dried egg yolk
30	火腿肠	pet ham
31	猫薄荷	catnip
32	小鱼干	dried fish
33	生骨肉	raw meat
34	多春鱼	capelin
35	鹌鹑	quail

续表

序号	中文名称	英文名称
36	羊奶布丁	goat milk pudding
37	卵磷脂	lecithin
38	鱼油	fish oil
39	诱食剂	phagostimulant
40	蛋白质	protein
41	粗脂肪	crude fat
42	粗灰分	crude ash
43	粗纤维	crude fiber
44	维生素	vitamin
45	矿物质	mineral substance
46	微量元素	microelement
47	氨基酸	amino acid
48	益生菌	probiotic
49	牛磺酸	taurine
50	处方饲料	veterinary diet

话术演练 Language Skills

产品规格介绍：

（1）The dimensions[1] of the product are 5.16×19×24 inches.

（2）This pack of ××× contains 48 (0.5 oz each) squeezable[2] cat treat tubes.

（3）We package ××× in convenient, easy-to-open pouches[3] that help preserve freshness. Just tear open an individual pouch and pour for a mess-free meal.

（4）The product contains one 24 count case of 3.5 oz easy peel trays of wet dog food: duck recipe, grilled chicken flavor, oven roasted, chicken flavor, turkey recipe.

（5）There are two shapes of kibbles[4]. One is almost triangle shaped and one is a little pebble shape. The triangular shape is about the thickness of a nickel[5] and is a little larger than the size of pinky fingernail. The pebble shape is a little smaller than a pencil eraser.

(6) You can slice or chop to use as a full feed or a treat, or grate[6] and use as a food topper! It is available in 4 lbs[7], 2.5 lbs, 1 lb, and 2.75 oz[8] sizes.

(7) Served in convenient trays with no-fuss, peel-away freshness seals, ××× adult dog food makes mealtime easy.

(8) The product is packaged in eco-friendly recyclable cans.

(9) ××× wet cat food contains twenty-four 2.6 oz twin pack trays (48 servings total) of wet cat food cuts in gravy perfect portions variety pack: 12 roasted chicken entree, 6 gourmet[9] salmon entree, 6 tender turkey entree.

(10) The chicken variety is 366 calories per cup.

(11) There approximately about 40 treats in each bag. Each treat is different sizes and can be easily broken up.

(12) This item requires vet authorization[10].

(13) Portable and small enough to fit in your pocket, these bite-size dog treats are perfect for on-the-go or anytime treating.

(14) Our organic catnip[11] comes in a resealable[12] bag or tub for maximum freshness.

单词解析：

1. dimension [daɪˈmenʃ(ə)n] n. 规模；尺寸

2. squeezable [skwizəb(ə)l] adj. 可压榨的；可压缩的

3. pouch [paʊtʃ] n. 小袋

4. kibble [ˈkɪbl] n. 磨碎食物（尤指狗食）

5. nickel [ˈnɪkl] n. （美国和加拿大的）5分镍币

6. grate [ɡreɪt] v. 磨碎；擦碎（食物）（近义词：grind）

7. lb abbr. 磅（拉丁语 libra 的书面缩略词，等同于 pound）

8. oz abbr. 盎司

9. gourmet [ˈɡʊrmeɪ] adj. 美味的

> 10. authorization [ˌɔθərɪ'zeɪʃ(ə)n] n. 授权(书)
> 11. catnip ['kætnɪp] n. 猫草;猫薄荷(同 catmint)
> 12. resealable [rɪsɪləb(ə)l] adj. 可重复封口的

产品质量与特色介绍:

(15) No grain, corn, wheat, artificial colors, flavors, or chemical preservatives[13] are added.

(16) Sustainably-raised salmon is the first ingredient; protein helps keep your dog at his bounding[14] best.

(17) Our recipes are formulated with the help of veterinarians and a pet nutritionist to provide your dog/cat with the optimal blend of protein and fat, without adding any grains.

(18) Each batch[15] is tested to ensure it meets our high standards.

(19) The ××× products by official testing at the same time in line with China, Europe, the United States three main food nutrition standards.

(20) Digestible ingredients and gentle cooking processes are used to ensure maximum digestibility.

(21) A wide variety of flavors and formulas are available.

(22) No cheap fillers[16] are added, such as potato or peas, which are linked to obesity, food allergies, and other health concerns.

(23) The ××× sources are 100% free-range, grass-fed meats, and wild-caught seafoods, all without added hormones, antibiotics[17], or growth promotants[18].

(24) These delicious chew treats are made from rawhide[19] and pork hide, then wrapped with real chicken, duck and chicken liver to create this truly delightful, long-lasting treat your dog will love.

(25) ××× requires all of our suppliers to sign a vendor promise that ensures quality and origin.

(26) ××× products are backed by high-quality nutritional standards and food safety requirements.

(27) All raw ingredients are tracked from time of receipt at our plants, through

their inclusion[20] in finished products, and on to retailers[21].

(28) Fresh ingredients preserved solely through refrigeration and raw ingredients frozen at the peak of freshness stay true to their natural form.

(29) This minimalist[22] processing approach preserves important nutrients and keeps closer to the diet your feline[23] evolved to eat.

(30) Dry roasted peanuts give this treat a real peanut butter flavor that your dog will love.

(31) The catnip is 100% organically grown, free from chemicals and pesticides[24], and a high-quality blend of leaf and flower tops for optimal potency[25].

单词解析：

13. preservative [prɪˈzɜːvətɪv] n. 防腐剂
14. bound [baʊnd] v. 跳跃
15. batch [bætʃ] n.（食物、药物等的）一批生产的量
16. filler [ˈfɪlər] n. 填料；填充物
17. antibiotic [ˌæntɪbaɪˈɔːtɪk] n. 抗生素
18. promotant [prəˈmɪtənt] n. 生长剂（由 promote 派生而来）
19. rawhide [ˈrɔːhaɪd] n. 生皮
20. inclusion [ɪnˈkluːʒ(ə)n] n. 被包括的人或物
21. retailer [ˈriːˌteɪlər] n. 零售商
22. minimalist [ˈmɪnɪm(ə)lɪst] n. 简约主义者
23. feline [ˈfiːˌlaɪn] n. 猫科动物
24. pesticide [ˈpestɪˌsaɪd] n. 杀虫剂
25. potency [ˈpəʊt(ə)nsi] n. 效力

产品功能介绍：

(32) To transition your dog to ××× products, mix your dog's current food with our product.

(33) This dog food features omega-6 fatty acids[26] and added vitamins and minerals to support a shiny coat and healthy skin.

(34) This weight management dog food contains 25% less fat and 15% fewer

calories than other similar products while still delivering a smart blend of ingredients for complete and balanced nutrition.

(35) This tasty kibble supports healthy digestion with a wholesome blend of fibers and prebiotics[27], plus antioxidants[28] to support a strong immune system.

(36) Deliciously crunchy[29] bites and tender meaty morsels[30] combine for a taste and texture dogs love and work with added calcium for a premium dog food that supports strong teeth and healthy gums.

(37) Along with a great taste cats love, this meal delivers 100% complete and balanced nutrition for maintenance of adult cats.

(38) The crunchy kibble helps reduce plaque[31] buildup and whiten teeth.

(39) Holistic ingredients help support digestion, healthy weight, reduced shedding[32], joint health, plus essential taurine[33] to promote heart and brain health.

(40) Crunchy texture of these irresistible cat snacks helps clean teeth, reduce tartar[34] buildup, remove plaque and freshen breath.

(41) ××× lickable treats have a thick and creamy texture ideal for handheld treating, making bonding with your cat super easy.

(42) ××× are fed as a treat, a training aid, or reward for your dog.

(43) ×××'s prescription diet dog food helps metabolize fat, maintain lean muscle, and maintain a healthy weight with added antioxidants to control cell oxidation and promote a healthy immune system.

(44) Moderately high fiber levels provide a feeling of fullness and help stabilize and minimize fluctuation[35] of blood glucose[36] levels in dogs requiring glucose management.

(45) Our food is intended as a complement to your senior cat's complete and balanced diet or a delicious treat after mealtime.

(46) Cat treats in creamy gravy is intended for intermittent[37] or supplement feeding only.

(47) The catnip can be added to food to entice[38] the fussiest[39] of felines.

单词解析：

26. omega-6 fatty acid ω-6 脂肪酸（身体必需的一种多元不饱和脂肪酸）

27. prebiotic [ˌpriːbaɪˈɒtɪk] *n.* 益生元

28. antioxidant [ˌæntɪˈɔːksɪdənt] *n.* 抗氧化剂

29. crunchy [ˈkrʌntʃɪ] *adj.* 爽脆的

30. morsel [ˈmɔːrsl] *n.* 少量；一块（食物）

31. plaque [plæk] *n.* 牙斑

32. shed [ˈʃed] *v.* 脱（毛）

33. taurine [ˈtɔːriːn] *n.* 牛磺酸

34. tartar [ˈtɑːrtər] *n.* 牙石；牙垢

35. fluctuation [ˌflʌktʃuˈeɪʃ(ə)n] *n.* 波动；起伏

36. glucose [ˈgluːˌkəʊz] *n.* 葡萄糖

37. intermittent [ˌɪntərˈmɪt(ə)nt] *adj.* 间歇性

38. entice [ɪnˈtaɪs] *v.* 引诱

39. fussy [ˈfʌsɪ] *adj.* 讲究的；挑剔的（fussiest 为最高级）

产品服务介绍：

(48) If for any reason you're not satisfied, simply let us know why or, feel free to contact us with your original receipt along with your feedback.

(49) We pour our heart and soul into each pet's bowl by thinking about the big picture but staying small and family owned to get it done right.

(50) We're proud of our products. If you aren't satisfied, we'll refund you for any reason within a year of purchase.

(51) × × ×'s alliance[40] with veterinarians puts them in a unique position finds a nutrition recommendation for your pet no matter what health issue your pet is facing.

单词解析：

40. alliance [əˈlaɪəns] *n.* 联盟

直播模板 Template

So right now the product We have here is the _____, with a couple of kinds with different flavors. We have the _____, _____, _____, and _____ flavors.

Each of these contain real meat including _____, _____, _____ or _____, and other meat by-products in them. The meats are minced into meat paste which offer a tender, tempting texture. _____ is formulated without grains, corn, wheat and soy. Plus, there are no artificial flavors or preservatives. _____ food is complete and balanced with the protein, essential vitamins, minerals and nutrients your _____ needs at any life stage. It's so delectable and easy to chew, your _____ will devour every tasty bite.

The tasty, fresh _____ are packaged in individual trays which means that you will have zero messy leftovers, unlike canned cat food. The plastic cups with peel-off lids make mealtime easy, no can opener required. You can just snap, peel and serve.

_____ food helps support and maintain lean muscle mass, and provides a complete source of nutrition. Another benefit is that _____ food can provide proper hydration to your _____.

As for the feeding guidelines, feed _____ the daily serving amount recommended on the product per 5 pounds of body weight _____ daily. Additionally, feed kittens/puppies up to _____ portions twice daily. For pregnant and nursing _____, feed them 2 - 3 times their normal amount. You can keep this up if you want to reduce some of the moisture, or if has been refrigerated, bring it down to temperature just a little if there are picky eater. But just keeping in mind that reducing the moisture levels too much by heating it up can also decrease the nutritional value your cat can get from it.

10.2　宠物日常生活及户外用品 Pet Daily and Outdoor Supplies

词汇积累 Vocabulary

序号	中文名称	英文名称
1	宠物屋	pet house
2	宠物床垫	pet cushion bed
3	宠物笼	pet cage
4	猫咪吊床	cat hammock
5	宠物围栏	pet playpen
6	宠物沙发	pet sofa
7	猫/狗碗	cat/dog bowl
8	自动喂食器	automatic feeder
9	喂水器	water fountain
10	宠物慢食碗	pet slow feeder
11	称重勺	scale cup
12	储粮桶	pet food container
13	冰垫	pet cooling mat
14	宠物垫	pet mat
15	毛毯	blanket
16	尿垫	pet pee pad
17	宠物厕所	pet toilet
18	全封闭式	totally enclosed type

续表

序号	中文名称	英文名称
19	半封闭式	semi-closed type
20	开放式	open style
21	猫砂	cat litter
22	膨润土猫砂	clay litter
23	豆腐猫砂	tofu litter
24	水晶猫砂	crystal cat litter
25	钠基矿石猫砂	sodium-based ore cat litter
26	可冲入厕所型	flushable
27	除臭剂	deodorizer
28	猫砂盆	cat litter box
29	猫砂垫	cat litter mat
30	无尘	dust-free
31	猫砂铲	cat litter scoop
32	宠物训练垫	training pad
33	罐头密封盖	can lid
34	宠物背包	pet backpack
35	航空箱	pet travel carrier
36	宠物手推车	pet stroller
37	宠物制热床垫	heating pad
38	宠物训练铃铛	training bell
39	牵引绳	pet leash
40	可伸缩	retractable
41	捡拾袋	pick-up bag
42	项圈	collar
43	除臭剂	pet odor eliminator

续表

序号	中文名称	英文名称
44	背带	pet harness
45	汽车座套	pet car seat cover
46	狗狗嘴套	dog muzzle
47	宠物摄像头	pet camera
48	宠物纸尿裤	pet diaper
49	宠物楼梯	pet stair
50	宠物追踪器	pet monitor/tractor

话术演练 Language Skills

产品规格介绍：

(1) The dimensions of the pad are 18×17×1.5 inches; weighs 2.05 pounds.

(2) Size of the cushion is 17″ plus 11″. The height from the floor to the top of the cushion is 9″.

(3) It is recommended for cats and small dogs like schnauzer[1], papillon[2], chihuahua[3], poodle[4], shih tzu[5], yorkshire terrier[6], pomeranian[7].

(4) Pet warming mat provides 6 temperature levels, from level 1 to level 6. It also equips with 5 timer modes: 4 h, 8 h, 12 h, 24 h or always on (default setting[8]).

(5) The blanket comes in colors of espresso, cozy denim, dove, and silver gray; it's also available in multiple sizes, like small, medium, large, and extra large.

(6) This red dog treat jar accommodates[9] up to 10 pounds of dog food or treats.

(7) Automatic pet feeder with a digital timer allows you to set certain time intervals between meals, up to 6 meals daily with 1 to 50 portions.

(8) This food dispenser[10] can store up to 16.9 cups of dry food, which can last feeding cats and small dogs for 20 days.

(9) This pet diner has a set of 2 bowls and each is 11 oz stainless steel bowl set

for feeding food and water, which is best for small dogs and cats.

(10) Our pet backpack can hold cats up to 17 pounds and dogs up to 13 pounds.

> 单词解析：
> 1. schnauzer ['ʃnaʊzər] n. 雪纳瑞狗(德国种刚毛犬的一种)
> 2. papillon ['pæpə,lɒn] n. 蝶耳狗(一种玩赏小狗)
> 3. chihuahua [tʃɪ'wɑːwə] n. 吉娃娃
> 4. poodle ['puːdl] n. 贵宾犬
> 5. shih tzu 狮子狗
> 6. yorkshire terrier [,jɔːrkʃər 'terɪər] 约克夏犬
> 7. pomeranian [,pɒmə'reɪnɪən] n. 博美犬
> 8. default setting 默认设置
> 9. accommodate [ə'kɔːmədeɪt] v. 容纳
> 10. dispenser [dɪ'spensər] n. 自动取物装置；饮用机

产品质量介绍：

(11) Electric pet warming pad utilizes chew resistant cord[11] and overheated protection, PVC[12] waterproof material and detachable[13] cover design to make it more convenient for daily use.

(12) Pet sofa is made of solid wood and plywood[14] frame, filled with high-density soft sponge and cotton, and covered with velvet[15].

(13) Made with 460 GSM premium[16] microfiber polyester[17], this blanket is soft, lightweight, durable, easy to care for and machine washable.

(14) Pet warming pad uses upgrading heating technology and advanced heating film[18] material, which is safer and more even heating than traditional heating pads.

(15) This unique modern decorative design will look gorgeous on your kitchen counter drawing compliments from your friends and family!

(16) The blanket is equipped with a layer of mylar[19] material that reflects body heat to create a warm sleep surface for dogs and cats to curl up in cozy comfort.

(17) The blanket features snuggly[20] soft terry[21] on one side and thick, insulating

sherpa[22] on the other; both materials are gentle on noses and paws for enhanced coziness.

(18) × × × product has patented airtight[23] structure, even if the feeder is moved or rocked[24], the dispenser will not drop extra food.

(19) This pet bowl is made of high-quality stainless steel with a unique resin[25] bottom.

(20) The stainless steel bowl is detachable, which is easy to take out to wash, keep clean, and convenient to add food or water.

(21) The bio-enzymatic[26] spray has no chlorine[27], no chemical propellants[28], and nothing that stains or fades colors.

(22) Our cat carrier adopts a larger elevation[29] angle design of the space capsule with a larger field of view, which greatly expands the height of the field of view, and adopts a three-sided transparent process.

(23) Low-dust cat litter enables a clean pour and forms tight, strong clumps[30] for easy scooping[31].

(24) The length of the rope is adjustable through the button on the rope and the standard size is from small kitten to large cat.

(25) The carrier is made of plastic with steel wire doors and screws that keep the top and bottom securely attached.

(26) The cat harness and leash set is escape-proof with durable, strong hook and loop fastener, no harsh webbing[32] or buckles[33].

单词解析：

11. cord [kɔːrd] *n.* (细)绳

12. PVC *abbr.* 聚氯乙烯(用于服装、管材、铺地材料等)

13. detachable [dɪˈtætʃəbl] *adj.* 可拆卸的;可分开的

14. plywood [ˈplaɪwʊd] *n.* 胶合板;夹心板

15. velvet [ˈvelvɪt] *n.* 天鹅绒;丝绒

16. premium [ˈpriːmɪəm] *adj.* 高昂的;优质的

17. polyester [ˈpɒlɪstər] *n.* 聚酯纤维

18. film [fɪlm] *n.* 薄膜

19. mylar ['maɪˌlɑːr] n. 密拉(一种聚酯薄膜)
20. snuggly [snʌglɪ] adj. 温暖舒适的
21. terry ['terɪ] n. 毛圈棉织物(多用以做毛巾)
22. sherpa ['ʃɜːrpə] n. 羊羔绒
23. airtight ['ertaɪt] adj. 密封的;密闭的
24. rock [rɔːk] v. 摇晃
25. resin ['rezɪn] n. 树脂;合成树脂
26. bio-enzymatic ['biːəʊenzaɪm'ætɪk] adj. 生物酶的
27. chlorine ['klɔrɪn] n. 氯气
28. propellant [prə'pelənt] n. 喷射剂;推进剂
29. elevation [ˌelə'veɪʃ(ə)n] n. 提升;升高
30. clump [klʌmp] n. 簇;堆;团
31. scoop [skup] v. 舀;挖
32. webbing ['webɪŋ] n. 带状结实织物
33. buckle ['bʌk(ə)l] n. 带扣

产品功能介绍:

(27) Pet heating pad is better for older pets, arthritis[34] pets, or the pets have recovered from injury or surgery.

(28) The terry fabric is designed with a waterproof interior coating to protect bed and living room furniture against dirt, spills, and accidents.

(29) The blanket can protect your couch, sofas, bed, and home goods from chewing, scratching, shedding and unwanted pet hair and fur while keeping your pet dry and comfortable.

(30) The waterproof thermal blanket can also be used as a car seat cover to protect the interior of your car from dirt, dander[35], and accidents, while providing your pup optimum snuggling comfort.

(31) Due to the airtight seal, the pet treats and food will remain fresh and crispy for a long time in this red treat jar.

(32) Many of our sofas are upholstered[36] with low profile, extra cushioned

arms, designed to offer a perfect place for those leaner dogs to rest their heads.

(33) When you plan to leave your cat for several days, an automatic feeder with battery backup will keep dispensing even if the power goes out and your cat won't starve.

(34) Mat textured surfaces promote pleasurable licking action, which generates saliva[37] helping protect your pet's teeth and gums.

(35) You can trust it on carpets, floors, furniture, clothing, litter boxes, kennels[38], carrier, anywhere pets can go and stains could happen.

(36) The field of view is expanded to 240°, bringing more fun to pet travel, and no longer have to worry about the pet's field of vision being too dark and fearful!

(37) Scented litter features a slow-release deodorizing[39] system for around-the-clock odor control and prevents ammonia[40] odor from forming for 14 days when used as directed.

(38) Made with a soft, breathable air mesh[41], this lightweight pet harness is perfect for walks all year round.

(39) Two reflective bands on the sides of this harness enhance pet's visibility for those early morning and late evening strolls.

(40) Hard-sided pet carrier is for transporting a dog or cat to the vet or for general travel.

(41) Indoor security camera can get crystal-clear video in 1080P full HD[42] with a 110° wide-angle lens to see every detail, day or night.

(42) A built-in speaker and microphone let you interact with your pets at home by talking via the Smart Life app.

(43) The dog vest harness has an adjustable chest strap[43] with snap[44] on buckle, enabling dog to move its body parts freely, and can customize fits for your puppy growth do not need to always change it.

单词解析：

34. arthritis [ɑrˈθraɪtɪs] n. 关节炎；风湿病

35. dander [ˈdændər] n. 头皮屑

36. upholster [ʌpˈhəʊlstər] v. 为（椅子等）装软垫

37. saliva [səˈlaɪvə] n. 唾液；口水
38. kennel [ˈken(ə)l] n. 狗舍
39. deodorizing [diˈəʊdəraɪzɪŋ] adj. 除臭的
40. ammonia [əˈməʊniə] n. 氨
41. mesh [meʃ] n. 网状物
42. HD (high definition) abbr. 高清晰度
43. strap [stræp] n. 带子
44. snap [snæp] n. 摁扣

产品服务介绍：

(44) We adopt customer satisfaction-worry-free 3-year warranty.

(45) We are committed to satisfying you with outstanding products and top-level customer service. Please do not hesitate to contact us if you have any concerns.

(46) The product comes with a 90-day limited coverage against material defects and may also qualify for our 60-day worry-free program.

(47) We have a 30-day return policy.

(48) Our factory directly provides good price, high quality and new design products for our customers.

(49) We offer OEM & ODM[45] and customize service.

(50) We are committed to providing customers for a better shopping experience and service level, you can contact us at any time, and we will give you the most satisfactory answer within 24 hours!

单词解析：

45. OEM&ODM 代工制造

直播模板 Template

This is a _____ bed. The _____ bed includes components of _____ and _____... The bed comes in colors of _____, _____, and _____. It has colorful patterns of _____, _____... It's also available in multiple sizes of small, medium, large, jumbo, and jumbo plus.

The external dimension of our sample product here is _____, internal dimension _____, weight _____ pounds. Please add extra 6-12" to the length of your _____(pet) in favorite sleeping position to confirm the bed size.

The material of the bed is _____, _____ and _____ for added durability and softness. It is filled with 100% recyclable eco-friendly _____. It uses premium _____ inserts which are much healthier to humans and _____. The surface is lined with _____ that is luxuriously soft and plush to the touch, a great complement to the equally smooth and downy _____ covering the sides and bolsters.

The _____ bed has _____ bottom which will be water resistant and will be non-slip which is great.

The cover is fully removable and washable. The durable _____ zips make it easy to unzip the bed and toss the outer cover into the washing machine for a deep clean.

Designed like a _____, this _____ bed provides a soft and cozy place for your pet to rest and relax. The classic _____ design promotes ultimate comfort and security, providing high-loft orthopedic cushion support as well as a super cozy nestling and burrowing space for _____.

This kind of bed may not be suitable for pets with excessive teething or destructive chewing behavior.

10.3 宠物清洁及医疗保健用品 Pet Cleansing and Healthcare Products

词汇积累 Vocabulary

序号	中文名称	英文名称
1	宠物除毛刷	pet hair brush
2	跳蚤梳	flea comb
3	针梳	stainless steel comb
4	除味喷剂	deodorizing spray
5	除毛手套	grooming gloves
6	宠物湿巾	cleansing wipe
7	宠物洗澡手套	pet bathing gloves
8	擦水毛巾	towel
9	洗耳液	ear wash
10	宠物牙刷	pet toothbrush
11	宠物牙膏	pet toothpaste
12	宠物沐浴液	pet shampoo
13	毛发柔顺液	pet conditioner
14	沐浴露起泡器	electric foam pump
15	宠物折叠浴盆	pet folding tub
16	沐浴刷	bath brush
17	洁足泡沫	cleansing foot foam
18	泡浴球	bubble bath ball
19	免水清洁液	waterless shampoo
20	洗澡袋	grooming bag

续表

序号	中文名称	英文名称
21	指甲剪	nail clippers/trimmers
22	指甲锉刀	nail file
23	电动磨甲器	electric nail grinder
24	宠物美容剪刀	pet grooming scissors
25	宠物智能烘干箱	pet intelligent drying box
26	宠物吹风机	pet hair dryer
27	宠物按摩器	pet massager
28	宠物美容吊床	pet grooming hammock
29	宠物剃毛器	pet hair shaver
30	宠物皮屑喷剂	dander reducing spray
31	泪痕清洁湿巾	tear wipe
32	宠物防抓指甲套	pet nail caps
33	跳蚤驱虫药	flea treatment medication
34	外驱	external deworming
35	内驱	internal deworming
36	耳螨药	ear mite drops
37	滴眼液	eye drops
38	猫癣药	cat ringworm treatment
39	猫癣灯（伍德氏灯）	Wood's lamp
40	情绪安抚剂	relaxant
41	营养补充剂	nutritional supplement
42	维生素片	pet vitamin
43	钙片	calcium tablet
44	营养膏	nutrition cream
45	药浴香波	medicinal bathing lotion

续表

序号	中文名称	英文名称
46	脱毛膏	hairball removal cream
47	软骨素	chondroitin
48	针筒推药器	pill shooter
49	伊丽莎白圈头套	remedy and recovery collar
50	宠物洁牙指套	dental care finger wipes

话术演练 Language Skills

产品规格介绍：

（1）The comb has strong stainless steel teeth, with only 0.15 mm needle pitch[1].

（2）The massager is sized to comfortably fit in the palm of your hand.

（3）There are 140 pieces cat nail tips in 1 pack with 7 adhesive[2] glues and 7 pieces of applicators[3].

（4）The package includes 1 pet pill tablet gun, 1 water feeding silica[4] gel[5] head, 1 pill feeding silica gel head.

（5）One box of pet dental care wipes contains 50 pre-soaked wipes.

> **单词解析：**
> 1. pitch [pɪtʃ] n. 间距
> 2. adhesive [əd'hɪsɪv] adj. 黏合的
> 3. applicator ['æplɪˌkeɪtər] n. 涂抹器
> 4. silica ['sɪlɪkə] n. 二氧化硅
> 5. gel [dʒel] n. 胶滞体

产品质量与特色介绍：

（6）The wire bristles[6] of our long hair cat brush made of stainless steel is 1.2 times as thick as bristles of other deshedding brush for cats.

(7) The metal pins on the cat brush for short haired cats have round rubber tips on the ends.

(8) The fine polished and rounded comb teeth are made of high-quality metal, which is smooth and durable.

(9) Pin head is rounded and gentle to skin that never scratch.

(10) It is made with the highest quality ingredients, including aloe vera[7] and oatmeal to moisturize and deeply condition[8] cat's dry skin and reduce redness and/or flakes[9].

(11) This dander[10] reducing spray is pH balanced for cats and can be used on all cats or kittens with dander.

(12) This formula is free of fragrances, sulfates[11], colorants[12], and harsh chemicals.

(13) Our soothing pet wash is effective yet extremely gentle, making it an excellent shampoo for animals with allergies and other sensitivities[13].

(14) Our all natural oatmeal shampoo is 100% detergent[14] and alcohol-free and 100% non-toxic.

(15) The towel is woven from high-quality combed cotton, with longer loops[15] to enhance absorbency[16] and performance.

(16) This nail file[17] provides a light touch in any direction for quick results.

(17) This deshedding brush is much stronger and not easy to break.

(18) The kitten brush is designed with a silicone[18] loop strap on the end of anti-slip handle, easily hanged on the wall and some other places.

(19) The button on the handle can make disposing of the shed hair one-handed without having to let go of the cat super easy.

(20) When grooming time is finished, simply push the button so the bristles retract[19], leaving you with a hair-free slicker[20] brush.

(21) The electric massager is equipped with 4 rotating heads with 96 soft massage nodes that are safe for their skin and fur.

(22) Wireless for easy use anywhere, our dog and cat massager is powered by a long-lasting rechargeable battery for 4 − 6 hours of use per charge.

（22）Claw caps are made from natural vinyl[21] resin and are non-toxic.

（23）Our claw scissors are fitted with razor sharp blades made out of stainless steel and an ergonomic[22] grip made out of a top-grade plastic.

（24）Our pet grooming hammock adopts double-layer fabric design, with the inner fabric using high-density knitted material, and the outer using 3D air-mesh technology.

（25）Pet grooming hammock is made of mesh textile material and the sling[23] is designed with a special craft sewing technique, no need to worry about tearing and falling off.

（26）This syringe[24] is made of high-quality food-grade material and soft silicone, non-toxic, reusable and washable.

（27）This flea[25] and tick[26] treatment is made with 2 tough killing ingredients, fipronil[27] and methoprene[28]—one to kill adult fleas and ticks and the second to kill flea eggs and larvae[29].

（28）Our proprietary blend includes thiamine[30], 3C (Colostrum Calming Complex)[31] and L-theanine[32] to produce a relaxed and calm state.

单词解析：

6. bristle [ˈbrɪs(ə)l] n. 鬃毛

7. aloe vera [ˌæləʊˈvɪrə] 芦荟汁

8. condition [kənˈdɪʃ(ə)n] v. 护理

9. flake [fleɪk] n. 皮屑；薄片

10. dander [ˈdændər] n. 头皮屑

11. sulfate [ˈsʌlˌfeɪt] n. 硫酸盐（同 sulphate）

12. colorant [ˈkʌlərənt] n. 颜料

13. sensitivity [ˌsensəˈtɪvəti] n. 敏感性

14. detergent [dɪˈtɜːdʒənt] n. 洗涤剂

15. loop [lup] n. 环；圈

16. absorbency [əbˈzɔːbənsi] n. 吸收力

17. file [faɪl] n. 锉刀

18. silicone [ˈsɪlɪˌkəʊn] n. 硅酮

19. retract [rɪ'trækt] v. 缩回;撤销
20. slick [slɪk] adj. 光滑的;圆滑的
21. vinyl ['vaɪn(ə)l] n. 乙烯基
22. ergonomic [ˌɜːgə'nɒmɪk] adj. 人体工程学的
23. sling [slɪŋ] n. 吊带;吊兜
24. syringe [sɪ'rɪndʒ] n. (皮下)注射器
25. flea [fliː] n. 跳蚤
26. tick [tɪk] n. 蜱虫
27. fipronil [fɪp'rɒnɪl] n. 氟虫腈
28. methoprene ['miːθəpriːn] n. 烯虫酯
29. larvae ['lɑːviː] n. 幼虫
30. thiamine ['θaɪəmɪn] n. 硫胺素;维生素 B_1
31. 3C (colostrum calming complex) 初乳镇静复合物
32. L-theanine 茶氨酸

产品功能介绍：

(29) Using this cat brush for long haired cats on a regular basis can gently and effectively remove loose hair, tangles[33], knots, dander and trapped dirt.

(30) 150° bent needles designed to penetrate deep into the coat are really easier to groom the undercoat[34] well.

(31) Regular combing and massaging can help improve blood circulation and relax your pet's mind while getting rid of loose fur to leave it a shiny coat.

(32) Comfortable half-arc handle offers your pet an easy combing experience.

(33) Cat dander remover spray reduces cat dander and flaking, leaving fur shiny and soft.

(34) This set of shampoo is specially formulated for pets with dry, itchy, sensitive skin.

(35) It works as a natural pet deodorizer[35] that neutralizes pet odor instantly and keeps pets fresher for longer after bath time.

(36) Your pet will enjoy a comfortable, smooth filing experience without the

harsh grinding sensation and physical discomfort of typical files.

(37) The unique inner groove[36] design and fine grit allows precision filing, target specific areas, shape and buff[37] claws with ease.

(38) As a cat deshedding brush, it's perfect for shedding and massaging your pets without scratching your pet's skin, even the sensitive skin.

(39) Keeping cats well-brushed can spare your kitties the ordeal[38] of throwing up hairballs.

(40) Our electric massager for cats and dogs provides therapeutic massage that aids in relieving tension and stiffness due to age, injury or stress while promoting bonding between you and your beloved pet.

(41) Our water-resistant handheld massager is great for working up a lather[39] and dislodging[40] dirt and grime[41] in your pet's fur.

(42) The claw caps can effectively prevent cat from scratching the affected area with skin disease, protect you when playing with them, and will not interfere with your cat's normal behavior.

(43) With this grooming[42] hammock[43], even at home, you can easily accomplish the same things as the pet hospital grooming table, such as trimming[44] nails, grooming, bathing.

(44) File your dog's nails to prevent rough edges.

(45) Dog and cat shampoo exfoliates[45] and moisturizes the skin to reduce shedding.

(46) Aloe, papaya[46], chamomile[47], kiwi, and mallow[48] extracts[49] leave the coat feeling silky soft.

(47) Frontline flea and tick treatment for cats kills fleas, flea eggs, lice, and ticks.

(48) Calming for cats is a veterinarian formulated product designed to assist in times of anxiousness or stress without producing a sedative[50] like effect or changing the personality of your pet.

(49) Omega fatty acids, cranberry, zinc[51], and biotin[52] help prevent, reduce, control, or even eliminate hairballs while supporting healthy skin.

（50）<u>Pet dental finger wipes</u> help to eliminate plaque build-up on teeth, remove tooth stains, massaging gums.

（51）<u>Peppermint</u>[53] scent helps to reduce bad breath and freshening breath.

单词解析：

33. tangle ['tæŋg(ə)l] n. 纷乱
34. undercoat ['ʌndərˌkəʊt] n. 内涂层
35. deodorizer [diˈəʊdəˌraɪzə] n. 除臭剂
36. groove [gruːv] n. 槽；沟；辙
37. buff [bʌf] adj. 浅黄色的
38. ordeal [ɔːrˈdɪl] n. 折磨
39. lather [ˈlæðər] n. 泡沫
40. dislodge [dɪsˈlɔdʒ] v. 去除
41. grime [graɪm] n. 尘垢
42. groom [gruːm] v. 擦洗；理毛
43. hammock [ˈhæmək] n. 吊床
44. trim [trɪm] v. 修剪
45. exfoliate [eksˈfəʊlɪeɪt] v. 去角质
46. papaya [pəˈpaɪə] n. 木瓜
47. chamomile [ˈkæməˌmaɪl] n. 洋甘菊
48. mallow [ˈmæləʊ] n. 锦葵
49. extract [ˈekˌstrækt] n. 提取物
50. sedative [ˈsedətɪv] n. 镇静药
51. zinc [zɪŋk] n. 锌
52. biotin [ˈbaɪətɪn] n. 生物素
53. peppermint [ˈpepərˌmɪnt] n. 薄荷

产品服务介绍：

（52）If <u>flea comb</u> does not meet your expectations, return it for a no-questions-asked refund of your purchase price.

（53）We believe the ingredients that touch your pet's coat and skin should be as naturally effective, non-toxic, and gentle as possible.

(54) As long as you have any dissatisfaction, we guarantee 100% return and 100% refund.

(55) Our pledge to you is that we will honor your trust in our product by standing by your side every step of the way as you use our tools on your quest to a healthier life.

(56) If the nail caps didn't fit your cat or you have any questions to victhy cat nail covers, we support replacement or 100% refund.

(57) These cat nail cutters are backed by a lifetime money-back guarantee.

(58) We are a cruelty-free brand. All our products are tested on humans first.

直播模板 Template

_____ shampoo and conditioner blend build a rich lather that rinses easily, leaving skin silky soft and shiny. _____ shampoo adopts a pH balanced formula, made with pure botanical extracts and natural conditioners like _____, _____, _____, _____, and _____. The _____ -based liquid is completely alcohol-free and made with _____ and _____ to make bath time a soothing experience. _____ is a natural deodorizer and it's safe for frequent use, even on puppies who know how to get dirty. _____ shampoo also features

_____ to give your smelly _____ a clean and refreshing scent.

The direction for use is as follows. First, shake well. Then wet the coat of your pet thoroughly. Rub a generous amount of _____ into your _____'s coat, building a rich lather. Rinse well and then dry your _____'s coat with a towel.

This soothing and cleaning bath wash is a great choice for pet parents and groomers to clean _____ of all ages, breeds, and sizes, and regardless or short, long, straight or course hair texture. The shampoo and conditioner can be used once every _____ weeks.

10.4 宠物服饰及玩具 Pet Apparels and Toys

词汇积累 Vocabulary

序号	中文名称	英文名称
1	宠物T恤	pet T-shirt
2	围嘴	bib
3	毛衣	sweater
4	针织背心	knitwear vest
5	连帽衫	hoodie
6	帽子	hat
7	雨衣	raincoat
8	防水肚兜	waterproof bellyband
9	披肩斗篷	cape
10	围巾	scarf
11	宠物羽绒服	puffer coat
12	狗狗背包	dog backpack
13	宠物颈圈	collar
14	领饰	neckwear
15	宠物袜子	pet socks
16	宠物术后绝育服	sterilization suit

续表

序号	中文名称	英文名称
17	宠物名字牌	ID tag
18	项链	necklace
19	宠物发夹	hair bow
20	领结	bow tie
21	结绳玩具	knotted rope toy
22	磨牙玩具	chew toy
23	毛绒玩具	plush toy
24	接抛玩具	flyer fetch toy
25	互动玩具	interactive toy
26	玩具收纳箱	toy storage bin
27	猫爬架	cat climbing frame
28	猫抓板	scratching board
29	猫抓柱	scratching post
30	逗猫棒	cat teaser stick
31	猫薄荷球	catnip ball
32	弹力球	bouncy ball
33	宠物跑步机	training treadmill
34	咬胶环	teething ring
35	橡皮球	rubber ball
36	宠物训练铃	pet training bell
37	木天蓼逗猫棍	polygonum cat teasing stick
38	剑麻绳	sisal rope
39	磨牙棒	teething stick
40	红外线逗猫笔	red laser light pointer
41	可折叠爬行隧道	collapsible tunnel
42	自嗨猫转盘	cat track
43	响纸球	crinkle ball

续表

序号	中文名称	英文名称
44	宠物益智藏食器	pet treat dispenser puzzle
45	狗狗飞盘	flying disc
46	宠物球发射器	ball launcher
47	不倒翁	roly-poly toy
48	漏食球	treat dispenser ball
49	交流发声按钮	communication button
50	塑料小弹簧	plastic cat spring

话术演练 Language Skills

产品规格介绍：

(1) It comes with 2 medium sticks—one is made from natural hemp[1] and the other has wag[2]-worthy original flavor.

(2) Interactive dog toy has a loud squeaker[3] inside and unique spiky[4] texture.

(3) It is perfect for small and medium dogs, and is available in different bright colors and sizes.

(4) This awesome plush[5] toy set includes three toys: a fox, a raccoon[6] and a squirrel, with two squeakers in each toy.

(5) Two-squeaker toy measures 14×6×2 inches; four-squeaker toy measures 18×6×2 inches.

(6) The package comes with 12 balls—each one measures between 1.5 – 2 inches, so even little kitties can enjoy a day of play.

(7) The costume is available in 6 sizes. XS is recommended for puppy or kitty weighing under 2.5 lbs. S is recommended for pet between 2.5 – 4 lbs. M is recommended for pet between 4 – 6.5 lbs. L is recommended for pets between 6.5 – 9.5 lbs. XL is recommended for dogs between 9.5 – 13 lbs. XXL is recommended for dogs between 13 – 17 lbs.

(8) Please measure your pet's size, then check size chart to choose the right

size to avoid return due to size issue.

(9) The neck girth[7] of the bib is 21.6 inches.

(10) The head girth of the hat is 19.6 inches, suitable for cats and small dogs.

(11) Our hoodies are made by hand, the size may be about 1 inch deviation[8], which is a normal phenomenon.

> **单词解析：**
> 1. hemp [hemp] *n.* 大麻
> 2. wag [wæg] *n.* 摇晃；摆动
> 3. squeaker [ˈskwiːkə(r)] *n.* 吱吱叫的东西
> 4. spiky [ˈspaɪkɪ] *adj.* 有尖刺的
> 5. plush [plʌʃ] *n.* 长毛绒
> 6. raccoon [ræˈkuːn] *n.* 浣熊
> 7. girth [ɡɜːθ] *n.* 围带
> 8. deviation [ˌdiːvɪˈeɪʃ(ə)n] *n.* 偏差

产品质量与特色介绍：

(12) ××× balls are solid, rubber, and will never pop, providing everlasting bounciness.

(13) Chew balls are dishwasher-safe and free of latex[9], vinyl[10] and phthalates[11].

(14) The teething stick has mold[12]-resistant filling which is perfect for freezing and washing.

(15) The ball toy is made of BPA-free, food-grade TPR[13] rubber so it's safe to play with every day.

(16) The squeaker football dog toy can stand up to tough play and rambunctious[14] rounds of fetch.

(17) It contains minimal filling for less mess around the house.

(18) Our plush snake features super-tough fabric over a dura-tuff lining[15] and reinforced double-layer seams for superior chew resistance.

(19) Innovative ball is super durable and double-molded to stand up to tough chewers.

(20) This product is tough enough to stand up to constant chewing, while being malleable[16] enough to be stretched and tugged[17].

(21) Glow-in-the-dark ball is made from a durable, easy-to-clean rubber and proprietary[18] glow pigment[19].

(22) Bright color gives increased visibility and helps prevent ball from getting lost.

(23) It delivers the natural wood flavor and texture that dogs can't resist and made without lead or phthalate for a toy you can trust.

(24) It comes with a safety release mechanism that's easy to operate; plus it has no exposed moving parts.

(25) The knot rope is made from 100% natural cotton.

(26) Crinkle ball delivers a satisfying crinkle sounds with every bat, pounce[20] and roll.

(27) This interactive triple-tiered tower equips each level with its own colorful rolling ball to provide three stories of stimulating play for cats.

(28) Irresistibly scratchable material is made with corrugated[21] cardboard that shreds easily without catching to satisfy your feline's urge to scratch.

(29) Soft and slightly stretchy fabric are used for a comfortable fit.

(30) The sweaters are made of premium acrylic[22] fabric which is soft and warm.

(31) The pet sweaters are easy to take on and take off just as human way of wearing.

(32) It is lightweight and foldable, perfect for daily use and store.

(33) The hat contains fillers and is not easily deformed.

(34) The embroidery[23] part of the bib uses environmentally friendly dyed cotton thread, which is long-lasting and durable.

(35) Unlike most dog raincoats, this long-sleeved design effectively isolates rain and snow from wetting over a large area, the inner layer of breathable mesh keeps dog's hair dry, but leaving the abdomen[24] empty does not affect dog to pee or poop.

(36) Button design make it easy to wear; lightweight material enables it to be foldable and can be put in a bag or backpack to carry around.

(37) Reflective strips are designed on this dog raincoat.

(38) High visibility allows dogs to ensure safety in rainy days, nights, and low-visibility environments.

(39) Trusted to be the leader of cosplay and general decor[25] items, ×××'s does not sacrifice quality for price.

(40) The hoodie is decorated with a windproof hat, and it has a drawcord[26], which can be tightly tied to the dog's head and will not fall off easily.

单词解析：

9. latex ['leɪˌteks] n. 乳胶；橡胶

10. vinyl ['vaɪn(ə)l] n. 乙烯基

11. phthalate ['θæleɪt] n. 邻苯二甲酸盐

12. mold [məuld] n. 霉菌

13. TPR (temperature programmed reduction) abbr. 热塑性橡胶

14. rambunctious [ræm'bʌŋkʃəs] adj. 喧闹的

15. dura-tuff lining 硬凝灰岩衬里

16. malleable ['mælɪəb(ə)l] adj. 可锻造的；易成型的

17. tug [tʌg] v. 拽；拉

18. proprietary [prə'praɪəˌterɪ] adj. 专营的

19. pigment ['pɪgmənt] n. 颜料；色素

20. pounce [pauns] n. 扑击；猛扑

21. corrugate ['kɔrəˌgeɪt] v. 揉皱

22. acrylic [ə'krɪlɪk] adj. 丙烯酸的

23. embroidery [ɪm'brɔɪdərɪ] n. 刺绣

24. abdomen [æb'dəumən] n. 腹部

25. decor [deɪ'kɔr] n. 装饰风格

26. drawcord ['drɔkɔrd] n. 抽绳

产品功能介绍：

(41) It helps keep your hound busy and satisfied with every chew—it can even help relieve anxious chewing habits.

(42) The ball is great for playing in the pool or at the beach.

(43) The teething stick also helps the dog keep cool during those hot summer days, just freeze and give it to your dog for an icy relief.

(44) Chewing helps puppies deal with teething pain, and it helps adult dogs keep their teeth clean and exercise their jaw, relieve anxiety, boredom and frustration.

(45) Pet chews help you create a safe and healthy outlet[27] for all your dog's chewing instincts.

(46) This plush dog toy is perfect for a game of fetch or as a comfort toy for your furry friend.

(47) Sturdy[28] nylon tabs[29] and handle give your dog a new way to play, and help the ball bounce.

(48) Proper supervision is advised when playing with all toys to ensure no accidental swallowing.

(49) Flyer fetch toy provides high-flying action to get dogs chasing after it.

(50) With ball launcher, there is no need to touch the ball to pick it up—simply use the end of the launcher and avoid a slobbery mess.

(51) Treat dispenser ball encourages slow eating by providing interactive obstacles for your pooch to overcome, extends playtime while limiting the number of treats.

(52) The rope features a convenient handle that makes tug-of-war easier on your hands.

(53) Erratic[30] bounce stimulates your kitty's hunting instincts to get them actively playing.

(54) The scratch board promotes nail health and positive scratching behaviors which are essential for a healthy and well-balanced kitty, and helps redirect scratching from furniture and other household items.

(55) Dress your pets in these delicate Halloween pumpkin sweaters to protect them from the cold and keep them free outdoor activities in the winter.

(56) The coat is a great outfit for holiday season, daily wear and special

occasion, such as Christmas, Halloween, theme parties.

> **单词解析：**
> 27. outlet ['aʊtˌlet] *n.* 专营店
> 28. sturdy ['stɜːdɪ] *adj.* 结实的
> 29. tab [tæb] *n.* 标签
> 30. erratic [ɪ'rætɪk] *adj.* 不稳定的；不确定的

产品服务介绍：

(57) Our team are professional and responsible pet lovers; plus, purchase our cat storm anxiety jacket with full confidence, we provide 30 days free return and 24 hours service for you.

(58) Purchases from unauthorized 3rd-party resellers may not be provided with after-sale services.

直播模板 Template

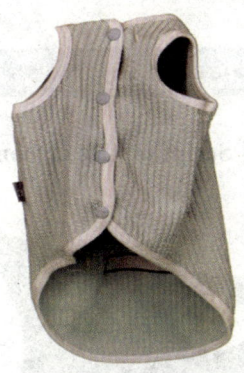

We all crave for warmth to endure the long and cold winter. In fact, even furry animals feel cold in the winter. If your _____ prefers to curl up, refuse to sleep and even get shaking in the cold weather, they need clothes to keep warm. Here, we have a _____ for _____ to wear in chilly fall and winter.

The _____ is _____-knitted by _____ with 100% natural, non-allergenic, organic _____ sourced from _____ with _____ standards. It uses only natural dyes from _____, with no harsh chemicals, artificial colors or plastics.

The turtleneck pullover sweater is made of high-density _____ that is comfortable, soft, warm and easy to care. It is easy to put on your pal for a comfy, snug fit thanks to the _____ design.

The pet's pretty _____ features classic _____ patterns and _____ cuffs and hem. It boasts chic looks and endless fashion, helps keep your _____ keep warm while staying breathable and stylish.

The _____ is available in different sizes and styles so you can find the perfect fit for your furry friend. It is particularly recommended for small sized dogs, cats and pups such as _____, _____, _____ etc.. Before purchasing, for the best fit, please match the dimensions to your pet's measurements as closely as possible.

This _____ is a perfect way for your pet to stay warm during the chilly days of fall and winter. Cozy _____ sweater combines the best of cuteness and comfort for _____. Great for fall get-togethers and themed photo ops and different occasions with your best fur friends.

10.5　实战脚本 Script

Live Streaming Script of Cat Grooming Hammock

Hi guys, welcome to our channel. I'm your host Joyce. If this is your first time to join our livestreaming, you can follow us and hit the subscription button. Today, we will bring some pretty good stuff for pet owners, a new range of pet supplies of wide applications.

Have you ever wanted to try to cut your cat's nails, but didn't have anyone to help you hold your pet? Trimming cats' nails and trying to groom them is a nightmare for many pet owners. Today we got a great unique item here to look at. This is a cat grooming hammock. It is like the function of grooming table, grooming arm. Even at home you can easily accomplish the same thing that groomers can accomplish for you with this incredible hammock and grooming kit.

As we can see here, there are four feet holes and an area for neck. The four holes have thickened edge, which is more comfortable for pet legs, and may alleviate emotional resistance and better cooperation. This cat hanger for nail trimming uses two layers of fabric. The inner fabric uses high-density knitted material so that makes it extremely breathable, and the outer uses 3D air-mesh technology. Between the two layers, there is a little bit of comfortable cushion inside. It is designed with double reinforced stitching to give them stronger durability and reliability. Besides, thickened edge of the front and rear legs and excellent breathability can reduce friction to protect pets, and keep cats calm and relaxed.

Our grooming hammock offers three sizes: S, L and XL. Size S is fit for cats whose spacing between legs is from 4.2 to 7.5 inches. Size X is fit for spacing from 5 to 9 inches. Size XL is fit for the spacing from 7 to 12.5 inches. The maximum loads for the three sizes are 15 lbs, 20 lbs and 30 lbs respectively. To choose the right size, so you need to measure the length between your cat's front and rear legs before purchasing.

It's also easy to put together and to use. It comes with four S hooks, two straps to securely hold the sling up. First slide your cat's legs through the holes, both the front and the back. Make sure that you have your cat face in the right direction. Use the straps provided and clip them onto anything that will support your cat's weight. You can screw the hooks into the ceiling and use ratchet straps to extend the length. The idea behind this is that you will hang this up from the ceiling and with your cat inside and then you can groom them, clip their nails. Cats will get calm and relax by hung in cat grooming harness.

It also comes with a premium package, including pet nail clippers, hanging straps kit, nail file, premium quality carabiner, and grooming scissors.

The market price is 31.99 \$ normally. But today, in our live show, we will give you 41% discount. The price for it is only 18.8 \$ for this incredible set of kit.

With this hammock, you can cut, paint or style your cat's nails with both hands. There will be no more wrestling, fighting or chasing your pet. We highly recommend this cat hammock to get all of your grooming needs taken care of.